SUSTAINABLE DEVELOPMENT

Sustainable Development
Economics and Environment in the Third World

David Pearce
Edward Barbier
Anil Markandya
London Environmental Economics Centre

EARTHSCAN PUBLICATIONS LTD LONDON

First published by
Edward Elgar Publishing Limited

First published in paperback in 1990 by
Earthscan Publications Limited
120 Pentonville Road, London N1 9JN

Reprinted 1994

A catalogue record for this book is available from the British Library

ISBN: 1 85383 088 7

Printed and bound in Great Britain by
Biddles Ltd, Guildford and King's Lynn

Earthscan Publications Limited is an editorially independent subsidiary of Kogan
Page Limited and publishes in association with the International Institute for
Environment and Development and the World Wide Fund for Nature.

Contents

Preface

'Sustainable development' is the fashionable buzzword in environmental conservation circles and in much of the world of international development. It received its most popular exposition in the highly influential Brundtland Report, in 1987, (World Commission on Environment and Development, 1987). The Brundtland Report was prepared by the World Commission on Environment and Development, created by the United Nations as a result of a General Assembly resolution in autumn 1983, and chaired by Mrs Gro Harlem Brundtland, Prime Minister of Norway. *Our Common Future* was the third in a series of UN initiatives; the first had been the Brandt Commission's *Programme for Survival* and *Common Crisis*. These were followed by the Palme Commission's work on security and disarmament, *Common Security*. Arguably, the Brundtland Commission's work has been the most influential of those initiatives.

But sustainable development as an idea had already been espoused in the World Conservation Strategy (WCS), produced by the International Union for the Conservation of Nature, World Wildlife Fund (now the Worldwide Fund for Nature) and the United Nations Environmental Programme in 1980. To social scientists the WCS was notable for its (virtually) total neglect of the main social science disciplines that should bear on issues of conservation, particularly economics. While this defect was remedied in the Brundtland Report which had a significant social science input, economists (as a profession) have paid little heed to the general theme of sustainable development. In part, this reflects the general lack of interest in environmental issues. Environmental economics plays a significant part in undergraduate and graduate economics courses in the USA and Canada; it is growing in importance in Europe. At the time of writing, however, there is not a single graduate course in environmental economics in the UK. Environmental economics as a discipline applied to problems of developing countries remains a specialism of fewer economists still; this may be due to its interdisciplinary nature. The need to know something about environment, about the developing world and about economics makes it a fairly daunting subject to pursue. It may also be due to the generally 'fuzzy' nature of the subject. There are no neat solutions, such as those that appear in the professional economics journals in respect of more abstract questions, and there are formidable problems of obtaining data and even greater ones of assessing the reliability of what there is.

This volume is an attempt on our part to give some structure to the concept of sustainable development and to illustrate ways in which environmental economics can be applied in the developing world. The subject is young and we therefore make no claim that what is in this book represents even the received wisdom of environmental economics, only a small part of which we have, incidentally, brought to bear on the problems. We are also aware that some of our colleagues do not agree with our interpretation of the meaning of sustainable development. What we have done is to look at how the term is being used, to ask what the common features of that language are in the belief that meaning is best discovered by the study of how we use words and to explore some of the implications of the meaning we discern in the literature.

The book is one of a number of products from many years of discussion and argument, and collectively of a great many visits to the countries we discuss. We cannot hope to indicate all the people whose ideas have influenced us over the years. But Jerry Warford of the World Bank's Environment Department must rank as a major influence not just on us, but on the environment and development debate in general. This is the second book to emerge from the London Environmental Economics Centre (LEEC).* The Centre was the brainchild of Richard Sandbrook, Executive Director of the International Institute for Environment and Development (IIED) London, and David Pearce. We are deeply indebted to Richard for his encouragement throughout. We owe a great deal to the enlightened and imaginative governments of Sweden, Norway and the Netherlands who have funded the Centre. Chapters 1 and 3 are developments of an earlier paper authored by all of us and presented to the Canadian Environmental Assessment Research Council's Conference on Integrating Economic and Environmental Assessment, in Vancouver, November 1988. We are grateful to the

*The first was Edward Barbier's *Economics, Natural Resource Scarcity and Development: Conventional and Alternative Views*, London, Earthscan, 1989.

members of that seminar for helpful comments. Chapter 2 is based on an extensive report prepared by two of us (D.W.P. and A.M.) for the UK Overseas Development Administration. Chapters 4 and 5 on Indonesia reflect work done by two of us for the World Bank (E.B. and D.W.P.) and by one of us (E.B.) for the US Agency for International Development. The views expressed in these chapters in no way reflect any official standpoint of either agency. Chapter 6, on Sudan, is partly based on a field mission by one of us (D.W.P.) to Sudan in 1987 and, to some extent, on continuing work by all of us in that tragic but beautiful country. Chapter 7 on Botswana reflects some earlier work for the international Union for the Conservation of Nature (IUCN) by one of us (D.W.P.), in association with several other researchers more than ably led by Charles Perrings. Chapter 8 on Nepal is based on collective work (but mainly by A.M. and E.B.) on several different missions. Chapter 9, on the Amazon, is based on thesis work (by E.B.) and on some joint work by one of us (D.W.P.) and Norman Myers. But the Amazon is the one case-study area that, at the time of writing, none of us has had the privilege of visiting. We therefore hope our reflections are not too divorced from reality.

Finally, we thank Jo Burgess, our researcher at LEEC, and Sue Pearce for assistance in the preparation of this volume. Despite this wealth of people to influence and advise us, mistakes there will be, and these remain entirely our responsibility.

EB. AM. DWP.
January 1989

1 Sustainable development: ecology and economic progress

Introduction

While 'sustainable development' is the acknowledged subject of much recent development thinking (see e.g. World Commission on Environment and Development, 1987; Repetto, 1986; Redclift, 1987; Turner, 1988; Stockholm Group, 1988), little headway appears to have been made in terms of a rigorous definition of the concept. Therefore, not surprisingly, efforts to 'operationalize' sustainable development and to show how it can be integrated into practical decision-making have been few and generally unpersuasive.[1] The use of the term 'development', rather than 'economic growth', implies acceptance of the limitations of the use of measures such as gross national product (GNP) to measure the well-being of nations. Instead development embraces wider concerns of the quality of life – educational attainment, nutritional status, access to basic freedoms and spiritual welfare. The emphasis on sustainability suggests that what is needed is a policy effort aimed at making these developmental achievements last well into the future. By implication, some at least of past development efforts have achieved only short-lived gains.

In this chapter we suggest a simple *definition* of sustainable development, and elaborate a set of *minimum* conditions for development to be sustainable, the conditions being based on the requirement that the *natural capital stock* should not decrease over time. Natural capital stock, in this context, is the stock of all environmental and natural resource assets, from oil in the ground to the quality of soil and groundwater, from the stock of fish in the oceans to the capacity of the globe to recycle and absorb carbon. We keep the definition of natural capital stock deliberately vague in order to capture the more general picture, and in the belief that a more detailed investigation will not raise insuperable problems. The meaning of a *constant* natural capital stock is more problematic, however, and we therefore devote a little time to alternative meanings.

1

2 *Sustainable development*

The idea that the natural capital stock should be held constant or improved, broadly reduces to an embodiment of the idea that resource and environmental degradation has gone 'too far'. This basic feeling is what we detect as the undertone to much recent environmental campaigning and discussion. In the language of economics, as degradation increases so the economic value of the next unit of environment at risk from destruction, whether tropical forest or wetland or whatever, is seen to be higher than the unit that has just disappeared or been degraded. Of itself, this idea of a rising 'marginal' economic value of natural environments the less there is of them will not justify maintaining what there is at any given moment of time. As we shall see, economists would typically argue that environmental degradation *should* take place so long as the gains from the activities causing the degradation (e.g. agricultural clearance of forests, development of wetlands) are greater than the benefits of preserving the areas in their original form. The idea that there is some 'optimum' stock of natural assets based on this comparison of costs and benefits needs to be addressed directly in order to see why the conservation of the existing stock should be elevated to be a goal of sustainable development. The rest of this chapter investigates this question.

Defining sustainable development
Since 'development' is a value word, implying change that is *desirable*, there is no consensus as to its meaning. What constitutes development depends on what social goals are being advocated by the development agency, government, analyst or adviser.[2] We take development to be a *vector* of desirable social objectives; that is, it is a list of attributes which society seeks to achieve or maximize. The elements of this vector might include:

- increases in real income per capita;
- improvements in health and nutritional status;
- educational achievement;
- access to resources;
- a 'fairer' distribution of income;
- increases in basic freedoms.

Correlation between these elements, or an agreed system of weights to be applied to them, might permit development to be represented by a single 'proxy' indicator, but this is not an issue pursued here.[3] *Sustainable* development is then a situation in which the development vector D does not decrease over time. However, such a simple definition is not problem-free. For example, use of the term implies the adoption of an infinite time horizon – i.e. that the aim is to achieve everlasting development – whereas practical decision-making requires adoption of some finite horizon. Nor does it tell us if the rate of change of D with respect to time t must be positive for each and every time period (which we might term *strong sustainability*), of whether only the trend of dD/dt must be positive (*weak sustainability*). One variant of the weak sustainability measure is that the *present value* of development benefits should be positive. A present value is a way of expressing a stream of benefits (or costs) that occur over time as a value perceived from the standpoint of the present. To do this future benefits and costs are *discounted* – i.e. given a lower weight relative to a similar benefit or cost in the present. Chapter 2 investigates the discounting issue in detail. For the moment, however, it is sufficient to note that present value maximization is consistent with the extinction of resources. How far those extinctions result in the development objectives themselves becoming unsustainable is open to question. But they lend some support to the idea that present value maximization is not a sufficient criterion for sustainable development. Sustainable development is better interpreted in its weak form – i.e. as saying that the rate of change of development over time is *generally* positive over some selected time horizon.[4]

Subject to the above caveats, we suggest that sustainability be defined as the general requirement that a vector of development characteristics be non-decreasing over time, where the elements to be included in the vector are open to ethical debate and where the relevant time horizon for *practical* decision-making is similarly indeterminate outside of agreement on intergenerational objectives. This level of generality may seem unsatisfactory, but the essential point is that *what* constitutes development, and the *time horizon* to be adopted, are both ethically and practically determined. Such an ethical debate can be illuminated by discussion of the alternative views on both issues, but it cannot be resolved other than by ethical consensus.

The conditions for sustainable development: constant capital stock
Much of the sustainable development literature has confused *definitions* of sustainable development with the *conditions* for achieving sustainability. The preceding discussion suggests that the definition, the meaning, of sustainable development, is evident from the phrase itself. We now consider a key necessary condition for achieving sustainable development. These conditions, elaborated below, are not sufficient, however. A sufficient set of conditions is likely to include, for example, institutional requirements for implementing sustainable development policy, and it may even require systematic changes in social values.[5]

We summarize the key necessary condition as 'constancy of the natural capital stock'. More strictly, the requirement is for non-negative change in the stock of natural resources and environmental quality. In basic terms, the environment should not be degraded further but improvements would be welcome.

The presumption that sustainability has something to do with non-depreciation of the natural capital stock is explicit in the Brundtland Report. Thus, 'If needs are to be met on a sustainable basis the Earth's natural resource base must be conserved and enhanced' (World Commission on Environment and Development, 1987, p. 57). It is somewhat more vaguely embraced in the World Conservation Strategy in terms of maintaining 'essential ecological processes and life support systems', 'preserving genetic diversity' and ensuring 'sustainable utilization of species and ecosystems' (IUCN, 1980, I). Both sources offer rationales for conserving natural capital in terms of moral obligation and the alleged mutual interdependency of development and natural capital conservation. A similar definition is advanced by economist Robert Repetto:

> sustainable development [is] a development strategy that manages all assets, natural resources, and human resources, as well as financial and physical assets, for increasing long-term wealth and well-being. Sustainable development, as a goal *rejects policies and practices that support current living standards by depleting the productive base, including natural resources*, and that leaves future generations with poorer prospects and greater risks than our own. (Repetto, 1986, p. 15)

Existing and optimal capital stock
Conserving the natural capital stock is consistent with several situations. The stock in question might be that which exists at the

point of time that decisions are being taken – the *existing* stock – or it might be the stock that *should exist*. The latter is clearly correct in terms of the application of neoclassical economic principles to resource issues. Economics would argue that there are costs and benefits of changing the natural capital stock. If it is reduced, it will be for some purpose; for example, much tropical forest clearance takes place for agricultural purposes. Similarly, wetlands are drained to gain the fertile soil for crop growing; natural habitats are reduced for housing development, and so on. Thus each destructive act has benefits in terms of the gains from the use to which the land is put. In the same way, using the atmosphere or the oceans as 'waste sinks' has benefits, in that alternative means of disposal are often more expensive. Thus the environment as a waste sink reduces production and consumption costs compared to what they would have been. Environmental destruction also has costs since a great many people use natural environments (for wildlife observation, recreation, scientific study, hunting, etc.). These 'use benefits' are lost (i.e. there are costs of destruction) if the land is converted for some other purpose. Similarly, one of the benefits of keeping the atmosphere unpolluted is that we avoid the damage that is done by pollution – e.g. better health and, globally, the avoidance of impacts such as global warming through trace gas emissions. Natural environments do not just have 'use values'. Many people like to think of environments being preserved for their own sake, an 'existence value'. These 'non-use' values need to be added to the use values to get the *total economic value* of the conserved resource or environment.[6]

Figure 1.1 depicts the cost–benefit comparison. The stock of natural assets is shown on the horizontal axis and costs and benefits are shown on the vertical axis. The cost curve shows that as the stock of natural capital (K_N) increases, there are increasing costs in the form of forgone benefits from *not* conserving the environment. The benefit curve captures the benefits to users and non-users of natural environments. Economic analysis would identify K_N* as the optimal stock of the environment. If the existing stock is to the right of K_N*, then it will be beneficial in net terms to reduce the stock – i.e. to engage in environmental degradation and destruction. If the existing stock is to the left of K_N*, then improvements in environmental quality are called for.

If our overview of the meaning of sustainable development is

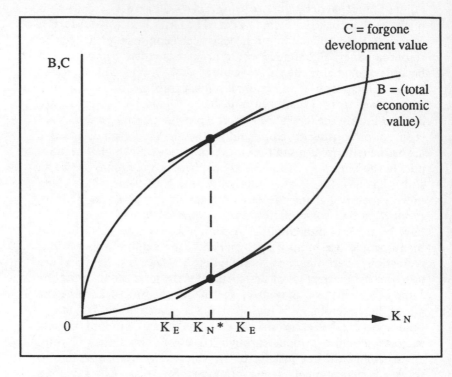

K_N is the natural capital stock; B shows the benefits from increasing it, benefits that accrue as use and non-use values; and C is the cost of increasing the natural capital stock, and these costs are the forgone benefits from using the natural assets for some other purpose. K_N^* is the optimal stock.

Figure 1.1   The costs and benefits of environmental change

correct, it appears to be inconsistent with the idea of maintaining optimal stocks of natural assets or, at least, it will only be consistent if we are to the left of the optimum depicted in Figure 1.1 (since sustainability is consistent with increasing environmental assets) or coincident with it. We therefore need to investigate further the rationale for maintaining and improving existing levels of environmental assets.

Several observations are in order. First, existing stocks would generally be regarded as being below optimal stocks in many developing countries. For some Sahelian countries they are significantly below the optimum, in that desertification and deforestation actually threaten livelihoods (Falloux and Mukendi, 1988). Nor is there evidence that the further reduction of soil quality, tree cover or water supplies will result in some form of surplus which can be re-invested in other man-made capital assets. Therefore, to some extent, deliberations about what precisely constitutes an optimum are redundant in the contexts of these countries.

The second observation relates to the identification of the 'optimum' in Figure 1.1. To say that capital stocks 'should' be optimal is tautologous. The interesting feature of optimality is how the benefits of augmenting natural capital are calculated. The critical factor here is that the *multifunctionality* of natural resources needs to be recognized, including their role as integrated life support systems. Thus a cost–benefit analysis that compares the 'value' of, say, afforestation with the opportunity cost of land in terms of forgone development values needs more careful execution than might otherwise appear to be the case. How far life support functions, such as contributions to geochemical cycles, can be captured by cost–benefit is open to question. In the face of uncertainty and irreversibility, conserving what there is could be a sound risk-averse strategy. Put another way, even in countries where it might appear that we can *afford* to reduce natural capital stocks further, there are risks from so doing because of (a) our imperfect understanding of the life support functions of natural environments, (b) our lack of capability to substitute for those functions, even if their loss is reversible in theory, and (c) the fact that losses are often irreversible. There is therefore a rationale in terms of *uncertainty* and *irreversibility* for conserving the existing stock, at least until we have a clearer understanding of what the optimal stock is and how it might be identified.

A third observation is that optimality tends to be defined in terms of economic efficiency, whereas conservation of the natural capital stock, as we shall see, serves other social goals. That is, Figure 1.1 is helpful as far as it goes, but it does not embrace the 'non-efficiency' benefits of natural capital stocks. As we shall see, these include serving certain distributional goals, both within current generations and between current and future generations. Of course, we have to be sure that these non-efficiency goals cannot be served better by converting natural capital into man-made capital, an issue we return to.

A fourth reason for supposing that existing stocks are important arises from recent research on the use of willingness-to-pay and willingness-to-accept measures of benefit.[7] A simple conceptual basis for estimating a benefit is to find out what people are willing to pay to secure it. Thus, if we have an environmental asset and there is the possibility of increasing its size, a measure of the economic value of the increase in size will be the sums that people are willing to pay to ensure that the necessary land or other asset is obtained. Whether there is an actual market in the asset or not is not of great relevance. We can still find out what people would pay if only there were a market.[8] In the same way, if there is to be reduction in the size of the asset, we can ask what people are willing to accept to give it up. Economic theory predicts that the difference between the willingness to pay and willingness to accept measures (the 'equivalent and compensating variation' measures of welfare gain) will not differ significantly. That is, a measure of willingness to pay for a small gain will be approximately equal to the requirement for compensation to give up a small amount of an asset. Empirical work suggests otherwise, with very large discrepancies between willingness to pay and willingness to accept being recorded. Prospect theory offers a rationale for compensation requirements being very much larger. Essentially, what exists is seen as a reference point and attitudes to surrendering some of what is already owned or experienced are quite different to those that come into play when there is the prospect of a gain. Put another way, the valuation function B in Figure 1.1 is 'kinked' at the existing stock of assets. The result of modifying Figure 1.1 is shown in Figure 1.2. The existence of the kink means that the optimal level of K_N is likely to be at the point of the kink: existing and optimal natural capital stocks coincide. In terms of the 'constant capital' idea in sustainable development, it implies that a high valuation should be placed on reductions in the existing capital stock, thus supporting the view that conservation of existing stocks itself has a high priority.

Overall, while there is a powerful case in analytical economics for thinking in terms of maintaining optimal rather than existing natural capital stocks as the basic condition for sustainability, there are also sound reasons for conserving at least the existing capital stock. For poor countries dependent upon the natural resource base, optimal stocks will in any event be above the existing stock. In other cases, there is a rationale in terms of incomplete information about the

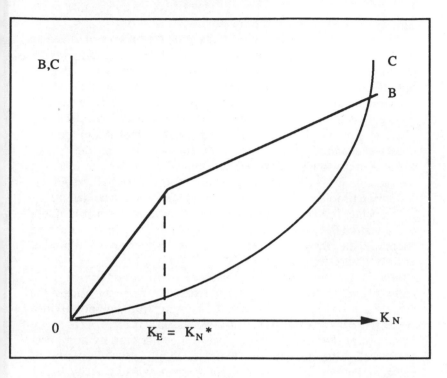

The benefit function of Figure 1.1 is now kinked at the existing stock of natural capital, making the existing and optimal stocks probably coincident.

Figure 1.2 Costs and benefits of conservation when the valuation function is kinked

benefits of conservation (the failure to appreciate and measure multifunctionality), uncertainty and irreversibility for conserving the existing stock. Additionally, resource conservation serves non-efficiency objectives, whereas optimality tends to be defined only in terms of efficiency. Finally, even in terms of efficiency, the existence of a valuation function which is kinked at the existing endowment of natural resources adds emphasis to the conservation of existing stocks.

The meaning of constant capital stock
Constancy of the natural capital stock can take on several different meanings. A common interpretation is in terms of constant *physical* capital stock. This is appealing for renewable resources, but, clearly, has little relevance to exhaustible resources since any positive rate of use reduces the stock. An alternative interpretation is in terms of a constant *economic value* of the stock. This allows for a declining physical stock with a rising real price over time, maintaining a constant economic value. The problem here is that the 'price' variable needs to be interpreted with considerable care to reflect all the economic values deriving from multifunctional resources. Valuation problems, especially with functions such as contributions to reducing future catastrophes, are formidable. An additional complication lies with the presence of discontinuities in the valuation function – i.e. threshold effects such that stocks below a minimum critical level result in major costs.[9]

A variant of the constant economic value concept is the view that a constant capital stock can be interpreted as one where the *price* of the stock remains constant over time.[10] The motivation behind this idea is that scarcity can often be effectively measured in terms of the price of a natural resource,[11] higher prices reflecting scarcity and lower prices reflecting abundance. This has some appeal in terms of exhaustible resources with uncertain reserves, where scarcity results in increased exploration effort or technological substitution. But for renewable resources, current prices are less likely to reflect future scarcity. As an example, fuelwood prices may remain constant in real terms, despite stock reductions, because the *flow* of harvest is not significantly affected. Price may then rise only as the last units of the resource are extracted.

A broader version of the constant value rule would require that the total value of *all* capital stocks be held constant, man-made and natural. Here the basic idea is that future generations would inherit a combined capital stock no smaller than the one in the previous generation. In this way, a depleted resource, say oil, would be compensated for by other investments generating the same income. This argument is considered in more detail shortly; but if it is to be advanced, it is clearly important that natural capital stocks be correctly valued, and that threshold effects be allowed for.

In general, there is no easy interpretation to the idea of a constant capital stock. Some combination of an equal value rule with indicators of physical stocks to allow for critical minimum stocks (which, in turn, might qualify as 'sustainability indicators') appears appropriate, but the issues have yet to be resolved.

More on the rationale for a constant capital stock

Conserving the natural capital stock serves goals which would command wide, though maybe not universal, assent.[12] Sustainable development based on this notion is consistent with:

- justice in respect of the socially disadvantaged;
- justice between generations;
- justice to nature;
- aversion to risk arising from our ignorance about the nature of interactions between environment, economy and society, and from the social and economic damage arising from low margins of resilience to external 'shocks' such as drought and plagues, or to 'stresses' such as soil erosion and agro-chemical residues;[13]
- economic efficiency.

As will become clear, the rationale for constant or increasing natural capital stock is likely to be stronger for some economies than it is for others at certain stages of development. We consider in turn each goal served by natural capital conservation.

Intragenerational equity

A constant or rising natural capital stock is likely to serve the goal of intragenerational fairness – i.e. justice to the socially disadvantaged both within any one country and between countries at a given point in time. The clearest evidence for this exists for poor developing economies in which direct dependence on natural resources is paramount. Examples include: reliance on biomass fuels such as fuelwood, crop residues and animal waste; reliance on untreated water supplies; dependence on natural fertilizers (organic materials) to maintain soil quality; fodder from natural vegetation for livestock; and wildlife meat for protein[14]. Table 1.1 illustrates this direct dependence.

The equity function of natural capital is less obvious for developed economies. Indeed the contrary view, that the demand for environmental assets is biased towards the rich, tends to define the

Table 1.1 *Direct dependence of selected developing countries on natural resources*

Country	Traditional fuel*	Irrigation water†	Drinking water‡
Ethiopia	89	n.a.	94
Nepal	93	n.a.	85
Sri Lanka	45	n.a.	64
India	n.a.	92	46
Indonesia	49	86	64
Philippines	n.a.	72	34
Bhutan	n.a.	n.a.	95

Notes:
*Traditional fuel consumption as a percentage of all primary energy consumption.
†Percentage of all water use accounted for by irrigation.
‡Percentage of population *without* access to drinking water.
Sources: UNICEF, *The State of the World's Children 1988*, Oxford, Oxford University Press, 1988; *Global 2000. Report to the President*, Harmondsworth, Penguin Books, 1982; World Bank/UNDP, *Energy Assessments*, for various countries.

conventional wisdom.[15] However, the evidence for supposing that there is a high income elasticity of demand – i.e. that the demand for environmental quality rises more than proportionately as income grows – is inconclusive.[16]

For the environment to be declared a 'pro-rich' good – i.e. one that the rich tend to consume proportionately more than the poor – we need evidence that the amount of environmental goods consumed tends to rise as a proportion of income as income increases. A feature of natural environments is that they tend to be 'public goods', goods that when supplied to one group of individuals are also supplied to others because of the inability to exclude the others from the benefits. Thus, if we improve air quality because one group of people mounts a campaign for a better environment, so others who may be indifferent to better air quality will also experience the improvement. There is no feasible mechanism for excluding them from the cleaner air. Public goods, then, have the attributes of 'jointness of supply' and 'non-excludability'. One implication is that if the rich wield more political power, they will 'force' more environmental quality on the poor than the poor wish to buy. Essentially, this is the argument of Baumol and Oates (1988). Many environmental assets tend to be 'local' rather than 'global' public goods. Air quality varies between areas, and one way in which the rich can buy higher air quality than the poor is to choose their work and housing locations accordingly. If everyone were free to move in response to regional variations in environmental quality, it seems more likely that each income group would consume the 'right' amount of environmental goods according to their preferences. In practice, we know that mobility is often limited by income and social constraints: the poor cannot move to more pleasant locations if they are away from business districts which, in turn, tend to be characterized by congestion, noise and pollution.

What little evidence we have tends to suggest that the *gross* benefits of environmental improvements are not systematically related to incomes. Reviewing the US literature, Pearce (1980) found that income elasticities for the benefits of the 1970 Clean Air Act in the USA were less than unity, implying that as income rose, so the proportion of environmental benefit to income fell. However, the costs of meeting the US air quality standards were *regressive* – i.e. the poor paid a greater proportion of their taxes in pollution abatement than did the rich, a reflection on the then US tax system. The net effect is that environmental quality does appear to be regressive in terms of the incidence of its *net* benefits; other studies, for example, of US water quality standards, offer no systematic pattern.

The evidence on the 'pro-rich' nature of localized environmental quality in the developed world is thus not compelling. For global environmental quality there is, as yet, no systematic study of the incidence of hypothesized impacts from, say, global warming, ozone depletion or ocean pollution. By the very nature of global pollution, it will be no respector of wealth or persons.

The general result therefore is that, as far as developing countries are concerned, environmental improvement is likely to be consistent with the goal of intragenerational equity, and very much so in the poorest agriculture-dependent economies. In the latter case, the 'environment-poverty trap' prevails: as poverty increases, natural environments are degraded to obtain immediate food supplies. As environments degrade, so the prospects for future livelihoods decrease: environmental degradation generates more poverty, thus accelerating the cycle. The provision of natural capital offers one way of breaking into the cycle. For the wealthy countries, the evidence for the positive equity function of environmental quality is inconclusive as far as localized environmental quality is concerned. For global pollution, the issue of the *incidence* of pollution has barely been studied.

Intergenerational equity

Although not intended for the purpose, Rawls's theory of justice offers a moral basis for arguing that the next generation should have access to at least the same resource base as the previous generation (Rawls, 1972; Page 1977). Rawls's 'maximin' strategy suggests that justice is to be equated with a bias in resource allocation to the least advantaged in society. Such a rule could emerge from a constitution drawn up by individuals brought together under a 'veil of ignorance' about where in society they would be allocated. Risk aversion dictates that the constitution-makers would avoid disadvantaging certain groups for fear that they themselves would be allocated to those groups. The intergenerational variant of the Rawls outcome simply extends the veil of ignorance to the intertemporal context in which each generation is ignorant of the time period to which it will be allocated.

Interpreted this way, there would appear to be no particular reason for focusing on *natural* capital as the instrument for achieving intergenerational equity. It might apply equally to man-made capital or to some composite of both types of capital. There are some reasons for supposing that natural capital is more important, however. First, natural capital may qualify as a Rawlsian 'primary good' – a good with the characteristic that any rational being would always prefer more of it to less. The life support functions of the natural environment would seem to fit this category since less of them would remove the very capability of choosing and having preferences. The ability to make a choice would, on this argument, have a higher ethical status than the rights and wrongs of making a particular choice. Secondly, natural capital differs from man-made capital in a crucial respect. Man-made capital is virtually always capable of symmetric variation – it can be increased or decreased at will. Natural capital is subject to *irreversibilities*, in that it can be decreased but often not increased if previous decrements lead to extinction. The primary good and irreversibility features of natural capital thus suggest that natural and man-made capital are substitutes only to a limited extent.

Natural capital and resilience
Both man-made and natural capital contribute to the resilience of an economy with respect to external acute or chronic shocks and stresses. At the starkest level, the larger the stock of natural capital, including working capital such as seed stocks and food security, the more likely it is that a poor agricultural country can withstand external shocks such as climatic variation and stresses such as international indebtedness. Man-made capital can serve these functions as well but tends to lack an important feature of natural capital – diversity. Some of the sustainable development literature stresses that resilience requires the adoption of 'ecologically sensitive' technologies adapted to local agro-ecological conditions (see especially Brown, 1981; World Commission on Environment and Development, 1987; IUCN, 1980). Therefore, animal draught power may be better than tractors. Organic fertilizer supplies nutrients and 'body' to the soil compared to the nutrient base only of artificial fertilizers. Run-off problems are risked with artificial fertilizers. In the poorest societies the man-made capital solution may not in any event be *feasible*, given the need to secure cash and foreign exchange. Natural capital augmentation then becomes the only route to sustainability and explains the current focus on agro-forestry, water harvesting techniques and 'socially relevant' technology.

Again, the rationale for natural capital conservation appears weaker for the developed world. Margins for flexibility are greater than in poorer countries where population growth and poor economic performance in general often produce very narrow risk margins in the face of external disturbances. But the comparative resilience of the developed world to such shocks and stresses may be illusory in the sense that the technologies used to advance economic progress have utilized *global common property* resources, notably the atmosphere and stratosphere for receiving air pollutants, and the oceans for liquid and solid effluents. The evidence of stress in those systems is now not disputed, as with ozone layer damage, the 'greenhouse effect', acid rain and major reductions in ocean biota diversity.

The resilience justification for conserving the natural capital stock is thus based on the idea that diverse ecological and economic systems are more resilient to shocks and stress. In turn, to maintain diversity it is essential to avoid irreversible choices. Since knowledge is rarely lost for ever, economic irreversibility is likely to be rare – a discontinued machine can be re-created, towns can be rebuilt, and so on. But ecological irreversibility is not unusual – natural species are lost every year, unique ecosystems are destroyed and environmental functions are irreparably damaged. All this suggests that we should only destroy natural capital stock if the benefits of so doing are very large. Put another way, destruction of irreversible natural capital stock should be avoided unless the social costs of conservation are unacceptably large. This basic rule defines the safe minimum standards (SMS) approach of Ciriacy-Wantrup (1952) and Bishop (1978). The SMS approach can be outlined as follows.

Consider a piece of land faced with two options: development (D) and preservation (P). If D occurs, the benefits of P (B_p) are lost forever. The benefits of preservation are uncertain, a feature of environmental assets that we have noted repeatedly. To make things simple, imagine that we can characterize this uncertainty by saying that 'yes' (Y) there are preservation benefits, and 'no' (N) there are no preservation benefits. The benefits of D (B_D) are known with certainty. The possibilities are given in the following matrix:

	Y	N	Maximum loss
D	B_P	o	B_P
P	$B_D - B_P$	B_D	B_D

For example, if we choose to develop the site (D) and the preservation benefits are positive, then we lose B_p. If we preserve (P) and there are positive preservation benefits, then we lose the development benefits but gain the preservation benefits. Thus the choice combination (P, Y) produces a maximum loss of $B_D - B_P$.

The idea underlying the calculation of the maximum losses, the last column in the matrix, is that we may wish to avoid these large losses. More formally, an attractive rule in the face of uncertainty and irreversibility is to minimize the maximum losses, or 'minimax'.

The SMS approach pays particular attention to the fact that the lower is B_D, the more is the minimax solution that is likely to be preferred. That is, we should ensure that B_D really is large before committing ourselves to irreversible losses of natural capital. The SMS approach thus urges caution about the alleged benefits of development, and 'raises the profile' of the environmental benefits of preservation. It thus reinforces the general idea developed in this chapter that conventional measures of costs and benefits need to be interpreted with caution because of the probable bias in favour of development benefits.

Economic efficiency
A superficial view of the comparative rates of return to augmenting man-made and natural capital suggests favouring the former. If the two forms of capital are substitutes, then this rate of return argument would imply expansion of the man-made capital stock at the expense of the environment. This view would characterize the traditional approach to economics and the environment in which economic change generally is at the expense of environmental quality.

Figure 1.3 suggests a way of conceptualizing the issue. The vertical axis shows K_M – man-made capital – while the horizontal axis shows K_N – natural capital. The 'trade-off' view is illustrated by curve AB: we cannot have more environmental capital without less man-made capital. Some of the sustainable development literature, however, argues that *Km* and *Kn* are *complements*. This idea is shown by the line OCD. It is likely that both characterizations of reality are false: it is difficult to see environment and development always as being in mutual harmony, and equally difficult to accept that environment always has to be sacrificed if we want economic progress. In so far as either is true, the complementarity hypothesis is more correct for countries at an early stage of development, and the trade-off approach is more correct for countries in the later stages.

The existence of a trade-off does not imply that a path of development from, say, C to A in Figure 1.3, is better than one from C to B. It simply illustrates possibilities. To obtain prescriptions we need some information on the productivity of each type of capital and on social preferences. None the less, some observations would appear to be in order.

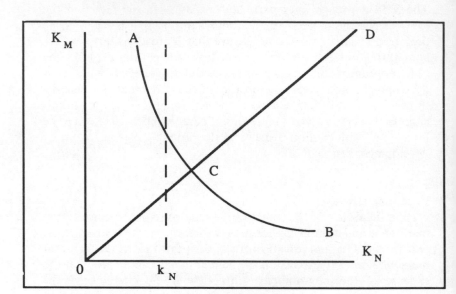

Figure 1.3   Environment and development trade-off and complementarity

For example, past development policy has been wrongly biased towards K_M. Man-made capital tends to be a marketed product whereas K_N tends to yield environmental services, for which there is no market and hence no perceived price. Since the price of K_N falsely appears to be lower than it should, more of K_N will be used relative to K_M. Nor is there adequate incentive to augment natural capital since increments in it will, partly, yield non-marketed outputs and services which have no price. Hence revenues will be associated with K_N investment which understate, often considerably, the rate of return to K_N augmentation. In part, this bias reflects the primacy of markets ('misplaced concreteness'), but it also reflects our ignorance of the multiple functions of natural systems. Investing in wetlands rehabilitation, for example, may yield cash flows for fisheries and recreation (to some extent), but it also yields non-marketed outputs such as hydrological protection, water purification, inland storm protection, etc. Efforts to put economic values on these non-marketed functions, and even to trace through otherwise disguised market functions of natural systems, demonstrate that the 'true' rate of return to investment in K_N is significantly higher than concentration of market outputs would suggest.[17]

The economic efficiency argument does not therefore favour K_M over K_N if the two compete for investment funds. What is needed is a more comprehensive valuation of the economic services provided by natural capital systems. There may also be some minimum stock of K_N below which no nation should go if it is to avoid major disruption – i.e. a point below which reductions in natural capital produce unacceptably large social costs. In Figure 1.3 this 'safe minimum standard' is illustrated by the line k_N.

Time and sustainable development

The emphasis on sustainability implies a greater concern for the future and for the inhabitants of the future than has characterized past models of the development process. It may not be too unfair to suggest that previous models of the development process have tended to assume that the 'future will look after itself', whereas the sustainable development approach acknowledges that the ability of the future to do this can be seriously impaired by actions taken now. In this sense, sustainable development does not give *greater* weight to the future than other development approaches: it simply points out that the *factual* assumption that future generations *would* be able to choose as freely as a current generation is not likely to be correct. None the less, a good deal of the sustainability literature focuses on the idea of weighting future generations' preferences more highly than the conventional political process might do. Because of this, it has targeted the practice of *discounting the future*, a standard feature of the economic approach to intertemporal decision-making, for special criticism. In view of that, then, we turn our attention in Chapter 2 to the rationale for discounting and the environmental critique of that rationale.

Notes

1. As an exception, we cite the work of Gordon Conway. Conway's approach has been applied at regional and local level in several developing countries and is based on the idea of sustainability as resilience within agroecosystems to external 'shocks' such as drought and pests; see Conway (1985, 1987).
2. For elaboration and further discussion, see Barbier (1987, 1988).
3. The measure most widely entertained as a single indicator is real income per capita. On this debate see Stewart (1985) and Lal (1988).

4. For the potential inconsistency between present value maximization and sustainability see Clark (1976) and Page (1977).
5. See e.g. O'Riordan (1988).
6. For discussion of the concept of total economic value see Pearce (1987).
7. See Knetsch and Sinden (1984) and Knetsch (1988). The psychological underpinnings of the disparity between the payment and compensation required measures of value lie in prospect theory: see Kahneman and Tversky (1979). For the view that the disparity is not as marked as might be thought see Brookshire and Coursey (1987) and Coursey, Hovis and Schulze (1987).
8. The techniques for doing this are reviewed in Pearce and Markandya (1989).
9. On the notion of 'safe minimum standards' for environmental capital see Bishop (1978).
10. See Page (1977).
11. For the rationale for using prices as a measure of scarcity see Barnett and Morse (1963) and Hall and Hall (1984).
12. A somewhat different rationale to that given here argues that it is the stock of assets rather than the flow of services from that stock that contributes to human welfare: see Boulding (1966).
13. On the distinction between shocks and stresses see Conway (1987) and Barbier (1988).
14. See Pearce (1986) for empirical evidence on direct dependence on natural resources.
15. For the conventional view see Baumol and Oates (1988, ch. 15).
16. The discussion that follows is based on Pearce (1980).
17. For a demonstration of this in the context of arid zone afforestation see Anderson (1987).

References

Anderson, D. (1987), *The Economics of Afforestation*, Baltimore, Md: Johns Hopkins University Press.
Barbier, E. (1987), 'The concept of sustainable economic development', *Environmental Conservation*, 14, 101–10.
Barbier, E. (1981), 'Sustainable resource management as a factor in international economic security', paper presented at Centre for Economic Policy Research Workshop on Economic Aspects of International Security, London, March.
Barnett, H. and Morse, C. (1963), *Scarcity and Growth: The Economics of Natural Resource Availability*, Baltimore, Md: Johns Hopkins University Press.
Baumol, W. and Oates, W. (1988), *The Theory of Environmental Policy, Cambridge*: Cambridge University Press.
Berry, R. J. (1977), *The Social Burdens of Environmental Pollution*, Cambridge, Mass.: Ballinger.
Bishop, R. (1978), 'Endangered species and uncertainty: the economics of a safe minimum standard', *American Journal of Agricultural Economics*, 60, 10–13.
Boulding, K. (1966), 'The economics of the coming Spaceship Earth', in H. Jarrett (ed.), *Environmental Quality in a Growing Economy*, Baltimore, Md: John Hopkins University Press, 3–14.
Brookshire, D. and Coursey, D., 'Measuring the value of a public good: an empirical comparison of elicitation procedures', *American Economic Review*, 77 (4), September, 554–66.
Brown, L. (1981), *Building a Sustainable Society*, New York: Norton.
Ciriacy-Wantrup, S. V. (1952), *Resource Conservation: Economics and Policies*, Berkeley, Calif.: University of California Press.

Clark, C. (1976), *Mathematical Bioeconomics*, New York: Wiley.
Conway, G. (1987), 'The Properties of Agroecosystems', *Agricultural Systems*, 24, 95–117.
Conway, G. (1985), 'Agroecosystem analysis', *Agricultural Administration*, 20, 31–55.
Coursey, D., Hovis, J. and Schulze, W. (1987), 'The disparity between willingness to accept and willingness to pay measures of value', *Quarterly Journal of Economics*, CII, 679–90.
Falloux, F. and Mukendi, A. (eds) (1988), *Desertification Control and Renewable Resource Management in the Sahelian and Sudanian Zones of West Africa*, World Bank Technical Paper No. 70, World Bank, Washington DC.
Hall, D. and Hall J. (1984), 'Concepts and measures of natural resource scarcity with a summary of recent trends', *Journal of Environmental Economics and Management*, 11, 363–79.
International Union for the Conservation of Nature (IUCN) (1980), *World Conservation Strategy*, Gland, Switzerland: IUCN.
Kahneman, D. and Tversky, A. (1979), 'Prospect theory: an analysis of decision under risk', *Econometrica*, 47, 263–91.
Knetsch, J. (1988), 'Environmental and economic impact assessments and the divergence between willingness to pay and compensation demanded measures of loss', paper presented at Canadian Environmental Assessment Research Council, Conference on Integrating Environmental and Economic Assessments, Vancouver, November.
Knetsch, J. and Sinden, J. (1984), 'Willingness to pay and compensation demanded: experimental evidence of an unexpected disparity in measures of value', *Quarterly Journal of Economics*, XCIX, 507–21.
Lal, D. (1988), 'Structural adjustment, the basic needs approach and development policy', *Estudios de Economía*, December.
O'Riordan, T. (1988), 'The politics of sustainability', in R. K. Turner (ed.), *Sustainable Environmental Management*, London: Belhaven Press, and Boulder, Colo: Westview Press, 29–50.
Page, T. (1977), *Conservation and Economic Efficiency*, Baltimore, Md: Johns Hopkins University Press.
Pearce, D. W. (1980), 'The social incidence of environmental costs and benefits', in T. O'Riordan and R. K. Turner (eds), *Progress in Resource Management and Environmental Planning*, Chichester: Wiley, Vol. 2.
Pearce, D. W. (1986), 'The economic consequences of natural resource degradation', Environment Department, World Bank, Washington, DC, mimeo.
Pearce, D. W. (1987), *Economic Values and the Natural Environment*, The Denman Lecture, University of Cambridge, February 1987.
Pearce, D. W. (1988), 'The sustainable use of natural resources in developing countries', in R. K. Turner (ed.), *Sustainable Environmental Management*, London: Belhaven Press, and Boulder, Colo: Westview Press, 102–17.
Pearce, D. W. and Markandya, A. (1989), *The Benefits of Environmental Policy*, Paris: OECD.
Rawls, J. (1972), *A Theory of Justice*, Oxford: Oxford University Press.
Redclift, M. (1987), *Sustainable Development: Exploring the Contradictions*, London: Methuen.
Repetto, R. (1986), *World Enough and Time*, New Haven, Conn.: Yale University Press.
Stewart, F. (1985), *Planning to Meet Basic Needs*, London: Macmillan.
Stockholm Group for Studies on Natural Resource Management (1988), *Perspectives of Sustainable Development*, Stockholm Group, Stockholm.

Turner, R. K. (ed.) (1988), *Sustainable Environmental Management*, London: Belhaven Press, and Boulder, Col: Westview Press.

World Commission on Environment and Development (1987), *Our Common Future* (The 'Brundtland Report'), Oxford University Press.

2   Discounting the future

Introduction

Chapter 1 has outlined an approach to economic and environmental stability based on the concept of 'sustainability', which was interpreted as requiring some constancy in the stock of natural environmental assets. The literature on sustainable development widely entertains an alternative notion, namely that conventional approaches to economic and social evaluation would be appropriate or, at least, more appropriate, if they dispensed with the notion of discounting future gains and losses. Not to discount effectively means that a unit of gain or loss in the future has the same weight as a unit of gain or loss in the present. In this way, future generations are not discriminated against, or so it seems. In this chapter, and in Chapter 3, we outline the rationale for using discount rates and the methods by which they are calculated; and re-evaluate them from an environmental perspective. The issues are complex, involving philosophical and economic considerations that cannot be simplified without danger of trivialization. However, they are important and lie at the centre of the intellectual debate on the balance between the needs of present and future generations, which is so critical to the issue of the environment. Hence it is important to consider them carefully and see how best they can be resolved.

We begin by explaining what discount rates are, why they arise and how they are determined. This is, of course, familiar ground to any economist and the treatment given here is very superficial. Any one who wants a more complete discussion of the issues in their own right should read Squire and van der Tak (1975) and Lind (1982). Our purpose is to explain the basic ideas sufficiently, so that we can examine the environmental critiques of discounting, and this chapter is devoted to doing just that. Overall, our conclusion is that – environmental considerations notwithstanding – the use of positive discount rates is justified. We do accept that such rates as are conventionally used in making investment decisions may be too high and some reduction in the discount rate may be justified. But this reduction is justified for *all* investments, not just those involving environmental costs and benefits. We would argue that there is no compelling case for treating the latter differently, and indeed there are better ways of dealing with environmental issues in investment and resource management policy than by adjusting the discount rate. These alternatives are discussed in Chapter 3.

Discount rates and resource allocation
Very broadly, discount rates are a mechanism by which we can compare the value of economic resources and services at different points in time. The basic premiss is that a certain resource utilized today (either in a production- or consumption-related activity) has a higher value than the same resource used at some point in the future. Two justifications are offered for this. One is that individuals are 'impatient' and would generally prefer a pound today rather than in, say, a year's time. Conversely, they would need more than a pound in a year's time in order to induce them to give up a pound today. This impatience, referred to by economists as 'time preference', is used as an argument in favour of placing a lower value on future goods and services than on present ones. The second argument for discounting is that since capital is productive, a pound's worth of resources will generate more than a pound's worth of goods and services in the future. Hence an entrepreneur would be willing to pay more than a pound to acquire a pound's worth of such resources now. This argument for discounting is referred to as the 'marginal productivity of capital' (the word 'marginal' indicating that *additional* units of investment have this property).

The percentage amount by which we reduce the value of a flow of income between two time periods is referred to as the *discount rate*. As a convention, this period is usually one year, and so if one dollar today is considered to be worth the same as 95 cents in one year's time, the discount rate is said to be 5 per cent.[1] For periods of more than a year, the formula is applied successively. So, if the discount rate is constant at 5 per cent, then a dollar today is worth 95 cents in one year's time and that, in turn, is worth 5 per cent less at the end of the second year – i.e. 95 × 0.95, or 90.25 cents. One can see that this successive application of the 'discount factor' is going to reduce the value of future incomes at a geometric rate. After 10 years the discount factor would be 0.95^{10}, or 0.60, and a dollar received then would be worth 60 cents. After 50 years, the factor would be 0.076, and after 100 years, 0.006. Moreover, the higher the rate of discount, the discount factor diminishes at a faster rate. It is this property of discounting that is the cause of more criticism than any other from the environmentalists.

The commonest (but by no means the only) use of discount rates is in appraising investments. By applying a discount factor to the difference between costs and benefits in each of the years one obtains a single value of the net benefits of the project, referred to as the 'net present value'. If we accept the validity of this discounting procedure, it is clear that a positive net present value is necessary for the project to be implemented.[2] In addition, discount rates have a number of other applications. The same kind of analysis can be carried out for evaluating regulatory policy (including conservation measures) in a fairly obvious way. It can also be used to decide on the rate of extraction of an exhaustible resource and the rate of exploitation of a renewable resource. The relationship between the management of these resources and the rate of discount is discussed later in this chapter.

The choice of the discount rate
What value the discount rate should take has been the subject of much debate among economists. Excluding questions of risk, which are discussed further below, the two basic candidates are the *consumption rate of interest*, which is based on the rate of time preference and the *opportunity cost of capital*, which is based on the marginal productivity of capital.[3] In the simplest of economies, with no taxes and no distortions in the capital markets, the levels of savings and investment would adjust, so that the two rates were equal. Then there would be difficulty in choosing between them. But real world economies are more complex than that and the two rates diverge, with the opportunity cost of capital being, in most cases, higher than the consumption rate of interest. In these circumstances, there is no generally agreed way of determining the discount rate. Much of the discussion is concerned with the *sources* from which the investment funds are drawn and the *uses* to which the benefits are put. This is not the appropriate place to go through these complex arguments, but it is worth noting that even before the environmental issues have been raised, there is a lack of agreement on how the discount rate should be determined. However, since it is precisely with the relationship between environmental considerations and

discounting that we are concerned, it is in the context of these that we will examine the arguments for the use of different (or indeed any) discount rates.

A re-analysis of the rationale for discounting

One important feature of the literature on environment, natural resources and development is its re-questioning of the fundamental arguments for discounting. This re-analysis arises partly because of the alleged 'discrimination' of conventional discount rate selection processes against the 'interests' of the environment, and partly because concern for natural environments is often (but not always) associated with an ethical stance on intergenerational justice. As an example of the former, high discount rates tend to encourage early, rather than later, depletion of exhaustible natural resources (this general proposition is further discussed later in this chapter). As an example of the latter, it is widely argued that, say, investment in nuclear power shifts forward in time the costs associated with that energy source, notably waste management and decommissioning. The use of positive discount rates, and particularly rates in the region of 10 per cent – a fairly typical practical rate – plays down future benefits that may be forgone, as well as future costs that may be incurred, to the detriment of future generations.

In fact there is no unique relationship between high discount rates and environmental deterioration, as is often supposed. High rates may well shift cost burdens forward to later generations, but if the discount rate is allowed to determine the level of investment, they will also slow down the general pace of development through the depressing effect on investment.[4] Since natural resources are required for investment, a relationship established in the environmental economics literature through the mass balance principle, the *demand* for natural resources is generally less with high discount rates than with low ones. High rates will also discourage development projects that compete with existing environmentally benign land uses – e.g. watershed development as opposed to an existing wilderness use. Exactly how the choice of discount rate impacts on the *overall* profile of natural resource and environment use in any country is thus ambiguous. This point is important since it reduces considerably the force of arguments to the effect that conventionally determined discount rates should be lowered (or raised, depending on the view taken) to accommodate environmental considerations.

None the less, it is the case that concern for the environmental dimension of development policy has led to a questioning of the basic rationale for discounting. We outline below some of the points that have been raised. *Note that what is being argued generally is that if we cannot substantiate the case for positive discounting, the presumption must be that a zero discount rate is, initially anyway, the more appropriate choice.* We consider the objections to the arguments in turn for discounting under four headings, as follows.

Pure time preference

As we have pointed out above, individuals are impatient and prefer the present to the future. Since it is further argued that society is no more than the sum of its individuals, it also prefers the present to the future. This temporal preference translates into a positive discount rate. As a fact of human nature, no one appears to deny the impatience principle. Furthermore, the dominant underlying value judgement of Western economic philosophy is that people's preferences should count. Hence it is difficult to argue with the proposition that if people prefer the present over the future, for whatever reasons, then pure time preference indicates that discount rates are positive.

Nevertheless, arguments against permitting pure time preference to influence social discount rates have been made and can be summarised as follows. First, individual time preference is not necessarily consistent with individual lifetime welfare maximisation (Strotz, 1956). The proof is complex, and a fairly intuitive version is given in Krutilla and Fisher (1985). This is a variant of the more general view that time discounting, because of impatience, is generally irrational (Jevons, 1871; Bohm-Bawerk, 1884; Ramsey, 1929; Pigou, 1932). Secondly, what individuals want carries no necessary implications for public policy. This amounts, of course, to a rejection of the underlying value judgement of the individualistic liberal economic tradition. Third, the underlying value judgement is improperly expressed. A society that elevates want-satisfaction to high status should recognise that it is the satisfaction of wants *as they arise* that matters. But this means that tomorrow's satisfaction matters, not today's assessment of tomorrow's satisfaction (Goodin, 1986).

What view is taken on the normative relevance of pure time preference depends on the acceptability of one or more of these objections. We would argue that to overturn the basic value judgement underlying the liberal economic tradition requires good reason: that is, the rationale for paternalism should be a strong one. We would surmise that such arguments do exist, but considering the context of development, one has to weigh carefully the contrasting forces of meeting basic needs and diverting resources to long-term development potential: the former might favour accepting pure time preference, the latter might not. Philosophically, the argument that the value judgement needs re-expressing in line with the third observation, above, is impressive. In practical terms, however, the immediacy of wants in many developing countries where environmental problems are serious might favour the retention of the usual formulation of the basic judgement.

Risk and uncertainty
Since Bentham in 1789, it has been argued that a benefit or cost is valued less the more uncertain is its occurrence. Since uncertainty is usually expected to increase with time from the present, this declining value becomes a function of time and hence is formally expressible in the form of an additional discount factor for risk and uncertainty.

The types of uncertainty that are generally regarded as being of relevance (although they are very often confused) are:

1. uncertainty about the presence of the individual at some future date (the 'risk of death' argument);
2. uncertainty about the preferences of the individual even when his existence can be regarded as certain;
3. uncertainty about the availability of the benefit or the existence of the cost.

The objections to using uncertainty to justify positive discount rates are several.

First, consider the uncertainty arising from not being sure that the individual will be present to receive a distant benefit – the 'risk of death' argument. This is often used as a rationale for the impatience principle itself, the argument being that a preference for consumption now rather than in the future is partly based on the fact that one may not be alive in the future to enjoy the benefits of one's restraint.

The criticism of this line of reasoning is that although the individual is mortal, and should properly take account of his mortality in his personal decisions, 'society' is not mortal in the same way. Hence its decisions should not necessarily be based on the same impatience principle.

Secondly, uncertainty about preferences is clearly relevant if we are talking about certain goods and, perhaps, even aspects of environmental conservation (as the 'environmentalism' of the 1970s and 1980s demonstrates), but hardly seem relevant if we are considering projects or policies whose output is food, shelter, water and energy. If anything, we can be more sure of future preferences for these goods, not less (Barry, 1977).

The third kind of uncertainty is generally acknowledged to be relevant, but the difficulty is that if it is allowed for by raising the discount rate, then this is tantamount to assuming a specific kind of relationship between time and uncertainty. In particular, it is being assumed that the scale of risk increases exponentially with time. There is no reason to believe that the risk factor takes this particular form and so the allowance for it through a single discount rate adjustment is invalid.

In conclusion, what is being argued here is not that uncertainty and risk are irrelevant to the *decision-guiding rule*, for resource allocation, but that their presence should not be handled by adjustments to the discount rate. For such adjustments imply a particular behaviour for the risk premium which it is hard to justify. This argument is in fact widely accepted by economists (Dasgupta and Pearce, 1972; Stiglitz, 1986), although it is still quite common among policy-makers. For example, there is a 2 per cent 'premium' attached to the officially recommended 5 per cent 'test discount rate' in the UK in the presence of 'benefit optimism' (UK Treasury, 1980).

If uncertainty does not take on a form consistent with exponential increase, the suggestion is that risk and uncertainty are better handled by other means – i.e. via adjustments to cost and benefit streams, leaving the underlying discount rate unadjusted for risk. This argument seems to us to be correct. It is worth noting, however, that adding a premium to the discount rate for risk *is* widely recommended. Annexe 2.1 outlines the formal procedure for making adjustments to discount rates for risk, but the calculation involved is complex, and requires information that could be directly used to evaluate the risk aspect of the project.

Table 2.1   Illustrative social time preference rates for sub-Saharan countries (based on 1973–83 data) (percentages)

	g	Social time preference rate for	
		$\mu = 1, \tau = 1$	$\mu = 1, \tau = 5$
Low-income countries	−1.9	−0.9	+3.1
Middle-income countries	−0.1	+0.9	+4.9

Source: Based on data in World Bank, *World Development Report 1985.*

Diminishing marginal utility of consumption
Earlier in this chapter we stated that there were two candidates for 'the discount rate'. One was based on the rate of time preference, and the other on the marginal productivity of capital. From the former is derived the *social rate of time preference*, which attempts to measure the rate at which the welfare, or utility, of consumption falls over time. Clearly this will depend on the rate of time preference, but it will also depend on how fast consumption is expected to grow, and on how fast utility falls as consumption grows. In Annexe 2.2 it is shown that the formula for the social time preference rate *i* is:

$$i = \mu g + \tau$$

Where τ is the pure time preference rate, g the rate of growth of real consumption per capita and μ the percentage fall in the *additional* utility or welfare derived from each 1 per cent increase in consumption. (Technically this is referred to as the elasticity of the marginal utility of consumption schedule.) With no growth in consumption, the social rate of time preference is equal to the rate of pure time preference, but if consumption is growing, the discount rate is higher than the rate of time preference. Intuitively, the reason for this is that the more one has in the future, the less one is willing to sacrifice today to obtain even more in the future. Moreover this impact is greater, the faster marginal utility falls with consumption.

What kind of discount rates would such a formula imply? It was conceived in the context of growing economies, but it is interesting and instructive to look at the implied rates for those countries where there have been severe environmental problems and where the growth rate has in fact been negative over the recent past. Data from the sub-Saharan countries as a group are presented in Table 2.1 for the period 1973-83. Two important points arise. First, growth in real consumption per capita was negative over this period both for the low- and middle-income countries. Taking a typical estimate of the elasticity of the marginal utility of consumption schedule as one, a pure time preference rate (τ) of 1 per cent yields a social discount rate which is negative for the low-income countries and only marginally positive for the middle-income countries.[5] The second point arises from the objective to the realism of such low rates: surely a value for τ of only 1 per cent is unrealistic? Such an objection arises from either the casual observation that individuals do not engage in e.g. sustainable farming practices, and hence have high implied personal time preference rates, or inspection of prevailing interest rates, particularly in rural areas. The final column shows the effect of raising the pure rate to 5 per cent. Note that even at this rate we are not close to the kinds of discount rate widely used for project appraisal in such countries. To get to rates of 10-15 per cent we require that τ increase to 12-17 per cent in the low-income case and 10-15 per cent in the middle-income case.

Assuming that it is legitimate to include pure time preference rates at all, are such rates realistic? Many would argue that they are because the mere presence of poverty itself induces high discount rates as concern is focused on food security over the next year or even few months rather than the long term. Proponents of the mortality-based time preference rates would argue that risk of mortality is also higher the poorer is the country, so that pure time preference will be high on these arguments.

There is, however, a problem with inferring high time preference rates from the observation of poverty, particularly so in the context of environmental problems. High discount rates are a *cause* of much environmental degradation as individuals opt for (totally understandable) short-term measures designed to satisfy immediate wants, and at the expense of sustainable practices. This much is established in the literature on resource degradation in poor countries (e.g. Pearce, 1987b). But, in turn, poor prospects arising from environmental degradation actually assist in generating the poverty that 'causes' high discount rates. The apparently high values of τ are not independent of the environmental conditions. To use those rates to *evaluate* environmentally oriented investments (e.g. soil conservation measures, afforestation, water harvesting, etc.) is to commit a basic error of analysis.

What can we conclude on diminishing marginal utility? Its suitability as a source of discounting appears to be reasonably unambiguous only in contexts where we can reliably expect sustainable changes in real consumption per capita. In countries where environmental damage is high, those conditions may well not pertain. The apparent rescue for the utility-discounting argument arises from inferring high pure time preference rates in those contexts, perhaps citing the argument that only high rates will explain some of the environmental degradation. But the discount rate in such circumstances is not independent of the conditions in question, so that one cannot infer the 'desirability' of such degradation from the inferred discount rates, nor the relative undesirability of conservation investment.

If high personal time preference rates are allowed to influence the value of i, the implication may therefore be that the discount rate unjustly reflects constrained activity, a situation where individuals are unable to act in a normal economic and environmental framework. This raises questions about the validity of such rates, perhaps abandoning the search for a social time preference rate altogether, or modifying the choice of rate to reflect the constraints on behaviour. The problem then is that there are no clear rules for choosing a discount rate. Essentially, g and τ in the social time preference rate formula are not independent: the lower are the expected values of g, the higher τ will be. At the very least, then, advocacy of the use of social time preference rates requires some downward adjustment of τ in contexts where the environment–poverty linkage is a strong one.

Opportunity cost of capital

The arguments in favour of using an opportunity cost of capital to determine the discount rate have already been discussed. In a practical sense, particularly in the context of project appraisal, the position taken by many economists is that the 'proper' social rate of discount is the rate of return on the best alternative project that is being displaced by the investment in question. In developing countries where there is a shortage of capital, these rates tend to be very high and this explains, in part, why institutions such as the World Bank use discount rates of 10 per cent and higher to decide on their lending policies in such countries.

The environmental literature has made some limited attempts to discredit discounting due to opportunity cost arguments (Parfit, 1983; Goodin, 1986). This literature is, however, confusing since most of the objections arise because the *implication* of opportunity cost discounting is that some rate greater than zero emerges and this is then held to be inconsistent with a concept of intergenerational justice. This aspect of the debate is considered in Chapter 3. However, there do appear to be two criticisms which are generally, but not wholly, independent of this wider concern.

The first arises because the discount *factor* arising from a constant discount *rate* takes on a specific negative exponential form. This is because discounting is simply the reciprocal of compound interest. In turn, compound interest implies that if we invest £100 today, it will compound forward at a particular rate, *provided* we keep not just the original £100 invested, but also re-invest the profits. Now suppose the profits are consumed rather than re-invested. The critics suggest that this means that those consumption flows have no opportunity cost. What, they say, is the relevance of a discount rate based on assumed re-invested profits if in fact the profits are not re-invested but consumed. Thus in the context of considering an airport that destroys beautiful countryside Parfit states:

> If we do not build the airport, such benefits would be enjoyed in each future year. At any discount rate, the benefits in later years count for much less than the benefits next year. How can an appeal to opportunity costs justify this? The benefits received next year – our enjoyment of this natural beauty – cannot be profitably reinvested. (Parfit, 1983)

If the argument is correct, it provides a reason for not using a *particular* rate – the opportunity cost rate – for discounting streams of consumption flows as opposed to streams of profits which are always re-invested. But, in that context, it would not provide a reason for rejecting *discounting* altogether since consumption flows should be discounted at a social time preference rate (or 'consumption rate of interest'). That is, the critics have not seen that a future loss of benefits *is* worth less than a current loss if we admit any of the arguments for a social time preference rate. As it happens, the particular critics in question would not admit to believing the arguments for time preference rates either, so their position would be consistent.

The second argument relates to intertemporal compensation. Consider an investment which has an expected environmental damage of £X in some future time period T. Should this £X be discounted to a present value? The argument for doing so on opportunity cost grounds is presumably something like the following. If we debit the investment with a social cost *now* of $£X/(1 + r)^T$, then that sum can be invested at $r\%$ now and it will grow to be £X in year T and can then be used to compensate the future sufferers of the environmental damage. Parfit (*ibid.*) states that this argument has confused two issues. The first is whether the future damage matters less than current damage of a similar scale. The second is whether we can devise schemes to compensate for future damage. The answer to the first question, he argues, is that it does not matter less than current damage, or if it does, it matters less only because we are *able* to compensate the future as shown. If we are not able to make the compensation, the argument for being less concerned – and hence the argument for discounting – becomes irrelevant.

The problem here is that actual and 'potential' compensation are being confused. As typically interpreted, cost–benefit rules, which guide investment decisions, require only that we could, hypothetically, compensate losers, not that we actually do. In this case, the resource cost to the current generation of hypothetically compensating a future generation is, quite correctly, the discounted value of the compensation. Really what Parfit is objecting to, we suggest, is the absence of built-in *actual* compensation mechanisms in cost–benefit appraisals. We have considerable sympathy with that view, but it is *not* relevant to the issue of how to choose a discount rate.

These particular arguments against opportunity cost related discounting are not, in our view, persuasive. It seems fair to say, however, they are not regarded by their advocates as the most forceful that can be advanced against discount rates *per se*. Those rest with arguments about intergenerational justice, and these are dealt with in Chapter 3.

Conclusions on the 'environmental critiques' of discounting
The environmental debate has undoubtedly contributed to intellectual soul-searching on the rationale for discounting. But, in our view, it has not been successful in demonstrating a case for rejecting discounting as such. It does raise issues of concern with respect to the use of rates of interest which reflect pure time preference, but it does not provide a case for rejecting pure time preference completely. It also raises further concerns about the compatibility of time prefer-

ence-based discounting and opportunity cost discounting, especially in the context of poor developing countries. For as we have seen, utility-of-consumption arguments may well suggest very low discount rates (ignoring pure time preference), whereas opportunity cost arguments might suggest very much higher ones. We further observed that traditional arguments for securing 'risk premia' on discount rates are fallacious: risk and uncertainty are properly handled in investment appraisal through adjustments to costs and benefits streams, not the discount rate. Lastly, we found environmental critiques of opportunity cost rates wanting (deferring consideration, however, of the wider intergenerational arguments until Chapter 3). As we shall argue, the environmental critique that discount rates are in some sense 'too high' reflects real concerns. But these are better dealt with not by adjusting discount rates, but through other means that we shall describe.

Discounting and natural resources

So far the discussion has been in terms of environmental effects, in general, and their impact on discount rates. However, there are one set of such effects that merit special consideration. These are the repercussions of the discount rate on the management of natural resources. The choice of the discount rate has a particular effect on the rate of exploitation of natural resources. The basic decision with regard to such resources is how much to consume now and how much to hold in store for future consumption. It is intuitively clear that this decision is going to be influenced by the price of present vs future consumption – i.e. the discount rate. In Annexe 2.3 (p. 51) we present a formal derivation of the two rules determining the optimal depletion of exhaustible resources (minerals, fossil energy) and the optimal use of renewable resources (a fishery, forest, hunting species, etc.). The rules are derived in a simple context. A fuller and more complex analysis can be found in Clark (1976).

The main point to note with regard to exhaustible resources is that the higher the discount rate, the faster is the rate of depletion of the resource in the earlier years, and the shorter is the interval before which the resource is exhausted. With a higher discount rate, a lower value is placed on future consumption relative to present consumption. Hence it is fairly clear that an optimal depletion policy, which seeks to maximize the discounted net benefits from a given stock of the resource, will prefer present consumption as the discount rate rises.

With renewable resources, the discount rate determines the rate of harvesting. It is shown in Annexe 2.3 that the higher this rate, the more intense is the harvesting effort, and so the smaller is the stock which will exist. In general the 'optimal' consumption of the resource requires a sustainable rate of use of the resource. This means that in the long run the rate of harvesting must equal the rate of regeneration. However, it is possible, if the discount rate rises above the maximum biological growth rate of the stock, that under certain conditions the resource will be depleted and extinguished altogether.

These features of optimal resource use have several implications for resource management policy. The first is that investments in the resource exploiting activity need to pay special attention to the effects of a chosen discount rate on the time profile of benefits and costs. The discount rate and the cost–benefit stream are no longer independent as in the other cases so far considered. For example, if one is evaluating two projects, one of which exhausts a resource in 10 years and the other does so over 25 years, then the higher the discount rate, the more likely one is to favour the former to the latter. High discount rates can prevail in capital markets for a number of reasons, such as macroeconomic policy and 'capital rationing'. These may be fully justified in those contexts but may have undesirable consequences for projects involving natural resources.

For renewable resources, a high enough discount rate can result in the resource being exhausted. Commercial logging operations evaluated at high discount rates could prove justified without replanting provisions (indeed this is more likely to be the case, given the normal time horizon over which such appraisals are made). As with exhaustible resources, this implies that the planning process can involve discount rates that do not pay adequate attention to the longer-term objectives of resource management.[6]

Apart from public investment appraisal, the exploitation of natural resources is also affected by the difference between the private rate of discount and the social rate. If the former is believed to be much higher than the latter, then resources in private hands will be overexploited. Methods for correcting this overexploitation have been discussed extensively elsewhere (see Pearce, 1987a; Repetto, 1986). In general, however, it does not involve changing the private discount rate. The reasons for this rate being too high are pervasive in the whole economy, and the rate itself is not easily manipulated. However, resource conservation can be achieved by the appropriate use of resource taxes, so that the government can 'capture' more of the economic rent arising from the resource development. Apart from slowing down this development where desirable, it also has the advantage of mobilizing resources for government use in a particularly efficient way.

Overall, the issue of discount rates is of particular importance with regard to natural resource management. High discount rates can result in policies that are not desirable from an intertemporal point of view. The question that follows, then, is should one use a lower discount rate in appraising these projects or not? And if not, then what other policies are available? In our view, the use of a lower discount rate is not the best policy to follow. To begin with, there is the question of which project should qualify. Inevitably there will be grey areas, causing further problems. Secondly, there are a number of situations in which private decisions are central to the resource exploitation problem, and discount rate changes for these groups are not a practicable or efficient policy. Thirdly, even if one used lower discount rates, there is no guarantee that some serious resource degradation might not occur.

As a result of these considerations we argue that, where natural resources are involved, some additional criterion is required. The one that we propose is *sustainability*. This is discussed in more detail in Chapter 3 but its appeal – particularly with regard to renewable resources – is evident. In many developing countries the stocks of such resources are below any reasonable estimate of what the long-run optimal stock is. In that event, it seems desirable that any investment policy that involves these resources should not permit a further fall in their stocks. These issues are discussed more fully elsewhere in this book.

So far much of the discussion on how to integrate environmental factors into investment appraisal and resource management has focused on making adjustments to discount rates. The two main kinds of adjustments that have been sought are:

1. Adding a premium to discount rates to reflect risk and uncertainty about environmental consequences of investments.
2. Lowering discount rates to reflect the interests of future generations.

We argue that neither argument constitutes a reason for adjusting discount rate. But because we will be arguing that these very relevant and important factors *do* need to be taken into account in the appraisal of investments, and in general policy, we need to be sure that we understand why the arguments for making adjustments to the discount rate are not persuasive.

The following sections examine these arguments more closely and look at alternative ways of dealing with the same issues – i.e. ways that do not involve adjusting the discount rate, but that achieve the objectives of dealing with the problems of:

* environmental risk;
* irreversible damage investment programmes;
* the interests of future generations.

Each of these is considered, in turn, below.

Environmental risk
We have argued that it is not advisable to adjust discount rates to reflect *environmental risk*. Essentially, this was because such an adjustment assumes risk to behave in a manner that is very unlikely to be realistic. For example, consider an investment which has a high environmental cost in the final years of the project, perhaps arising because of the need to dismantle equipment which contains toxic materials. Now assume that we are uncertain about the size of this cost. The uncertainty ought to make the investment less attractive compared to a situation in which we knew the dismantling costs with certainty. If we raise the discount rate, this will be the effect (see Annexe 2.1, p.49). However, while the *direction* of adjustment is correct, we have no foundation for believing that the present value of the dismantling cost has been accurately represented by the adjustment to the discount rate. In theory, it is possible under special circumstances to obtain a discount rate which reflects the risk. In practice, we argue that adjusting discount rates for risk is not an efficient procedure because it imposes a time profile for risk on to the project which has no particular justification, and because it requires information on certainty equivalence (see below) that is more effectively used directly in the valuation of the project.

The problem of accommodating risk can be overcome by using *certainty equivalence* procedures. A simple example will suffice here. Table 2.2 gives a cost–benefit profile for an hypothetical project.[7] The second column shows the expected net benefits. These are the *average* values arising from assessing the chances of the benefit occurring. For example, if the net benefit in year two is a 50 per cent chance of £200 and a 50 per cent chance of nothing, the expected value is £100 ((0.5 × 200) + (0.5 × 0)). The third column contains the adjustment to risk (sometimes confusingly termed the 'risk discount factor'). What this adjustment shows is the way in which attitudes to risk modify the expected values. Thus in year 2 the expected net benefit is 100. This might be compared to a return of 90 that is expected with complete certainty. Thus we should be indifferent between the 'gamble' of the 100 and an absolutely certain return of 90. This adjustment converts the expected net benefits to their *certainty equivalents*. For example, the expected value of £100 in year 2 is risky. We are likely to prefer a smaller but certain sum of money to this risky £100. This smaller sum is shown as £90 in column 4 and hence 0.1 is the risk adjustment. (Note that in this example the risk adjustment has nothing to do with time). This should be sufficient to differentiate adjustments for risk from adjustments for time discounting. This is shown in column 5 of the table using an hypothetical 5 per cent discount rate.

Table 2.2   Risk adjustment and discounting: an example

Year	Expected net benefit	Risk adjustment	Certainty equivalent	Discount factor	Adjusted flows
1	− 100.0	1.0	− 100.0	1.0	− 100.0
2	+ 100.0	0.9	+ 90.0	0.95	+ 85.5
3	+ 100.0	0.8	+ 80.0	0.91	+ 72.8
4	+ 100.0	0.75	+ 75.0	0.86	+ 64.5
5	− 80.0	1.20	− 96.0	0.82	− 78.7
[Sum]					+ 44.1

Irreversibility

One special environmental consideration that might, *prima facie*, imply the adjustment of the discount rate is that of irreversibility. The issue, as the term implies, is that the costs associated with a large number of decisions are *irreversible*: a valley that is flooded for a dam cannot be restored to its original state; ancient buildings that are pulled down for a road development may be reproducible if dismantled and moved, but invariably are lost forever; and radioactive waste, once produced, cannot be destroyed, it must be stored somewhere and no storage option is without risk (that risk is then present for hundreds of years, maybe more). Clearly, any policy of *not* developing a valley, of not building the road and of not building nuclear power stations involves a forgone benefit. The damage avoided by not taking a development decision has to be weighed against the benefits that the development would have conferred. But the 'no development' decision at least leaves the option to develop at a later stage, whereas the development decision leaves no option to reverse irreversible damage. One approach which goes some way towards building these problems into a benefit–cost methodology has been developed by Krutilla and Fisher (1975) and conveniently extended and formalized by Porter (1982). We outline the basic ideas below. A former model of the Krutilla–Fisher–Porter approach is given in Annexe 2.4.

Consider a valley containing unique natural assets and for which a hydroelectric development is proposed. Such a proposal was mooted for part of the Gordon River, in Tasmania, in the late 1970s, but the area to be flooded included areas of great natural beauty and of anthropological interest, together with a religious significance for aborigines. In 1976 the World Wildlife Fund urged Australia to protect the ecosystems of south-west Tasmania, for once flooded, this wilderness area would be lost forever and the wilderness benefits lost. Whatever the benefits of hydroelectricity generation, then, these forgone benefits must be counted as part of the costs of the development. The net benefits of development could thus be written:

$$\text{Net benefits} = B(D) - C(D) - B(P)$$

where $B(D)$ are the benefits of development, $C(D)$ are the development costs and $B(P)$ are the net benefits of preservation (i.e. net of any preservation costs which are likely to be positive, namely damage costs). All the benefit and cost items need to be expressed in present value terms – i.e. they need to be discounted. As noted above, some would argue that the discount rate itself should be set very low for projects with long-term environmental benefits or costs. In this case, it would have the effect of making $B(P)$ large because they are forgone for ever, whereas the net benefits of development will be dissipated once the life of the dam is finished – perhaps 50 years after its construction. *In the Krutilla–Fisher approach, how-*

ever, the discount rate is 'conventional', in that it is set equal to some measure of the marginal productivity of capital. We therefore proceed on this assumption.

The next thing to consider is that the benefits of preserving the area are likely to increase with time relative to other benefits in the economy. The reasons for thinking this are that (a) the overall supply of natural wilderness is decreasing in every country in the world; (b) the demand for 'wilderness experience' tends to be increasing with income growth and with population growth which generates 'crowding' effects; and (c) the demand for wilderness to remain in its natural state, even without it being directly experienced also appears to be growing (i.e. we surmise that existence values are increasing). The net effect is to raise the 'price' of the wilderness asset through time. In a cost–benefit analysis this is simply included by allowing benefits to increase at some rate of demand growth, say g. The net effect of letting preservation benefits grow at $g\%$ per annum and then discounting them back again at the discount rate of $r\%$ is to discount the benefits by a rate $(r - g)\%$. In other words, the effect is very similar to using a lower discount rate for preservation benefits. In this sense, the Krutilla–Fisher approach is not markedly different to manipulating the discount rate, but it does preserve the use of a 'conventional' discount rate which has the attraction that the procedure cannot be criticized for distorting resource allocation in the economy by using variable discount rates.

Krutilla and Fisher engage in a similar adjustment for development benefits, but in reverse. They argue that technological change will tend to reduce the benefits from developments such as hydroelectricity which will be reduced because superior electricity generating technologies will take their place over time. The example quoted in their work is nuclear power. Clearly the empirical relevance of this argument can now be disputed, but it is useful to develop the analysis on the assumption that development benefits will be subject to this technological depreciation. Let this rate of depreciation be $k\%$ per annum. Then the effect is to produce a net discount rate on development benefits of $(r + k)\%$. That is, the discount rate applied to development benefits has increased.

This, in essence, is the basis of the Krutilla–Fisher approach. It is in fact far more complicated than this because it is extended to allow for limits to the rate of growth of preservation benefits, ways of estimating the rate of technological change, and an analysis of the benefits and costs of postponing decisions, so that further information about the gains and losses can be obtained. The important point, however, is that the procedure does not actually require that benefits be estimated. Instead the procedure is to calculate the net benefits of development – i.e. the value of the output of electricity minus associated costs – and then to ask what the value of preservation benefits *would have to be* for the development not to take place. As a check, however, it should be possible to estimate *user* benefits by adopting the travel cost method of recreational benefit analysis. On a grander scale, the contingent valuation method could be used to obtain preservation benefits overall. These could then be compared directly with the development benefits.

The Krutilla–Fisher approach was used by Saddler *et al.* (1980) in their evaluation of the proposed Gordon River hydroelectricity development. They report various results according to different assumptions about the rate of growth of preservation benefits and different discount rates. With a discount rate of 5 per cent, a value for $g = 4\%$, and an assumed capacity to absorb visitors such that g applied only for 30 years, Saddler and his colleagues obtain the following result: $A1 of preservation benefits in the initial year will have a present value of $A260. (*Note*: there are additional parameter values relevant to this calculation. It is not a simple matter of summing the discounted value of $A1 each year for 30 years). Now, Saddler *et al.* estimate that the hydroelectric option would be cheaper than an alternative coal-fired option for generating electricity. The difference between the two is a present value of cost savings of $A189 million. Dividing the $A189 million by $A260 gives some $A725,000. What this means is that if the preservation benefits are $A725,000 in the first year, then the present value of preservation benefits will exceed the difference in the cost of the coal-fired and hydroelectric schemes. Expressed differently, the preservation benefits outweigh the cost differential, and hence they justify the adoption of the more expensive electricity generation scheme (coal) which does not involve the destruction of the wilderness area. The only issue remaining, then, is to ask whether the preservation benefits are likely to be $A725,000 in the first year. The answer could be judgemental – i.e. simply letting decision-makers decide if this is below what they think the first year preservation benefits are. Or user benefits could be estimated using one of environmental benefit estimation techniques. In the Saddler *et al.* study the result is left to judgement, and for a unique wilderness area it is more than unlikely that preservation values lie below this figure.

The Gordon dam was never built, in large part because of the worldwide outcry against the proposal. This example shows how the problem of irreversibility can be handled through adjustments to costs and benefits and does not need the discount rate to be changed, although the effects are similar. The numbers that actually emerge from the Gordon River application show that even if preservation benefits cannot be measured, the method offers some help in deciding on the desirability of the project. On the other hand, it is also significant that a benefit estimate would help to 'clinch' the analysis. For example, while in this case it is self-evident that preservation benefits are larger than the minimum required amount, it is perfectly possible to imagine cases where the analysis would not be so clear-cut.

Future generations
The question arises as to why market rates of discount are thought to be inappropriate in a context where the interests and rights of future generations are accepted as legitimate factors in the selection of a social discount rate. This section briefly surveys the arguments relating to this issue.

The higher the rate of discount, the greater will be the discrimination against future generations. First, projects with social costs that occur well into the future and net social benefits that occur in the near term will be likely to pass the standard cost–benefit test the higher is the discount rate. Thus future generations may bear a disproportionate share of the costs of the project. Secondly, projects with social benefits well into the future are *less* likely to be favoured by the cost–benefit rule if discount rates are high. Thus future generations are denied a higher share of project benefits. Thirdly, the higher the discount rate, the lower will be the overall level of investment, depending on the availability of capital, and hence the lower the capital stock 'inherited' by future generations. The expectation must be, then, that future generations will suffer from rates of discount determined in the market-place since such rates are based on current generation preferences and/or capital productivity which is not associated with the general existence of future markets.

It has been argued, however, that existing preferences do take account of future generations' interests. The way in which this might occur is through 'overlapping utility functions'. What this means is that my welfare (utility) today includes, as one of the factors determining it, the welfare of my children and perhaps my grandchildren. Thus if i is the current generation, j the next generation and k the third generation, we may have:

$$U_i = U_i(C_i, U_j, U_k)$$

where U is utility and C is consumption. In this way, we could argue that the 'future generations problem' is automatically taken account of in current preferences. Notice that what is being evaluated in this process is the current generation's judgement about what the future generation will think is important. It is not therefore a discount rate reflecting some broader principle of the rights of future generations. The essential distinction is between generation i judging what generation j wants (the overlapping utility function argument) and generation i engaging in resource investment so as to leave generation j with the maximum scope for choosing what it wants.

The issue is whether such an argument can be used to substantiate the idea that current, market-determined rates reflect future generations' interests. The basic reason for supposing that the argument does not hold is that market rates are determined by the behaviour of many individuals behaving in their own interest. If future generations enter into the calculus, they do so in contexts when the individual behaves in his/her 'public role'. Here the idea is that we all make decisions in two contexts – 'private' decisions reflecting our own interests and 'public' decisions in which we act with responsibility for our fellow beings and for future generations. Market discount rates reflect the former context, whereas social discount rates should reflect the public context. This is what Sen (1982) calls the 'dual role' rationale for social discount rates being below the market rates because of the future generations' issue. It is also similar to the 'assurance' argument, namely that people will behave differently if they can be assured that their own action will be accompanied by similar actions by others. Thus we might each be willing to make transfers to future generations, but only if we are individually assured that others will do the same. If we cannot be so assured, our transfers will be less. The 'assured' discount rate arising from collective action is lower than the 'unassured' discount rate.

There are other arguments that are used to justify the idea that market rates will be 'too high' in the context of future generations' interests. The first is what Sen (*ibid.*) calls the 'super-responsibility' argument. Market discount rates arise from the behaviour of individuals, but the state is a separate entity with the responsibility of guarding collective welfare and the welfare of future generations as well. Thus the rate of discount relevant to state investments will not be the same as the market discount rate, and since high rates discriminate against future generations, we would expect the state discount rate to be lower than the market discount rate.

The final argument used to justify the inequality of the market and social rate of discount is the 'isolation paradox' (Sen, 1961, 1967). This is often confused with the assurance problem (see above), but the isolation paradox says that individuals will not make transfers, *even if* assurance exists. Demonstrating the difference between market and social discount rates in this context is not straightforward. Here we present the results; for proofs, see Sen (1967). Pursuing the argument above that individuals will place some weight on the consumption of future generations, especially on consumption of direct descendants, assumes that the following weights are placed on consumption:

> own consumption $= 1$
> others' consumption in current generation $= b$
> consumption of descendants $= c$
> consumption of others in future generation $= a$

If £1 of saving today yields a return that is shared in the proportions h and $1 - h$ between descendants and others in the future generation, then the market rate of discount is:

$$\pi = \frac{1}{ch + (1 - h)a} - 1$$

Now suppose that individuals agree to make a collective saving contract for £1 of additional saving by all n persons in the current generation, and that the return is enjoyed by descendants and others in the ratio 1 to $n - 1$. Then the social rate of discount is:

$$p = \frac{1 + (n) - (1)b}{c + (n - 1)a} - 1$$

The possibility exists that π and p are the same, but as long as the current individual fails to capture the entire investment returns for his descendants ($h < 1$), or as long as the individual's selfishness *vis-à-vis* others today is stronger than concern for his descendants *vis-à-vis* others in the future generation ($c < a/b$), then p is less than π.

Any positive social rate of discount will discriminate against future generations' interests. This suggests that the social discount rate is to be determined in the context of collective decision-making rather than some aggregation of individuals' decisions. This might mean looking at individuals' 'public role' behaviour, leaving the choice of discount rate based on a collective savings contract. None of these options offer a theory of how to determine a discount rate in quantitative terms. What they do suggest is that market rates will not be proper guides to discount rates once future generations' interests are incorporated into the social decision rule. The view taken here is that these arguments can be used to justify rejecting the market rate of interest as a social discount rate *if it is thought that the burden of accounting for future generations' interests should fall on the discount rate*. As we argue, however, we consider this an unnecessarily complex and almost certainly untenable procedure. It is better to define the rights of future generations and use these to circumscribe the overall cost–benefit rule, leaving the choice of discount rate to fairly conventional current generation orientated considerations. We suggest that it is better to adjust other aspects of the investment appraisal to account for future generations' interests. A telling reason for this is that lowering rates will encourage more investment overall, and this will increase the demand for resources and environmental services. A lowering of rates across the board could thus have counter-productive results if the aim is to accommodate environmental concerns. One alternative, of course, is to lower discount rates for 'environmental' projects, but not for other projects. In practice, this is likely to be impossible to do because of the problems of deciding which is an environmental project and which is not. Is any rural development investment, for example, an environmental project? Since most projects will have an environmental dimension – they will all impact positively or negatively on the environment – the analyst would have to have some idea of the *scale* of the environmental dimension before deciding which discount rate to choose. Then he would need a cut-off point in order to decide which projects qualify for the lower rate and which for the higher one. Altogether the procedure has large arbitrary features.

We suggest, then, that while there are attractive features in the future generations argument, they may either backfire in the sense of not accommodating the concerns that motivate a reduced discount rate or they will result in largely impractical procedures. How might future generations' interests be taken into account? This issue requires some discussion.

The intergenerational problem
This is not the place to survey the various theories of inter-generational justice. It is, in any event, a complex and much disputed area of philosophy. We shall assume that the future has, at least, some claim on the present simply because they have an *interest* in the present. This interest, arising from the fact that what we do now affects the future, regardless of the fact that we do not know who future people will be, confers rights on future generations (Feinberg, 1980; Goodin, 1986). For our purposes, we accept that a case for intergenerational justice exists, and that the process of discounting appears to discriminate against it.

How might these future rights be protected in practice? Certain minimum requirements emerge with respect to any investment appraisal. Above all, it is essential that any investment appraisal should check on the resource and environmental consequences of the investment. This much has been recommended as standard procedure by the OECD (1986) and is an OECD Council Recommendation.

A second requirement is that efforts should be made to *measure* environmental damage. To some extent, this might be guaranteed by the use of *environmental impact assessment* procedures, but we would go further and suggest that attempts be made to identify the monetary cost of resource and receiving environment damage. The rationale here is to demonstrate the economic importance of natural environments and natural resources.

The procedures identified above are, of course, essential whether the environmental considerations are located in the current or the future. The interests of the future require something more, however, and this is captured in the idea, which is the theme of this book, of *sustainable development*. The basic notion has been outlined in this chapter and in Chapter 1 and it is formalized in Chapter 3. What is required is to define a set of *compensating investments* that maintain the flow of services from a given stock of environmental goods, and to include the costs and benefits of such investments along with the investment under consideration. The problems of defining, and choosing, such a set of compensating investments are discussed in Chapter 3. What is of interest, however, is the implication for the discount rate. For what this procedure suggests is that we do not need to adjust the discount rate for the interests of future generations. They are met by the sustainable use constraint and hence the changed cost profile for the project. The discount rate that is used can then be the opportunity cost of capital, adjusted if necessary for any consumption displacement effects. Moreover, it is in keeping with the arguments made earlier that adjusting the discount rate for future generations' interests is both clumsy and inefficient.

Notes
1. Technically the discount rate r, calculated on the initial value of £1, is given by solving for r in the equation $\{1/(1 + r)\} = 95$. This gives a value of r of 5.26.
2. Although a positive net present value is necessary, it is not sufficient. This is because there may be a shortage of capital resource to undertake all the investments that have a positive net present value.
3. The terms 'rate of interest' and 'rate of discount' are often used interchangeably, as is the case here. However, some caution is needed as the rate of interest is a more general term, referring to all market rates as well as social ones. The rate of discount as we define it here refers only to the social rate of interest. Note also that when we speak of discount rates, we are referring to *real* rates of interest – i.e. they are net of any rate of increase in the price level.
4. This relationship between the level of investment in the economy and the rate of interest is one of the 'macroeconomic' relationships referred to at the beginning of this chapter. In general, as the rate of interest rises, so it has a depressing effect on investment, as fewer projects can compete with the returns offered to investors in the financial markets.
5. These values of μ and τ are typical in much of the economic analysis carried out in this field. For other examples, and a discussion of the introspective arguments on which they are based, see Stern (1977).
6. It is not true, however, that all long gestation projects suffer with high discount rates. As Anderson (1986) has shown, forestry projects can yield very high rates of return when the benefits are properly measured.
7. This example looks at the risk of the project by looking at only the *variance* aspect of that risk. In non-technical terms, this means that the risk is assumed to lead to the net return in each period being uncertain, but that uncertainty is not correlated across periods. So, if the return in one period is low, we do not say that this tells us anything about the return in other periods. If risks in different periods are correlated, we need to look at the *covariance* of the risk as well. Discussion of this issue can be found in Lind (1982).

Annexe 2.1: The treatment of risk premia in discount rate estimation
In this chapter it has been argued that risk and uncertainty about the availability of future benefits should not be a reason for adjusting the discount rate to include a 'risk premium'. None the less, such a procedure is widely recommended. In this annexe we show how it would be calculated and what the objections to using it are.

Let an individual have an initial income endowment of Y. An environmental 'bad' has a distribution B and an expected value $E(B)$. Hence the individual's expected income is:

$$E(Ye) = Y - E(B) \tag{A1.1}$$

Assuming that individuals are risk-averse, the utility of the expected income has the relation:

$$E(U(Ye)) < U(E(Ye)) \tag{A1.2}$$

By von Neumann–Morgernstern utility theory there must be an income $Y^* < E(Ye)$ such that:

$$U(Y^*) = E(U(Ye)) \tag{A1.3}$$

Hence the individual is willing to pay $Y - Y^*$ to avoid the loss $E(B)$; thus:

$$[Y - Y^*] > [Y - E(Ye)] = E(B) \tag{A1.4}$$

or:

$$Y_t^* < [Y_t - E_t(B_t)] \tag{A1.5}$$

where t indicates the time period for which the relationship holds.

Equation (A1.4) says that the individual is willing to pay an insurance premium $(Y - Y^*)$ greater than the expected cost of the environmental bad, $E(B)$. Equation (A1.5) re-expresses the relationship in terms of a certain income (Y^*) and *net benefits*. The discounted value of the net benefits can be calculated at the *riskless rate of discount* in which case Y^* is relevant; hence:

$$NPV = \sum (1 + r)^{-t} Y_t^* \tag{A1.6}$$

Alternatively, discounting can take place at a rate k inclusive of a risk premium, in which case $[Y_t - E_t(B_t)]$ is relevant and:

$$NPV = \sum (1 + k)^{-t}[Y_t - E_t(B_t)] \tag{A1.7}$$

Since Y_t^* (A1.6) is equal to (A1.7) and $Y^*_t < [Y_t - E_t(B_t)]$, then $k > r$.

However, it is clear from the way the problem is set up that k can only be calculated by equating (A1.6) and (A1.7) and solving for k. This requires, of course, that Y^*_t be calculated first, in which case the second calculation is redundant. Furthermore, although a value of k can be found that satisfies equations (A1.6) and (A1.7), it does not generally ensure that:

$$\sum [Y_t - E_t(B_t)] \cdot (1 + k)^{-t} = \sum Y_t^* \cdot (1 + r)^t \qquad (A1.8)$$

that is, the discounted present value of expected future benefits is not equal to the discounted present value of the certainty equivalent. Equation (A1.8) will only be true if the ratio of the certainty equivalent to the expected value increases exponentially over time, thus:

$$\{Y_1^*/[Y_1 - E_1(B_1)]\}^t = \{Y_t^*/[Y_t - E_t(B_t)]\} \qquad (A1.9)$$

It should also be noted that although the above example shows a *risk premium* added to the risk-free discount rate, this only applies when discounting net benefits (Fisher, 1973). When net costs are being discounted, a *risk discount* applies (Brown, 1983; Prince, 1985).

Annexe 2.2: The consumption rate of interest
In this annexe we show the relationship between the consumption rate of interest and the rate of pure time preference.

The welfare associated with an individual who has a level of consumption c at time t is given by:

$$W(c) = c^{(1 - \mu)}e^{-\tau t}/(1 - \mu) \qquad (A2.1)$$

This welfare function is concave in c and assumes that utility declines over time (for given c) at a rate τ. The marginal welfare for this person is given by differentiating equation (A2.1) with respect to c:

$$W_c(c) = c^{-\mu}e^{-\tau t} \qquad (A2.2)$$

The consumption rate of interest, i, is defined as the rate of fall over time of the marginal welfare of consumption – i.e. – $d/dt(W_c(c))/W_c(c)$. Hence from equation (A2.2) it follows that:

$$d/dt(W_c(c))/W_c(c) = (d/dt(c)/c) \cdot \mu + \tau \qquad (A2.3)$$

$(d/dt(c)/c)$ is the rate of growth of consumption. Defining this as g, gives:

$$i = \mu \cdot g + \tau \qquad (A2.4)$$

Annexe 2.3: Discount rates and the depletion of natural resources
We begin by showing the case of a renewable resource such as a fishery. Then the relationship between the harvest rate, the stock and the change in the stock can be written as:

$$dX/dt = F(X) - H(t) \qquad (A3.1)$$

where X = stock of the resource;
H = harvest;
$F(x)$ = the natural growth function;
dX/dt = the rate of growth over time of the stock.

The harvest rate will depend on the effort put into it and on the stock, that is:

$$H = \phi(E,X) \qquad (A3.2)$$

where E = effort in harvesting. For convenience equation (A3.2) is written as:

$$H = E \cdot G(X) \qquad (A3.3)$$

Then the profit (rent) from the fishery is:

$$\pi = P.H - C.E \qquad (A3.4)$$

where P is the price of the natural resource and C is the cost per unit of effort. From equations (A3.3) and (A3.4):

$$\pi = P.H - C.H/G(X) \qquad (A3.5)$$

Let $C/G(X)$ be defined as $C(X)$. Equation (A3.5) then reduces to:

$$\pi = [P - C(X)].H \qquad (A3.6)$$

The problem then is to maximize the present value of profits $PV(\pi)$, or:

$$\text{max.} \int_0^\infty [P - C(X)].H.e^{-\tau t}dt \qquad (A3.7)$$

where τ is the discount rate. From equation (A3.1):

$$H = F(X) - (dX/dt) = F(X) - X \qquad (A3.8)$$

where X is dX/dt. Substituting equation (A3.7) into (A3.8) gives:

$$\text{max} \int_0^\infty [P - C(X)].[F(X) - X].e^{-\tau t}dt \qquad (A3.9)$$

The solution to equation (A3.9) is:

$$F'(X) - (C'(X) \cdot F(X))/(P - C(X)) = \tau \qquad (A3.10)$$

where prime ' indicates a derivative with respect to X. Equation (A3.10) is the fundamental rule of optimal renewable resource use. It is more readily understood if we modify it further. Rearrange equation (A3.10) as:

$$F'(X)[P - C(X)] - C'(X).F(X) = \tau.[P - C(X)] \quad (A3.11)$$

Consider the expression $[P - C(X)].F(X)$. Differentiate it to get:

$$(d/dX)\{[P - C(X)].F(X)\} = F'(X).[P - C(X)] - C'(X).F(X) \quad (A3.12)$$

The solution of equation (A3.12) is the same as the left-hand side of equation (A3.11). So (A3.11) can be written as:

$$(d/dX)\{[P - C(X)].F(X)\} = \tau.[P - C(X)] \quad (A3.13)$$

Since it can be shown that at the optimum $H(t)$ is also equal to $F(X)$ – i.e. the fishery should be used sustainably – we can replace $F(X)$ in (A3.12) by $H(t)$. However, $[P - C(X)].H(t)$ is the sustainable rent or profit from the activity. Call this $R(X)$; then equation (A3.13) simplifies to:

$$(dR/dX).(1/\tau) = P - C(X) \quad (A3.14)$$

which is a restatement of the fundamental rule for the optimal use of a renewable resource. This rule changes when prices change. The solution to equation (A3.9) then becomes:

$$F'(X) - (C'(X).F(X))/P - C(X)) = \tau - \dot{P}/[P - C(X)] \quad (A3.15)$$

where $\dot{P}$ is dP/dt. The meaning of equation (A3.14) is best understood by pretending that fishing is costless – i.e. that $C(X)$ is zero and hence $C'(X)$ is also zero. Then equation (A3.15) becomes:

$$F'(X) = \tau - \dot{P}/P$$
$$\text{or } F'(X) + \dot{P}/P = \tau \quad (A3.16)$$

$F'(x)$ is the marginal productivity of the stock, and $\dot{P}/P$ is the rate of price appreciation of the unharvested stock – i.e. the capital gain. The left-hand side of equation (A3.16) is then the combined value of a unit of stock. If this is less than τ, the stock should be exploited further. If it is more than τ, the stock should be harvested less.

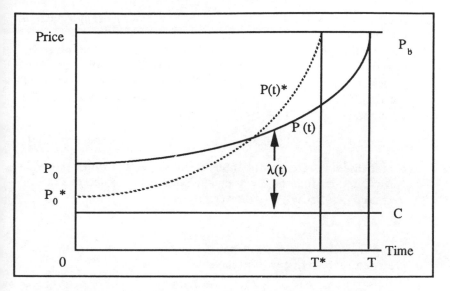

Figure A2.1   Effect of increasing discount rate

Note that an *exhaustible resource* can be defined as one where $F'(X) = F(X) = 0$. Then equation (A3.16) becomes:

$$\dot{P}/P = \tau \qquad \text{(A3.17)}$$

Equation (A3.17) is known as Hotelling's Rule (Hotelling, 1931). It says that an exhaustible resource should be depleted at a rate consistent with the rate of price increase being equal to the discount rate.

What happens if the discount rate rises? This is shown in Figure A2.1, which has the resource price on the vertical axis and time on the horizontal axis. $P(t)$ is then the price path consistent with Hotelling's Rule, C is the unit extraction cost (assumed constant) and $R(t) (= P(t) - C)$ is the royalty. P_b is the price of some substitute resource, known as the 'backstop' technology. Now, since $P(t)$ rises at the discount rate, a rise in that rate must alter the price path (and hence the time path of the extraction rate). In fact the *initial* price P_0 falls and the new path of $P(t)$ is shown as $P(t)^*$. The effect of a rise in the discount rate is therefore to lower early period prices, increase extraction rates in the early period, raise prices in later periods, lower extraction rates in later periods and exhaust the resource earlier (T' instead of T).

Annexe A2.4: A simplified model of the Krutilla–Fisher approach to irreversibility
This outline of the Krutilla–Fisher approach follows that given by Porter (1982). It uses perpetuities rather than finite periods. Consider a development project costing £1. Let the net benefits of the development be £D_t in year t. Then the present value of the development is $PV(D)$ where:

$$PV(D) = -1 + \int_0^\infty D_t \, e^{-rt} \, dt \qquad (A4.1)$$

r is the discount rate and the integration is over an infinite interval. Next we assume that the development benefits are subject to a rate of 'technological decay', k (see text), so that:

$$D_t = D_0 \, e^{-kt} \qquad (A4.2)$$

where D_0 is the development benefit in year 0. Now turning to the preservation benefits, we will have:

$$PV(P) = \int_0^\infty P_t e^{-rt} \, dt \qquad (A4.3)$$

and:

$$P_t = P_0 \, e^{gt} \qquad (A4.4)$$

where g is the rate of growth of preservation benefits. Bringing equations (A4.1) to (A4.4) together and solving the integrals gives:

$$NPV(D) = -1 + D_0/(r + k) - P_0/(r - g) \qquad (A4.5)$$

Equation (A4.5) implies that the net present value of development benefits will be positive if, and only if, the discount rate lies in a particular range. At low rates, g tends to push the preservation benefits up high, so that the development project is not worthwhile. High rates tend to discriminate in the usual way, by reducing the development benefits. Porter (*ibid.*) shows that comparatively low values of g and k have the effect of pushing the development project into the region of being unacceptable.

References
Anderson, D. (1986), *The Economics of Rural Afforestation in Ecologically Threatened Areas*, Baltimore, Md: Johns Hopkins University Press.
Baier, A. (1980), 'The rights of past and future persons', in E. Partridge (ed.), *Responsibilities to Future Generations*, Buffalo, NY: Prometheus, pp. 171–83.

Barry, B. (1977), 'Justice between generations', in P. Hacker and J. Raz (eds), *Law, Morality and Society*, Oxford: Clarendon Press, pp. 268-84.

Bentham, J. (1789), *An Introduction to the Principles of Morals and Legislation*, London: Athlone Press.

Bohm-Bawerk, E. C. (1884), *The Positive Theory of Capital*, New York: Stedard.

Brown, S. (1983), 'A note on environmental risk and the rate of discount', *Journal of Environmental Economics and Management*, 10, pp. 282-6.

Clark, C. W. (1976), *Mathematical Bioeconomics*, New York: Wiley.

Dasgupta, A. and Pearce, D. W. (1972), *Cost-Benefit Analysis: Theory and Practice*, London: Macmillan.

Feinberg, J. (1980), *Rights, Justice and the Bounds of Liberty*, Princeton, NJ: Princeton University Press.

Fisher, A. C. (1973), 'Environmental externalities and the Arrow-Lind public investment theorem', *American Economic Review*, 63, pp. 722-5.

Goodin, R. (1982), 'Discounting discounting', *Journal of Public Policy*, 2, pp. 53-72.

Goodin, R. (1986), *Protecting the Vulnerable*, Chicago: University of Chicago Press.

Hotelling, H. (1931), 'The economics of exhaustible resources', *Journal of Political Economy*, 39, pp. 137-75.

Jevons, W. S. (1871), *The Theory of Political Economy*, London: Macmillan.

Krutilla, J. and Fisher, A. C. (1985), *The Economics of Natural Environments*, 2nd edn, Resources for the Future, Washington, DC.

Lind, R. (1982), 'A primer on the major issues relating to the discount rate for evaluating national energy options', in R. Lind (ed.), *Discounting for Time and Risk in Energy Policy*, Baltimore, Md: Johns Hopkins University Press.

OECD (1986), *Environmental Assessment and Development Assistance*, Paris: OECD.

Olson, M. and Bailey, M. (1981), 'Positive time preference', *Journal of Political Economy*, 89, pp. 1-25.

Page, T. (1983), 'Intergenerational justice as opportunity', in D. MacLean and P. Brown (eds), *Energy and the Future*, Totowa, NJ: Rowman and Littlefield.

Parfit, D. (1983), 'Energy policy and the further future: the social discount rate', in D. MacLean and P. Brown (eds), *Energy and the Future*, Totowa, NJ: Rowman and Littlefield, pp. 31-7.

Pearce, D. W. (1987), Foundations of an Ecological Economics', *Ecological Modelling*, 38, 9-18.

Pearce, D. W. (1988), 'The economics of natural resource degradation in developing countries', in R. K. Turner (ed.), *Sustainable Environmental Management: Principles and Practice*, London: Francis Pinter, 102-17.

Pigou, A. C. (1932), *The Economics of Welfare*, London: Macmillan.

Porter, P. (1982), 'The new approach to wilderness preservation through benefit-cost analysis', *Journal of Environmental Economics and Management*, 9, pp. 59-80.

Prince, R. (1985), 'A note on environmental risk and the rate of discount: comment', *Journal of Environmental Economics and Management*, 12, pp. 179-80.

Ramsey, F. P. (1929), 'A mathematical theory of saving', *Economic Journal*, 38, pp. 543-59.

Repetto, R. (1986), *Natural Resource Accounting in a Resource Based Economy: An Indonesian Case Study*, Washington, DC: World Resources Institute.

Saddler, H., Bennett, J., Reynolds, I. and Smith, B. (1980), *Public Choice in Tasmania: Aspects of the Lower Gordon River Hydro-electric Development Proposal*, Centre for Resource and Environmental Studies, Australian National University, Canberra.

Sen, A. (1961), 'On optimizing the rate of saving', *Economic Journal*, 71.

Sen, A. (1967), 'Isolation, assurance, and the social rate of discount', *Quarterly Journal of Economics*, LXXXI, 112-24.

Sen, A. (1982), 'Approaches to the choice of discount rates for social benefit-cost analysis', in R. Lind (ed.), *Discounting for Time and Risk in Energy Policy*, Baltimore, Md: Johns Hopkins University Press.

Squire, L. and Van der Tak, H. (1975), *Economic Analysis of Projects*, Baltimore, Md: Johns Hopkins University Press.

Stern, N. (1977), 'The marginal valuation of income', in M. J. Artis and A. R. Nobay (eds), *Studies in Modern Economic Analysis*, Oxford: Blackwell.

Stiglitz, J. (1986), *Economics of the Public Sector*, New York: Norton.

Strotz, R. (1956), 'Myopia and inconsistency in dynamic utility maximization', *Review of Economic Studies*, 23 (3), pp. 165-80.

UK Treasury (1980), *Investment Appraisal and Discounting Techniques and the Use of the Test Discount Rate in the Public Sector*, UK Treasury, London.

3 Economic appraisal and the natural environment

Introduction

In Chapter 2 we investigated the rationale for discounting costs and benefits in the future. While much of the environmental critique of discounting is understandable, in that chapter we suggested that altering discount rates to give a greater weight to temporally distant environmental costs, and to reflect the probable preferences of future generations, is fraught with difficulty. Making such modifications should not be ruled out, but the essential argument is that by espousing the philosophy of sustainable development as natural capital conservation, the problems of adjusting discount rates can – to a considerable extent – be avoided. By adopting the goal of sustainable development discounting procedures can be adopted much as conventional economics would dictate. But discounting then occurs *within the bounds* of sustainability requirements.

This chapter explores the way in which sustainability criteria would alter economic appraisal. We show the effects on economic appraisal of requiring that the natural capital stock be at least constant. The appraisal technique chosen to illustrate the approach is *cost–benefit analysis*.

Cost–benefit analysis

Cost–benefit analysis (CBA) embodies intuitive rationality, in that any course of action is judged acceptable if it confers a net advantage – i.e. if 'benefits' outweigh 'costs'. What constitutes a gain or loss depends on the objective function chosen. Most CBA operates with a function based on economic efficiency – i.e. on the basis that a benefit is anything whereby more is preferred to less, and a cost is anything whereby less is preferred to more. But this is only *one* objective function. It is widely used because economic efficiency is embodied in the very structure of the welfare economics developed over the last century. In principle, however, any other objective function can be chosen or, more profitably, a *set* of objectives can be chosen. Common parlance has it that CBA using more than one objective is termed 'extended' CBA. Such terminology is neutral if the idea is to compare multi-objective CBA with the 'norm' – i.e. CBA based on economic efficiency alone. It is misleading terminology if it is meant to imply that the basic structure of CBA is somehow overturned by the inclusion of other objectives.[1] Indeed integrating the sustainability objective into CBA can be shown to leave the basic structure of CBA intact, but the resulting modifications to the basic theorems are of interest and, we suggest, of importance.

The formal cost-benefit rule can be written as follows. Ignoring time for the moment, the requirement for an action, policy, investment or other decision to be socially worthwhile is:

$$(B - C) > 0 \qquad (3.1)$$

where B refers to benefits and C to costs. Benefits are anything that people prefer. Costs are anything that people do not like ('disprefer'). Environmental damage is a cost as long as there are people who are upset by it. Therefore, we might distinguish two types of cost: non-environmental costs (keeping C for this), and environmental costs (E). The basic rule thus becomes:

$$(B - C - E) > 0 \qquad (3.2)$$

Chapter 2 has provided the rationale for discounting benefits and costs. So if we write the *discount factor* as:

$$d^t = e^{-rt}$$

where r is the *discount rate*,[2] the underlying formula becomes:

$$\sum_t \{(B_t - C_t - E_t) \cdot e^{-rt}\} > 0 \qquad (3.3)$$

where the subscript t now denotes the time period and $\sum_t$ denotes the summation of benefits and costs over time.

Sustainability and cost–benefit analysis

Sustainability can be introduced into CBA by setting a constraint on the depletion and degradation of the stock of natural capital. Essentially, the economic efficiency objective is modified to mean that all projects yielding net benefits should be undertaken subject to the requirement that environmental damage (i.e. natural capital depreciation) should be zero or negative. However, applied at the level of *each project* such a requirement would be stultifying. Few projects would be feasible. At the *programme* level, however, the interpretation is more interesting. It amounts to saying that netted out across a set of projects (programme), the *sum* of individual damages should be zero or negative. That is, if E_i is the value of the environmental *damage* done by the ith project, we require that:

$$\sum_i E_i \leq 0 \qquad (3.4)$$

Rather than show here how the time dimension is integrated, Annexe 3.1 addresses the time question directly and shows that two formulations of the sustainability constraint emerge. Under *weak sustainability*, it is the present value of E_i, $PV(E_i)$, which is constrained to be non-positive. Under *strong sustainability*, each E_i is constrained to be non-positive *for each period* of time.

Since it is not feasible to set $PV(E_i)$ to be zero or negative for each project, but it is feasible to set E_i to be non-positive, the sustainability constraint amounts to including within any portfolio of investments one or more *shadow projects* whose aim is to compensate for the environmental damage from the other projects in the portfolio.[3] The conventional CBA rule would then apply to the *environmentally depleting* projects – i.e. these would be evaluated using equation (3.3), above.

The *environmentally compensating* project(s), j, would be chosen such that:

$$\sum_j PV(A)_j \geq = \sum_i PV(E_i) \qquad (3.5)$$

for the weak sustainability criterion, and:

$$\sum_j A_{jt} \geq \sum_i E_{it} \text{ for all } t \qquad (3.6)$$

for the strong sustainability criterion, where the jth project is designed to compensate for the damage done by the other projects. For the compensating projects, then, the normal CBA decision rule does not apply, although we would wish to minimize the cost of achieving the sustainability criterion.

One alternative approach to adopting environmentally compensating projects is widely suggested, as we have discussed in Chapter 2, namely lowering the discount rate for environmentally beneficial projects relative to those that generate environmental damage. It is possible to show that adjusting discount rates for some 'environmental risk premium' can produce similar results to those suggested here, but the adjustments are complex and actually determining the risk premium for damaging projects (or the discount for beneficial projects) is liable to generate impossible informational demands. Yet another suggestion that *all* projects should attract a lower discount rate, can actually be counterproductive of the basic idea of maintaining natural capital stocks. This is because lower discount rates encourage a larger *total* of investment and this will 'drag through' the system more materials and energy and hence more waste (by the laws of thermodynamics). We conclude therefore that the compensating project approach is more profitable as a way of practically modifying CBA.

Notes
1. Thus it is sometimes suggested that incorporating a distributional objective into CBA leads to fundamental modification. But this is not so. See Pearce (1986) and, in the developing country context, Little and Mirrlees (1974) and Dasgupta, Marglin and Sen (1972).
2. Readers may be more familiar with the discount factor in discrete time as: $d^t = 1/(1 + r)^t$.
3. The shadow project idea is suggested by Klaassen and Botterweg (1976) in what appears to be a neglected paper.

Annexe 3.1: A formal analysis of sustainability and cost–benefit analysis

The traditional project appraisal criterion is that the discounted net benefits of each project *i* should be non-negative, that is:

$$\sum_{t=0}^{t=T} \delta^t \cdot [B_{it} - C_{it}] \geq 0, i \epsilon \mathbf{P} \qquad (A3.1)$$

where B_{it} is the benefit of the *i*th project in time period *t*, C_{it} is its cost in that time period and δ is the discount factor. $\mathbf{P}$ is the collection of primary projects available to the decision-maker. If in addition to the normal costs of the projects, there are also some environmental costs, then the criterion becomes:

$$\sum_{t=0}^{t=T} \delta^t \cdot [B_{it} - C_{it} - E_{it}] \geq 0, i \epsilon \mathbf{P} \qquad (A3.2)$$

where E_{it} is the cost of the environmental damage generated by project *i* at time *t*. Criterion (A3.2) is insufficient for overall environmental sustainability. For example equation (A3.2) could hold while, at the same time, the total environmental damage costs generated by the portfolio of projects are greater than zero, in some time periods, namely:

$$\sum_{i \epsilon \mathbf{P}} E_{it} > 0, \text{ some } t \qquad (A3.3)$$

That is, the portfolio as a whole is continuing to degrade the environment. Over the long run, the cumulative degradation (e.g. soil erosion, deforestation and waste accumulation) may severely degrade or deplete the resource base.[1] Consequently, to ensure that a portfolio of projects does not undermine the sustainability of the resource requires the adoption of an explicit constraint on the above appraisal process (rule A3.2). There are two possibilities: a weak and a strong sustainability criterion.

The weak sustainability criterion states that the *discounted present value of the* environmental damage costs across all projects is non-negative, whereas the strong sustainability criterion requires that the net environmental costs across all projects be non-negative *for each and every time period.* These are represented mathematically below.

The planning criteria for each of the sustainability conditions can be expressed as follows. For each of the projects, i, in the portfolio **P**, there is an indicator of the level of activity for that project for every time period; this is called Q_{it}. At the same time, there is a portfolio of environmentally mitigating or shadow projects s. Each project j in this set has associated with it a cost profile, $C_{j1}, C_{j2} \ldots C_{jT}$; a benefit profile, $B_{j1}, B_{j2} \ldots B_{jT}$; and a set of net environmental benefits, $A_{j1}, A_{j2} \ldots A_{jT}$. As before, each project is defined in terms of its activity level by the variable Q_{jt}, $t = 1, 2 \ldots T$. For the sustainability criterion to be met in an optimizing framework the set of projects have to be chosen such that the sum of the returns from *all* projects is maximized, subject to the net environmental damage being non-positive. If the total net returns are defined as *TNR*, then the planning problem with sustainability becomes:

$$Maximize\ TNR = \sum_{t=0}^{T} \delta^t \sum_{i \in P} [B(Q_{it}) - C(Q_{it}) - E(Q_{it})] +$$
$$\{P, S, Q, Q_i, Q_j\}$$

$$\sum_{t=0}^{T} \delta^t \sum_{i \in S} [B(Q_{jt}) - C(Q_{jt}) + A(Q_{jt})] \tag{A3.4}$$

subject to:

$$\sum_{t=0}^{T} \delta^t [\sum_{i \in P} E(Q_{it}) - \sum_{j \in S} A(Q_{jt})] \leq 0$$
(*weak sustainability*) (A3.5)

or:

$$[\sum_{i \in P} E(Q_{it}) - \sum_{j \in S} A(Q_{jt})] \leq 0, \text{ all } t$$
(*strong sustainability*) (A3.6)

The optimization problem characterized above can be formidable as it involves the choice of projects, shadow projects and their activity levels by time period. Some insight into the maximization problem can be gained if the projects selected are fixed and the functions $B(\cdot)$,

$C(\cdot)$, $E(\cdot)$ and $A(\cdot)$ are differentiable in Q.[2] Then if the functions $A(\cdot)$ and $B(\cdot)$ are concave and the functions $C(\cdot)$ and $E(\cdot)$ are convex, the overall problem becomes one of concave programming and can be represented for the weak sustainability criterion as:

$$\text{Maximize } \mathbf{L} = \sum_{t=0}^{T} \delta^t \sum_{i \in P} [B(Q_{it}) - C(Q_{it}) - E(Q_{it})] +$$

(A3.7)

$$\sum_{t=0}^{T} \delta^t \sum_{i \in S} [B(Q_{jt}) - C(Q_{jt}) + A(Q_{jt})] -$$

$$\lambda \left\{ \sum_t \delta^t \left[\sum_{i \in P} E(Q_{it}) - \sum_{j \in S} A(Q_{jt}) \right] \right\}$$

where $Q_{it} \geq 0$, $Q_{jt} \geq 0$, all i, j, t and $\lambda \geq 0$. λ is the Lagrange multiplier whose value will depend, in general, on all the Qs and δ. It can be interpreted as the 'price' of the sustainability constraint. Its value is equal to the decrease in net present value of all the projects when the maximum permitted net environmental damage (set at zero in the base camp) is reduced further by a small amount.

An analogous expression holds in the case of strong sustainability and its interpretation is discussed further below. From the Kuhn--Tucker maximization conditions for equation (A3.7) the following expression can be obtained:

$$\frac{dB}{dQ_{it}} - \frac{dC}{dQ_{it}} - \frac{dE}{dQ_{it}} = \lambda \frac{dE}{dQ_{it}}, \text{ all } t$$

(A3.8)

if $Q_{it} > 0$. Rearranging equation (A3.8) yields:

$$\frac{dB}{dQ_{it}} - \frac{dC}{dQ_{it}} = (1 + \lambda) \frac{dE}{dQ_{it}}, \text{ all } t$$

(A3.9)

Equation (A3.9) states that the net marginal benefit from the project should be equal to the net marginal environmental damage cost, *plus a factor* λ, which represents a premium due to the sustainability criterion. If there were no such constraint, it would be rational to equate the net benefits of the project to its environmental costs; for if the latter were greater than the former, total gains could

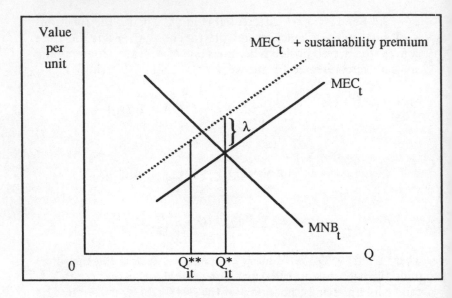

Figure A3.1   Effect of a sustainability premium

be increased by reducing Q_{it}, and if they were less than the former, total gains could be increased by increasing Q_{it}. This is shown in Figure A3.1, with net marginal environmental costs represented by MEC_t and net marginal benefits by MNB_t. Total benefits are maximized at Q_{it}^*. But if the factor λ is positive, this implies that benefits have to be reduced slightly as a result of the sustainability constraint. Hence a new curve is drawn, which represents the environmental costs, plus a 'sustainability premium'.[3] The new optimum is to the left of the unconstrained one, implying a lower level of activity (Q_{it}^{**} against Q_{it}^*).

Two points should be noted about the above analysis. First, the premium λ need not be positive. It is possible to envisage a set of shadow projects, whose returns would be sufficient to net out all environmental damage, even when they have been selected to operate at their unconstrained maximizing levels. In that event, there would be no need for the shadow projects to be justified as 'shadow projects', but ones that were valid in their own right. The second point is that where the sustainability premium is positive, the shadow projects individually may not satisfy the traditional appraisal criterion, as given in equation (A3.1). This is clear from an inspection of

(A3.7). A shadow project could have a negative net present value but its output of A_{jt} could be so great as to justify the project in terms of its contribution to fulfilling the sustainability constraint.

It can also be seen, from a figure analogous to the one shown here, that if λ is positive, the value of Q_{jt}, the shadow project's activity level, will be greater than it would be if λ were zero. Under strong sustainability the first-order conditions can be rearranged to yield:

$$\delta^t \cdot \frac{dB}{dQ_{it}} - \frac{dC}{dQ_{it}} - \frac{dE}{dQ_{it}} = \lambda(t) \cdot \frac{dE}{dQ_{it}}, \text{ all } t \qquad (A3.10)$$

if $Q_{it} > 0$. This rearranges to give:

$$\delta^t \cdot \frac{dB}{dQ_{it}} - \frac{dC}{dQ_{it}} - \frac{dE}{dQ_{it}} = \lambda(t) \cdot \frac{dE}{dQ_{it}}, \text{ all } t \qquad (A3.11)$$

Equation (A3.11) is analogous to (A3.9) but states that the sustainability premium grows exponentially with time. The equations in (A3.11), together with the constraints themselves, are a system of equations that determine the values of $\lambda_1, \lambda_2 \ldots \lambda_T$; Q_{i1}, $Q_{i2} \ldots Q_{iT}$; $Q_{j1}, Q_{j2} \ldots Q_{jT}$ for all i and j. In order to find out how the values of the λs change with δ and how the sustainability premium changes with δ, one has to carry out a full comparative statics exercise on this system of equations. Unfortunately, no general results appear to be available, and more structure would have to be put on the problem before results of this kind could be obtained.

Notes

1. Here the constraint is formulated in value terms for environmental damage. This may not be the relevant concept if it is in fact the physical damage that one wants to restrict for each type of degradation. The analysis presented here can easily be extended to the case of several environmental constraints, but the only implication as far as this presentation is concerned is that the mathematics would become more cumbersome.
2. In general, the values of Q will not be free to vary from period to period and so the domain over which the maximization is being carried out will not be $\mathbf{R}_+{}^n$. However, for expository purposes the assumption of a freely variable Q is convenient.
3. On the idea of a sustainability premium see Pearce (1988).

References

Dasgupta, P., Marglin, S. and Sen, A. (1972), *Guidelines for Project Evaluation*, New York: UNIDO.

Klaassen, L. and Botterweg, T. H. (1976), 'Project evaluation and intangible effects: a shadow project approach', in P. Nijkamp (ed.), *Environmental Economics*, Leiden: Martinus Nijhoff, Vol. 1.

Little, I. M. D. and Mirrlees, J. (1974), *Project Appraisal and Planning for Developing Countries*, London: Heinemann.

Pearce, D. W. (1986), *Cost–Benefit Analysis*, London: Macmillan.

Pearce, D. W. (1988), 'Optimal prices for sustainable development in D. Collard, D. W. Pearce and D. Ulph (eds.), *Economics, Growth and Sustainable Environments*, London: Macmillan, 59–66.

4 Sustainable development in the upper watersheds of Java

Introduction

The current natural resource and environmental problems confronting Indonesia reflect the impacts of four important economic trends: (1) rapid population growth; (2) rapid economic growth over the past two decades, fuelled mainly by oil but also by other natural resource exports; (3) considerable expansion of food production, the beginnings of industrialization and regional economic development off Java; and (4) extensive land opening, often under marginal environmental conditions in both upland and lowland areas (Hanson, 1987).

A distinction is usually made between Indonesia's smaller Inner Islands of Java, Madura, Lombok and Bali and the larger Outer Islands that comprise the remainder of the country (Figure 4.1). Whereas land on the Outer Islands is abundant (albeit consisting mostly of low-fertility converted or existing forest land), on densely populated Java virtually all the high-quality arable land of the lowland areas is already under cultivation. The only land available for further agricultural extensification is the often erodible, low-yielding upland areas of upper watershed catchments. A significant number of rural farming households already depend on these lands for their livelihoods. The crucial question is whether it is possible to improve the productivity of existing upland farmlands by intensification rather than by encouraging further extensification on fragile catchment areas or by accelerating problems of soil erosion on these lands. If intensification is feasible and sustainable, the policy issue is how to achieve it. That issue is the main focus of this chapter.

Figure 4.2 illustrates the specific economic-environmental linkages associated with Indonesia's uplands erosion problems. In Indonesia, as noted above, 36 watershed areas totalling 10.4 million ha are classified as critical lands. On Java the area of critical upland is increasing at the rate of 1–2 per cent per annum and now totals over 2 million ha, approx. one-third of Java's cultivated uplands.

Key:
1 Daerah Istimewa Aceh
2 Sumatera Utara
3 Sumatera Barat
4 Riau
5 Jambi
6 Sumatera Selatan
7 Bengkulu
8 Lampung
9 DKI Jakarta

10 Jawa Barat
11 Jawa Tengah
12 Daerah Istimewa Yogyakarta
13 Jawa Timur
14 Bali
15 Nusa Tenggara Barat
16 Nusa Tenggara Timur
17 Timor Timur
18 Kalimantan Barat

19 Kalimantan Tengah
20 Kalimantan Selatan
21 Kalimantan Timur
22 Sulawesi Utara
23 Sulawesi Tengah
24 Sulawesi Selatan
25 Sulawesi Tenggara
26 Maluku
27 Irian Jaya

Figure 4.1   Indonesia (BPS, 1985)

Estimated sedimentation rates of rivers in Java from erosion vary from 10–40 tonnes per hectare per year, which is about average for most tropical upland areas (Barbier, 1987; World Bank, 1987b).

With population densities in these areas averaging 600–700 people per square kilometre, and with holdings averaging 0.4 ha or less and 20–25 per cent of the population being landless in some areas, together with yields for upland rice and corn averaging 0.9–2.5 tonnes ha^{-1}, the general pattern is one of poor, predominantly subsistence households seeking to increase their immediate basic food requirements by using inappropriate cropping patterns that result in high soil erosion levels from their rain-fed lands. In addition, significant erosion problems are caused by absentee and better-off farmowners cultivating highly profitable but erosive crops, such as vegetables, and by the failure to police state-owned tree plantations properly, particularly the failure to prevent illegal fuelwood collection and agricultural conversion (*ibid.*).

Although there are numerous donor-financed projects for rehabilitating degraded upper watersheds, and the government of Indonesia (GOI) has its own Regreening and Reforestation programme for critical lands, long-run concern over sustainable development of upland agriculture has yet to become a policy priority. The current economic strategies for achieving export promotion and agricultural diversification in Indonesia tend to be more narrowly focused on maximizing short-run gains with very little regard to proper resource management. For example, in agriculture, the overwhelming policy objective is to increase production, especially of certain targeted secondary crops (e.g. cassava, maize, soybeans, sugar and groundnuts) and export estate crops (e.g. palm oil and rubber). The issues of whether current patterns of resource use in upland areas on Java can sustain increased production, or whether current investment programmes and incentive schemes to boost production either ignore the problems of upland soil erosion, even contribute to them, receive little attention.

As the two following sections indicate, the costs of continuing this policy approach (or lack of one) for the uplands of Java may be quite high – in terms of lost potential production and the actual on-and off-site impacts of soil erosion and runoff. Moreover, the overall policy goals of agricultural diversification and increased employment opportunities for rural populations on Java may not be achievable without attention to the development of more sustainable

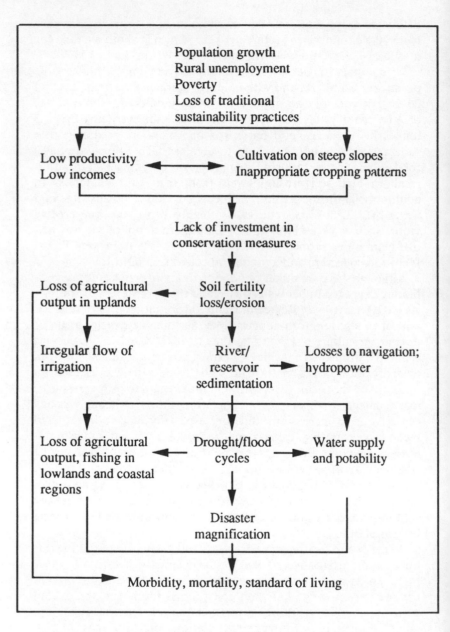

Figure 4.2   Indonesia: uplands erosion

agriculture in the uplands. This is reflected in several trends, as follows.

1. Although between 1971 and 1980 agriculture in Indonesia accounted for only 16 per cent of the jobs created, declining oil revenues and slower manufacturing growth have since placed renewed pressure on agriculture to absorb surplus labour. Thus over 1980–5 agriculture was forced to absorb approx. half of new entrants and maintained a constant employment share of 55 per cent (Douglass, 1987).
2. The scope for further intensification of rice on lowland, irrigated areas, especially on Java, is limited, with 94 per cent of wet paddy fields planted with high-yielding varieties (HYVs) and with yields stagnating in recent years. Moreover, the farmer terms of trade for rice on Java has deteriorated and is significantly less attractive than for other crops (World Bank, 1987b).
3. Although there is scope for diversifying production to increase total output on lowland areas on Java, there is little room for increased absorption of labour. If surplus Javanese labour is to be absorbed in agriculture, it will be through expansion on to marginal lands, especially upon the drylands of upper watersheds. For example, on Java during 1973–83 the average annual rate of expansion of dryland cultivation was 1.8 per cent, whereas for wetland it was 1.1 per cent (Douglass, 1987).

It follows that sustainable agricultural development of the uplands of Java is required to generate future growth and employment in agriculture. Although past agricultural policies may have been appropriate for achieving the objective of rice self-sufficiency and rural and agricultural development of the irrigated lowlands, a similar approach is not suitable for the more highly diversified soils, topography and agro-ecological conditions that characterize the upland areas. Matching the appropriate land management skills, technical packages and farming systems to these varied conditions must therefore be the cornerstone of a sustainable agricultural policy for the uplands. The rest of this chapter discusses the actual and potential economic contribution of the upland areas on Java, the costs of their mismanagement and the factors contributing to it, and the policy direction for a more sustainable development of the uplands of Java.

The economic contribution of the Javan uplands

In Indonesia extensive conversion of land for agriculture is seen to be a priority both because of geographically concentrated food production and population. Around 63 per cent of the total population is concentrated on Java, Madura and Bali – the so-called inner islands, which comprise just over 7 per cent of Indonesia's total land area (BPS, 1986, tables 3.1.1–3.1.3). Similarly, Java and Sumatra account for over 80 per cent of total food production in Indonesia, with Java accounting for over 60 per cent of the rice production and over 70 per cent of corn and soybean output. Rice production, which accounts for 69 per cent of the total food crop area harvested, already occupies the most fertile lowland areas on Java, Bali, southern Sulawesi and southern Sumatra. About 87 per cent of rice areas in Indonesia are irrigated, with Java accounting for 57 per cent of the total irrigated area (*ibid.* tables 5.1.2 and 5.1.26).

However, as noted above, there is little scope for increasing harvesting areas, even sustaining high rates of growth in yields and output of rice on Java. As the average area planted with higher-yielding varieties (HYVs) of rice on Java reached 94 per cent in 1981–5, and on East Java 99 per cent, yields were nearly constant over 1983–6. In recent years a quarter of the increased rice production has already come from extending rice cultivation to marginal lands, in particular, the tidal swamps of Sumatra and Kalimantan (Barbier, 1987; World Bank, 1987a). Moreover, rice is facing increasing competition for irrigated and other land on Java from other crops, whose growth and income prospects are much brighter. Finally, if diversification into secondary food crops and estate crops is meant to complement rather than displace rice production, then increased output of the former will mean intensifying production, and extending the area of cultivated marginal lands, such as the upland farming areas on Java.

The limits on expanding irrigated rice production and increasing yields on the fertile lowlands of the Inner Islands suggest that these resources are already being exploited at or near their full potential production level. In contrast, agricultural production on Java's uplands are epitomized by low yields stemming from cropping systems, land management techniques, input packages and, above all, research and extension advice that are inappropriate for the more diversified and fragile agro-ecological conditions found on

Table 4.1   Area planted of paddy and secondary crops: Java, 1985

	Wetland (ha)	Dryland (ha)	Total (ha)	Total Indonesia (ha) (area harvested)
		('000 units)		
Paddy	4,756.5	329.7	5,086.2	9,902.3
Maize	541.9	1,403.6	1,945.5	2,439.9
Cassava	25.6	766.9	792.5	1,291.8
Sweet Potatoes	40.4	58.8	99.2	256.1
Peanuts	123.8	245.7	369.5	510.1
Soybeans	378.6	238.9	617.5	896.2
Total	5,866.8	3,043.6	8,910.4	15,296.4

Sources: BPS, *Production of Cereals in Java*, 1985; and *Costs Structures of Farms Paddy and Palawija*, 1985.

these lands. Thus the potential economic contribution of cultivated upland areas could be signficantly improved.

Nevertheless, dryland (mainly upland) food production accounts for approx. two-thirds or more of maize, cassava, sweet potato and peanut production and around 40 per cent of soybean production on Java. The total dryland area planted to paddy and secondary crops on Java amounts to about one-fifth of total harvested food production area in Indonesia (see Table 4.1). Thus food production alone on the marginal drylands of Java may contribute to over 3 per cent of GDP and about 15 per cent of agricultural GDP in Indonesia. Moreover, Table 4.2 indicates that yields in food production could be substantially increased, particularly on dryland areas, by overcoming land management and other constraints. This suggests that the potential food production on Java's drylands could be almost 25 per cent greater than current output (see Table 4.3). On highly erodible soils (e.g. limestone clays), and on slopes greater than 50 per cent, switching out of annual food cropping altogether into perennial tree crops and livestock-based systems would significantly increase the economic potential of these severely degraded uplands.

The costs of upper watershed degradation in Java

Java has one of the highest natural erosion rates in the world. Volcanic eruptions cause extensive mudflows, landslides and other

Table 4.2   Indonesia Agricultural Incentives Policy Study:

Commodity	Provinces with major smallholder activities in order of importance	Main constraints to increasing smallholder production
(1)	(2)	(3)
Paddy (rice) (dry gabah)	W. Java, E. Java, C. Java, S. Sulawesi, N. Sumatra, S. Sumatra, W. Kalimantan, S. Kalimantan, W. Sumatra, Aceh, Lampung, NTB, Bali, Riau, Jambi, NTT*	Pests (chiefly brown planthopper and rats); diseases; limited periods of water supply or flooding; lack of upland blast-resistant varieties
Corn (dry seed)	E. Java, C. Java, S. Sulawesi, NTT, N. Sulawesi, W. Java, N. Sumatra, Bali, SE Sulawesi, Yogyakarta, C. Sulawesi, Lampung, NTB	Downy mildew and insufficient good seed of mildew-resistant variety; yield closely linked to rainfall; risk factors and unreliable marketing discourage farmers from using cash inputs
Cassava (fresh root)	E. Java, C. Java, W. Java, Yogyakarta, Lampung, NTT, S. Sulawesi	Poorly developed marketing system and low farmgate price; inadequate supply of improved planting material; crop management poor due to lack of incentives and knowledge
Groundnut (shelled)	E. Java, D. Java, W. Java, Yogyakarta, S. Sulawesi, N. Sumatra, NTB	Marketing system and price fluctuation; inadequate supply of good seed of improved planting material; crop management poor due to lack of incentives and knowledge
Soybean (dry seed)	E. Java, C. Java, NTB, Lampung, W. Java, Yogyakarta, N. Sumatra, Mali	Pod-boring insects uncontrolled; intermediate fruiting pattern; cercospora rust disease; rather poor quality due to lack of effective pest control and low standard of management
Sweet potato (fresh root)	E. Java, W. Java, C. Java, Irian Java, N. Sumatra, NTT, Bali, NTB, Maluku	Lack of effective marketing system and adequate improved planting material; limited use of case inputs due to lack of market and price level

*NTT = Nusa Tenggara Timor and NTB = Nusa Tenggara Barat

Source: World Bank, *Indonesia – Agricultural Policy: Issues and Options*, Technical Annexe, table 2; and World Bank, Washington, DC, 17 July 1987.

main constraints on production and potential for increasing the yields of major food crops

Key points for emphasis in extension	Present average smallholder yield†	Agronomically feasible average yield†	Expected yield with improved extension†
(4)	(5)	(6)	(7)
Selection of varieties resistent to local pests/diseases; improved nursery management; timing, rate and method of application of fertilizers and pesticides; correct time of transplanting; pest surveillance; communal rat control; water management including draining in maturity period	Java: 4.5 ton ha^{-1} Other islands: 3.0 ton ha^{-1}	Java: 6.0 ton ha^{-1} Other islands: 4.5 ton ha^{-1}	Java: 5.0 ton ha^{-1} Other islands: 3.5 ton ha^{-1}
Introduce short duration HYV in E. Java and in other provinces mildew-resistant HYV; correct time of planting and pest control; rate, time, method of application of fertiliser; improved processing and storage	Java: 1.7 ton ha^{-1} Other Islands: 1.6 ton ha^{-1}	Java: 2.75 ton ha^{-1} Other islands: 2.3 ton ha^{-1}	Java: 2.1 ton ha^{-1} Other islands: 1.9 ton ha^{-1}
Selection of high-yielding, bacterial blight-resistant varieties; improved processing to achieve better quality and price; promote use of fertilizer; better plant spacing; erosion control measures	Java: 9.9 ton ha^{-1} Other islands: 9.8 ton ha^{-1}	Java: 20 ton ha^{-1}	Java: 12.3 ton ha^{-1} Other islands: 12.2 ton ha^{-1}
Introduce improved HYVs; use of good seed rate; improved time, method of applying fertilizer; improved pest and disease control and post-harvest handling; improve sowing timing and land preparation; liming where necessary	0.94 ton ha^{-1}	1.5 ton ha^{-1}	1.25 ton ha^{-1}
Introduce improved varieties; improved seed and preparation/planting techniques, pest control, and post-harvest handling; rhizobium inoculation; basal phosphatic and initial nitrogen fertilizer applications	0.90 ton ha^{-1}	1.50 ton ha^{-1}	1.1 ton ha^{-1}
Introduce improved planting materials; improved rate, time and method of applying fertilizer and post-harvest handling	7.8 ton ha^{-1}	20 ton ha^{-1}	10 ton ha^{-1}

†Metric tons

Table 4.3   Actual and potential production of major food crops: Java, 1985

	Dryland area ('000 ha)	Actual yield (ton ha^{-1})	Potential yield (ton ha^{-1})	Actual production ('000 ton)	Potential production ('000 ton)
Paddy	329.7	1.75*	1.94†	576.975	639,618
Maize	1,403.6	1.7	2.1	2,386.12	2,947.56
Cassava	766.9	9.9	12.3	7,592.31	9,432,87
Sweet potatoes	58.8	7.8	10	456.64	568
Peanuts	245.7	0.95	1.25	233.415	307.125
Soybeans	238.9	0.9	1.1	215.01	262.79
Total	3,043.6	–	–	11,462.47	14,177.96

Notes:
*From Frederick C. Roche, Sustainable Farm Development in Java's Critical Lands: Is a Green Revolution Really Necessary?, Cornell University, Division of Nutritional Sciences, 1987, table 12, p. 46.
†Assumes an 11 per cent increase, as suggested by Table 4.2.
Sources: As Table 4.2, except where indicated.

forms of mass movements of soil and rocks, yet at the same time provide new soil materials of great potential fertility. In the long run natural erosion is roughly in balance with new soil formation. In practice, though, natural erosion rates measured over the short term are very high, between 1.2–12 tonnes ha^{-1} in volcanic areas and 19–60 tonnes ha^{-1} in limestone/marl areas. The total soil loss per year for Java is some 7–8 thousand million tonnes, of which the vast majority is believed to be due to accelerated erosion of dryland farming in upland areas. However, such accelerated erosion varies with slope, soil type and depth and the nature of the tillage and crop cover. On Java the recent volcanic soils are generally less erodible than the more shallow, poorly drained sedimentary (limestone/ marl) soils.[1]

Two types of costs are incurred from soil erosion: on-site losses in agricultural productivity, and off-site costs in the form of siltation of irrigation channels, harbour and reservoirs, increased flooding due to siltation, damage to coastal fisheries, disruptions to urban and industrial water supplies and increased damage due to fertilizer and pesticide runoff (see Table 4.2). A recent study by the World

Table 4.4   Soil erosion: losses and costs in Java ($m. per annum)

On site	324
Off site:	
irrigation system	8–13
harbour costs	1–3
reservoirs	16–75
Total	349–415

On-site soil losses (figures rounded)

Type of land use	Land area (16^6 ha)	Soil loss (10^6 ton)	Soil loss (ton ha^{-1})
Sawah	4.6	2	0.5
Forest	2.4	14	5.8
Degraded forest	0.4	35	87.2
Wetlands	0.1	–	–
Tegal (rain-fed)	5.3	737	138.3
Total	12.9	787	61.2

Source: W. B. Magrath and P. Arens, *The Costs of Soil Erosion on Java – A Natural Resource Accounting Approach*, World Resources Institute, Washington, DC, November 1987.

Resources Institute for Java estimated the total costs of (human-induced) accelerated erosion $349–415 million annually, which amounts to 0.5 per cent of Indonesian GDP (see Table 4.4). The authors stress, however, the difficulty of accurate estimation of the off-site impacts, particularly in separating out sedimentation from natural and non-farm erosion from erosion caused by upland dryland farming.

The overwhelming proportion of soil loss occurs on the *tegal* (dryland farming) lands. Productivity losses are estimated to lie in the range of 4.4 per cent per annum (for less sensitive crops such as cassava) to 6.8 per cent per annum for the more sensitive crops. The total cost of accelerated erosion in terms of forgone productivity is estimated to be approx. $324 million per annum, or some 4 per cent of the value of the six major rain-fed crops on Java (see Table 4.4).[2] A calculation of the loss in farmers' incomes from the failure to control soil erosion on the 903,092 ha of severely degraded upland farming area on Java suggests an annual on-site cost of around $140 million for these 'critical' lands (Barbier, 1987).

The World Resources Institute study estimated the off-site costs of damage to irrigation systems, sedimentation of reservoirs and harbour dredging. Those totalled $25–$91 million annually (see Table 4.4); insufficient information was available to assess other off-site effects. Nevertheless, as a rough order of magnitude, these estimates suggest that the downstream costs of upper watershed degradation on Java are relatively less important currently than the on-site productivity costs.

Key factors in upper watershed degradation
With such high population densities in the upland areas of Java, demographic pressures are inevitably a major factor contributing to land degradation in upper watersheds. Population growth rates appear lower, however, in those upper watersheds for which statistics are available, being close to 1 per cent per annum compared with a 1.81 per cent growth rate for Java as a whole (BPS, 1985; World Bank, 1987b). On the other hand, as noted earlier, the scarcity of arable land on Java is increasing the extensification of agriculture into upland areas that are highly marginal for resource production and, in many cases, already severely degraded.

One of the long-standing responses to the high population density on Java has been to move families to the Outer Islands for permanent resettlement. It is estimated that, measured over a 50-year period, spontaneous migration occurs at the rate of 2.5 families for every government-sponsored migrant family. Since 1950 approx. 560,000 families have been officially transmigrated – suggesting a total migration of 1.4 million families. However, this amounts to only about 5 per cent of the current population of Java and Bali. There is also some doubt as to whether a large proportion of the migrants originate from those areas of Java, such as the uplands, where the effective population pressure on resources is greatest. In addition, the official transmigration programme has been severely cut back in recent years, mainly due to financial pressures on the government. This is threatening planned programme targets, and as a result, eliminating any remaining hope that transmigration can be used to control population pressures on Java (Hardjono, 1986; World Bank, 1986).

However, there have been significant investments in the upper watersheds of Java through GOI and donor-assisted programmes that combine upland agricultural development with soil conservation. From 1972 to 1986 these investments amounted to an estimated $224 million, of which the majority were spent by GOI on Regreening grants.[3]

The donor-assisted projects have included substantial components for the development and extension of integrated packages of improved farming systems suitable to upland conditions. The UN Food and Agriculture Organization (FAO) Solo Project (1972–8) initially developed the integrated tree–fodder–animal husbandry system to replace annual cultivation on steep slopes that subsequently became the model for the other upland projects, including the Regreening programme. Bench terracing for slopes of 50 per cent or less with annual cultivation has also become standard practice. The general approach of all projects has been to subsidize bench terrace construction through cash wages, free agricultural inputs and/or in-kind inputs of food (Solo Project only) for farmers' labour. Demonstration or model farms are used in the dissemination of techniques, inputs and extension advice. Check dams and gully plugs have also been used by some projects, notably in the Regreening programme.

The evolution in approach by these programmes reflects the realization that a key factor contributing to soil erosion and low productivity on upland farmlands is the failure of farmers to adopt the appropriate farming and cultivation systems for the diverse agro-ecological conditions found on these lands. For example, a study of bench terracing and related farming practices in the Citanduy basin revealed that model farms based on recent and Pliocene volcanic soils have the lowest soil relative erodibility index and highest net returns, whereas the model farms located on the sedimentary derived (limestone) soils have low, and in some cases negative, net returns. This is due not only to the generally lower fertility of the limestone soils, but also to the higher labour inputs required for implementation and maintenance of terracing and the higher rate of topsoil loss due to greater soil erodibility.[4] In addition, bench terraces may have a high risk of collapsing after a long period where there is high limestone content of the subsoil and the bentonite clay mineral causes instability. Similarly, during periods of peak rainfall inappropriately bench-terraced fields can lose just as much if not more soil than adjacent fields cultivated using traditional methods (nearly similar to ridge terracing) (Fagi and Mackie, 1987).

Farmers are also encouraged, through extension support, to adopt improved cropping patterns, which together with the introduction of new varieties, increased inputs (e.g. fertilizer and pesticides) and better technical information are intended to improve the net returns from cultivation. For example, in the Citanduy II Project in West Java, farmers were advised not to monocrop corn and cassava, but switch to growing higher-value crops. As a result, increased returns from terracing have been largely associated with changing crop patterns: cassava production fell from 42.4 to 12.4 per cent of the average value per plot, while rice production increased from 7.1 to 26.8 per cent and peanut production rose from 3.4 to 17.8 per cent (Saragih, Huszar and Cochrane, 1986). Finally, on steep uplands livestock and agro-forestry based systems are found to be more appropriate than cultivation of annual crops. On slopes greater than 50 per cent the basic approach has been to discourage farmers from growing annual crops and instead to plant tree crops for cash income such as cloves, fruits, coffee, cocoa and tea, fuelwood for domestic consumption and sale, fodder trees and grass under the canopy for livestock.

Hence, given that upland farmers face significant costs in adopting soil conservation measures and changes in farming systems, they are unlikely to make changes in their land management unless there is a perceived economic advantage in so doing. In addition, the more productive or profitable the land use, the more farmers will be willing to maintain and invest in better land management and erosion control practices. Higher productivity and returns will also mean that farmers can afford to maintain terraces and other conservation structures and to continue with labour-intensive erosion control measures. On the other hand, poorer upland farmers, dependent on low-return cropping systems, such as maize or cassava, may be aware that soil erosion is reducing productivity but may not be able to afford to adopt conservation measures. At the other extreme, farmers with very profitable crops that are extremely erosive, such as temperate vegetables on steep upper volcanic slopes, may not consider soil conservation measures if their returns do not appear to be affected by soil erosion losses. Thus the relationship between the erodibility and profitability of different farming systems on different soils and slopes is an important determinant of whether upland farmers adopt a soil conservation strategy.[5]

Other important factors may also be significant, such as the ability to earn greater returns from off-farm employment, insecurity of land tenure, poor transportation and marketing facilities and inadequate information on available technology, inputs and farming methods. For example, the lack of secure land tenure prevents many farmers on steep slopes from adopting agro-forestry systems, as they have no incentive to bear the 3–5-year 'waiting cost' before harvesting trees. Similarly, the landowners who lease the land often hold it for speculative purposes – and hence are only interested in maximizing the yields of the crop in the ground (Barbier, 1988; Sumitro, 1983).

Current GOI pricing policies and general market trends have a significant influence on the economic incentives for upland farmers to improve their cropping systems and land management. Although there are important regional variations in trends, on the whole over the period 1976–86 across Java, the farmer terms of trade for paddy rice have declined sharply. For secondary food (*palawija*) crops, such as cassava, maize, soybeans, groundnuts and other legumes, the terms of trade have risen only marginally, except for more significant increases in central Java. Recently also the price of cassava has rebounded, doubling in 1985 and again in 1987, largely reflecting GOI's targeting policy of overcoming domestic shortages and procuring sufficient supplies to meet the EEC export quota.[6] For commercial crops as a whole (e.g. coffee, tea, cloves, pepper and other tree crops), the decline in world commodity prices has generally depressed farmer terms of trade, although the devaluations in 1983 and September 1986 have restored Indonesia's competitiveness in many tree crop exports. For both tropical and temperate fruits, high effective protection has meant that the farmer terms of trade on Java have increased dramatically in recent years.[7]

With the exception of the recent price rise for cassava, these price trends for Java may over the long run encourage upland agricultural production to move from less profitable cultivation of relatively inelastic basic starchy staples to more profitable, income-elastic commodities such as fruits, animal products and tree crops. As noted above, although increased profitability alone may not be sufficient for inducing conservation, increasing profitability of agriculture provides an important incentive for upland farmers to invest in soil conservation measures and improved land management techniques (Barbier, 1988; Roche, 1987; and Saragih, Huszar and Cochrane, 1986).

On the other hand, the higher farmer terms of trade and thus profitability of vegetable crops and sugarcane – due to highly protected domestic pricing, and in the case of sugar, stringent area targeting – may actually be a disincentive to soil conservation in the uplands of Java. As the average returns to these highly commercialized and input-intensive crops increase share tenancy and absentee ownership become more common, which can reduce the incentives for long-term investments in improved land management if tenancy arrangements are insecure, and if the objectives of absentee owners is short-term profit maximization or land speculation. In addition, the increased profitability of vegetable crops means that farmers are encouraged to cultivate them on steep-sloped volcanic soils, where water runoff and hence soil erosion are enhanced. The recent and rapid rise of cassava prices is also worrying, as some upland farmers are switching from farming systems more protective of erosive soil, such as those based on livestock rearing, agro-forestry and multi-cropping annual crops, to growing just cassava which can lead to increased erosion (World Bank, 1987b).

There is also concern that some improvements in terms of trade are not directly benefiting farmers needing to make investments in land management, farming system improvements and soil and water conservation. Current evidence suggests that the considerable market power of exporter associations, licensed exporters and approved traders and other marketing intermediaries is ensuring that farmers are receiving relatively few of the benefits of devaluation with respect to coffee, corn, cassava, spices, pepper and other smallholder commodities. In general, farmers growing crops on rain-fed drylands, which predominate in the uplands of Java, tend to have lower producer margins than farmers growing crops on the irrigated lowlands. For example, farmers receive 80–85 per cent of the retail price for soybeans and only 60–65 per cent of the final price of corn, which is predominantly a dryland crop (World Bank, 1987a).

Moreover, whereas farmers in lowland irrigated areas of Java have benefited substantially from the disproportionate investments in marketing and transportation going to these areas as part of the past policies to boost rice self-sufficiency, marketing and transportation facilities in many upland areas are still inadequate. In the uplands farmers tend to have holdings that are small in scale and scattered on small and isolated plots, which increase transportation and marketing inefficiencies. In addition, as they have limited labour and capital, very limited market information and more mixed cropping systems yielding smaller volumes of individual crops, upland farmers are less likely to engage in marketing activities and are more prone to price discrimination by marketing intermediaries. In the Citanduy River Basin, West Java, only 10–20 per cent of clove and peanut farmers perform marketing activities, such as drying, transporting the commodities to subdistrict sellers, or a combination of these two activities.[8] The inability of upland farmers to receive sufficient returns from their marketing efforts may deter them from investing in improved farming systems or in soil and water conservation techniques that also boost yields.

The hallmark of the past policy to achieve rice self-sufficiency in Indonesia was generous input subsidies, which have substantially benefited farmers in the lowland irrigated areas of Java, southern Sumatra, southern Sulawesi and Bali. In 1985 total agricultural input subsidies were at approx. $725 million to $220 million for fertilizer, $25 million for pesticides, $30 million for irrigation operation and maintenance (O & M), and $370 million for irrigation capital expenditures and $80 million for credit. The current effective subsidy for fertilizers to farmers is about 38 per cent of the farmgate price; for pesticides more than 40 per cent; for irrigation as much as 87 per cent; and for credit an implicit rate of 8 per cent (World Bank, 1987a).

There is considerable evidence that these input subsidies are encouraging wasteful and inefficient use. For example, the current rate of fertilizer application is two to three times higher in Indonesia than in comparable Asian countries. If application levels were reduced by one-third, savings of some $150 million per annum could be achieved. Similarly, subsidized pesticides encourage inappropriate and excessive use, discourage traditional methods of eradicating pests and make integrated and biological pest control methods relatively less attractive to farmers. A complete withdrawal of the pesticide subsidy is likely to reduce rice output by only 0.7 per cent while saving the government $25 million annually. Inadequate irrigation charges and generous subsidies have contributed to excessive use of water in many areas, and the failure to cover O & M costs is preventing needed investments in the irrigation network to improve supply. And finally, over 50 per cent of the subsidized credit goes to sugar producers, even though sugar accounts for only 3.3 per cent of the value of the total crop production in Indonesia (*ibid.*).

However, with the current policy emphasis on agricultural diversification, these subsidies are increasingly being used to stimulate production of non-rice crops, notably sugar, cassava, maize, palm oil and soybeans. Although these subsidies are gradually extending to farmers in upland farms, rain-fed and mainly upland crops on Java, with the exception of high-valued vegetables, fruits and commercial crops, still tend to use relatively less subsidized inputs than irrigated rice and sugar. On the other hand, rain-fed crops appear to use relatively more organic fertilizers (Roche, 1987).

Supplying subsidized inputs to upland farmers will not only increase the total costs of this policy at a time of economic austerity for the government, but it may also prove to be counterproductive. For example, fertilizer subsidies are a disincentive, at least in the short run, for upland farmers to face the full economic costs of declining soil fertility, particularly from soil erosion, and to respond with sound land conservation techniques. In Ngadas, East Java, farmers are presently using over 1,000 kg of subsidized chemical fertilizers per hectare to produce two 10-tonne potato crops. These yields are less than half of what could be attained with improved soil management and green manuring techniques. Recently farmers have increased their use of organic fertilizers, as they came to realize that increased fertilizer use was no longer offsetting yield reductions (Carson *et al.*, 1987).

Although in Indonesia inputs are generously subsidized, expenditure on agricultural research is below the target level of 2 per cent of agricultural GDP of comparable countries. The GOI's Agency for Agricultural Research and Development's (AARD) total research budget amounted to only 0.3 per cent of agricultural GDP in 1986-7. Although about 65 per cent of this budget is allocated to Java, the main focus has been on rice. For example, 60 per cent of the staff with graduate training in food crop research work on rice (World Bank, 1987a). More investment and reallocation of priorities in agricultural research to farming systems and land management techniques appropriate for upland areas is required. Similarly, there needs to be improvements in the links between this upland-oriented farming systems research and the agricultural and forestry extension services.

Policies for sustainable uplands development

Isolated soil and water conservation projects are not sufficient to deal with the problem of upper watershed degradation on Java. Sustainable development might be better served by complementary economic policies and investment strategies that both enhance agricultural development in the uplands through increasing incomes and productivity and, at the same time, reduce the economic pressures on farmers to deplete the land and accelerate soil erosion. To do this, however, may require a re-orientation of agricultural policies and resources away from their current bias towards lowlands rice production, to meet the very specific needs of upland agriculture. It is also clear that for such a reallocation of resources to be successful, it must also be efficient. This implies that the input-subsidized and production-oriented targeting approach for each commodity that, as part of the Green Revolution, was successful in achieving rice self-sufficiency by the early 1980s would be a costly – and perhaps counterproductive – approach to replicate for the uplands of Java. There are basically two reasons, as follows.

First, the highly diversified soil conditions, topography and agro-ecological zones that comprise the uplands, which are often characterized by non-contiguous small holdings with mixed cropping patterns, require a more flexible farming systems approach. Instead of attempting to direct cropping patterns and areas to be harvested on a single commodity basis, this approach should be orientated towards both effectively controlling soil erosion and boosting productivity of the varied and appropriate mixed cropping, agro-forestry and silvo-pastoral systems that would be appropriate under these diverse upland conditions. The immediate priority areas for investment in the uplands therefore are for research and extension to support this new farming systems approach, and for building up the physical infrastructure of the uplands, such as rural transport, integration of markets, and post-harvest technology and processing.

Secondly, although past agricultural policies may have achieved the objective of rice self-sufficiency and general rural and agricultural development of the lowlands of Java, there are indications that a similar approach applied to stimulate agricultural diversification – and particularly development of upland dryland agriculture – would be highly costly. It would also encourage inefficient and wasteful use of subsidized inputs and may even exacerbate problems of land degradation. With Indonesia now producing rice surpluses that have resulted in high storage costs of excess stocks and subsidized exports, there is clearly a case for introducing a phased reduction of those subsidies favouring irrigated rice production and reallocating funds towards the more prioritized upland investment needs of research and extension and infrastructure.

Reducing or eliminating input subsidies and reallocating research and extension funds could in the short-term release US $275 million annually for investment in more sustainable agriculture.[9] Assuming over time a complete phasing out of the fertilizer subsidy and a fourfold increase both in research and, extension budgets, this could increase to as much as US $525 million per year. Thus the following investment programme would be feasible:

1. Integrated pest management (IPM) for brown planthopper control to be gradually extended to IPM for other pests.
2. Increasing the availability of general rural credit, particularly to marginal farmers, at affordable rates and with multiple terms.
3. Research and extension to develop and support new farming systems and land management techniques appropriate for the marginal (mainly dryland and swampland) sedentary agriculture in the Outer Islands and the uplands of Java, as well as shifting cultivation. This would include the development and dissemination of new varieties appropriate to diverse agro-ecological conditions, research into past and disease outbreaks and improvements in smallholder estate crop systems.
4. Investment in:
    (a) further improvements in farming systems for specific agro-ecological zones;
    (b) improvements in the physical infrastructure serving these zones, including rural transport, integration of markets, credit facilities, post-harvest technology and processing, and produce quality.

Such an agricultural strategy does not necessarily mean sacrificing the overall government objectives of food self-sufficiency and agricultural diversification. On the contrary, it may be crucial for achieving these objectives.

In addition, a major reason for the failure of the current strategy is its distortion of the incentives for upland farmers to invest in improvements in their management of their land and in agricultural systems and soil and water conservation techniques that control erosion. Removing these distortions requires:

1. eliminating high effective protection rates for vegetables and sugar;
2. ending procurement policies for cassava that artificially increase its relative price;
3. removing monopolistic trading and marketing practices to allow the benefits of improved terms of trade of commercial tree crops to reach upland smallholders;
4. ensuring the availability of general rural credit in the uplands at affordable interest rates;
5. overcoming the bottlenecks in the production and dissemination of seeds of HYVs crucial to improve diverse farming systems for variable upland conditions.

Finally, the experience gained from upper watershed projects and programmes indicates that there is a need to strengthen the technical capacity of local and regional staff and to develop the effective interaction between agencies providing technical planning and supervision and local bodies participating to set development priorities. Such institution building is essential to improve the technical capability of local and regional government for farm and village planning, conservation and land use planning and implementation, and watershed management.

In effect, these policies and strategies have as their objective comprehensive rural development in the uplands of Java, with a strong emphasis on infrastructure investments and balanced regional development. The additional value of such physical infrastructure investments in rural areas is their potential for direct and indirect generation of off-farm employment. For example, the increased investment in rural infrastructure in the lowlands of Java that accompanied the rice-based development strategy expanded off-farm employment opportunities in trade, transportation, private construction and services that especially benefited the landless and those with marginal holdings (Collier *et al.*, 1982; Hedley, 1987). Greater infrastructure investments in the uplands of Java would also have important income-generating and multiplier employment effects, as would the establishment of some processing and transformation in rural areas to allow produce to be stored, moved to nearby or distant markets, sorted, graded and packed for domestic and export markets, and processed into both food and industrial products.

Although there is some evidence that the availability of off-farm income may lessen farmers' attachment to the land and hence their willingness to invest in improved land management, the effective co-ordination of physical infrastructure investment with agricultural and rural development activities should expand overall incomes and employment opportunities sufficiently to ensure that the majority of households would use these additional resources to invest in and improve their land.

Notes

1. See Magrath and Arens (1987). Erodibility is often defined as 'the ease with which soil particles are being detached and carried away by the impact of falling rain' (World Bank, 1987b). The major soils of Java are commonly divided into four susceptibility classes: recent volcanic (low erodibility), Pliocene volcanic (low to medium), Pliocene sedimentary (high) and Miocene sedimentary (very high): see Kucera *et al.* (1986).

2. On the methodological approach to calculating these costs see Magrath and Arens (1987).

3. World Bank (1987b). Regreening funds are for privately owned land, as distinct from Reforestation grants, which are for replanting state-owned forests. Total expenditures for Regreening on Java over 1976–86 amounted to $166 million. Whereas donor-assisted watershed projects tend to combine the objectives of increasing the productivity and incomes of upland farms, soil conservation and, in some cases, local institution building, Regreening has been seen as a vehicle for employment creation in underdeveloped rural areas, asserting the central government's presence in peripheral regions and distributing funds to these locations to stimulate more balanced regional demand.

4. Kucera *et al.* (1986). Bench terracing often requires a significant input of human labour, ranging from about 750 to over 1800 man days (MD) per hectare, depending on the slope. This implies construction costs of between $40–$2,060 ha^{-1} (1979 prices), or $560–$2075 ha^{-1} for total labour and material costs. These estimates do not include the additional costs to the farmer of periodic maintenance of terraces, waterways and drop structures. For farmers to add an intensive livestock system, the cost of establishing a grass cover on terraces is approx. $72 ha^{-1} for material (1979 prices) and an extra 2–5 MD ha^{-1}, if 20 per cent of the hectare is in terrace risers and lips. A mature female sheep or goat costs about $70: see Bernsten and Sinaga (1983).

5. For further discussion and analysis of these economic incentives see Barbier (1988).

6. Although only 10 per cent of the cassava produced in Indonesia is exported, 97 per cent of exports are to the EEC: see Kasryno (1987).

7. For further discussion see World Bank (1987b).

8. Irawan (1986); on the role of marketing and transportation infrastructure investments in stimulating further agricultural diversification and upland development: see Hedley (1987).
9. This amounts to US $150 million from a reduction in the fertilizer subsidy, US $25 million and US $40 million from the abolition of the pesticide and sugar credit subsidies respectively, and US $30 million each for reallocation of research and extension funding.

References

Barbier, E. B. (1987), 'Natural resources policy and economic framework', in J. Tarrant *et al.*, *Natural Resource and Environmental Management in Indonesia*, Jakarta; USAID, October.

Barbier, E. B. (1988), *The Economics of Farm-level Adoption of Soil Conservation Measures in the Uplands of Java*, Environment Department Working Paper No. 11, World Bank, Washington, DC.

Bernsten, R. and Sinaga, R. (1983), 'Economics', Technical Appendix VI, in GOI/ USAID, *Composite Report of the Watershed Assessment Team*, 3 vols, USAID, Jakarta, May.

Biro Pusat Statistik (1986), *Statistik Indonesia 1985*, Jakarta: BPS.

Biro Pusat Statistik (1985), *Statistik Indonesia 1983*, Jakarta: BPS.

Carson, B. and KEPAS East Java (1987), *A Comparison of Soil Conservation Strategies in Four Agroecological Zones in the Upland of East Java*. KEPAS, Malang, Indonesia, July.

Collier, W. L., Soentoro, Wirandi, Pasandaran, E., Santoso, K. and Stepanek, J. F. (1982), 'Acceleration of rural development on Java', *Bulletin of Indonesian Economic Studies*, **18**, November, 1-12.

Douglass, M. (1987), 'Changing patterns of access to agricultural land on Java and the Outer Islands', Department of Urban and Regional Planning, University of Hawaii, Honolulu, October.

Fagi, A. M. and Mackie, C. (1987), 'Watershed management in upland Java – Past Experience and Future Directions', paper presented at Soil Conservation Society of America Conference on Soil and Water Conservation on Steep Lands, San Juan, Puerto Rico, 22-27 March.

Hanson, A. J. (1987), 'Environmental management development in Indonesia', paper presented at IIED Conference on Sustainable Development, London, 28-30 April.

Hardjono, J. (1986), 'Transmigration: looking to the future', *Bulletin of Indonesian Economic Studies*, **22**, August, 28-53.

Hedley, D. D. (1987), 'Diversification: concepts and directions in Indonesian agricultural policy', Workshop on Soybean Research and Development in Indonesia, CGPRI Centre, Bogor, Indonesia, 24-26 February.

Irawan, B. (1986), 'Executive summary: marketing analysis for dryland farming development in Citanduy River Basin', USESE, Ciamis, Indonesia.

Kasryno, F. (1987), *Analysis of Trends and Prospects for Cassava in Indonesia*, Center for Agroeconomic Research, Agency for Agricultural Research and Development, Bogor, Indonesia, April

Kucera, K. *et al.* (1986), *Micro Model Farm Assessment of Land Resources*, Department of Forestry and USAID, Citanduy, Ciamis, Indonesia, May.

Magrath, W. B. and Arens, P. (1987), *The Costs of Soil Erosion on Java – a Natural Resource Accounting Approach*, Washington DC: Resources Institute, November.

Roche, F. C. (1987), 'Sustainable farm development in Java's critical lands: is a "Green Revolution" really necessary?, Cornell University Division of Nutritional Sciences.

Saragih, B., Huszar, P. C. and Cochrane, H. C. (1986), 'Model Farm Program Benefits: the Citanduy watershed', USAID, Jakarta, July.

Sumitro, A. (1983), 'Tree crop management', Technical Appendix V, in GOI/USAID *Composite Report of the Watershed Assessment Team*, 3 vols, USAID, Jakarta, May.

World Bank (1986), *Indonesia – Transmigration Review*, Washington, DC: World Bank, October.

World Bank (1987a), *Indonesia – Agricultural Policy: Issues and Options*, Washington DC: World Bank, July.

World Bank (1987b), *Indonesia – Java Watersheds: Java Uplands and Watershed Management*, Washington, DC: World Bank, November.

5 Sustainable forest management in the Outer Islands of Indonesia[1]

Introduction

In Chapter 4 we have discussed policies and approaches for sustainable development of agriculture in the upper watersheds of Java. This chapter explores the need for sustainable forest management as a response to land use conflicts on the Outer Islands of Indonesia, and asks whether current Indonesian policies are encouraging sustainable management of Indonesia's production forests. Although increased economic exploitation of forest resources has been achieved in the short run, it is questionable whether the current strategy is very efficient or sustainable in the long run. There is also increasing concern over the loss of forest areas to agriculture and other uses.

In Indonesia the problem of proper management of forest resources stems less from lack of funds than from a need to change fundamental attitudes. In the past the Indonesian forests 'have been regarded primarily as a reserve of land for conversion to other uses and a storehouse of raw materials to be converted to ready cash, rather than a valuable renewable resource and production system in their own right, which could be managed for the sustained long-term production of a variety of goods and services' (GOI/IIED, 1985, p. 21). Changing this attitude is crucial if forestry policy is to develop appropriate approaches to management of production forest, assign and protect conservation areas, establish plantations, and clear land for other uses.

On paper forest policy appears to be well thought-out. Indonesia's forest lands are divided into protection forests intended primarily to maintain watersheds; national park and reserve forests; limited production forests in which restrictive felling is allowed; full production forests which can be commercially exploited or converted to plantations; and conversion forest areas that can be cleared for agriculture and other use. Guidelines exist for selective cutting of production forests, and a reforestation fund exists for replanting cut stands. Nature conservation targets in the current five-year plan, Repelita IV (1984-9), include establishing 12 tourism forests, 10 nature reserves, and 16 protection forests. There is also a significant Regreening and Reforestation Programme that aims to rehabilitate and establish forests to protect critical watershed catchment areas (see Chapter 4).

However, in practice, implementation of forestry policy has run into many difficulties. A major problem has been the lack of reliable data on the actual utilization patterns of forest land. Only half of Indonesia's production and conversion forests have been subject to aerial photo surveys; preliminary ground surveys have covered only 60 million hectare of forestry areas; and only 0.2 per cent of forest land has been intensively surveyed. The result is that there is insufficient and uncertain information on forest degradation, conversion and deforestation on which to base policy. What information does exist from independent research conducted by donor agencies, university research stations, private industry and provincial authorities is neither well co-ordinated nor analyzed for policy-making purposes. In addition, decisions concerning forestry policy implementation are invariably taken by central government, often without any reference to the special forestry requirements of each province.

In addition, there are increasing demographic and economic pressures to 'open up' forest lands. Indonesia's population of 104.2 million is not evenly distributed (Table 5.1). Approximately 60 per cent of the total population is concentrated on the so-called Inner Islands of Java and Bali, which comprise just over 7 per cent of the country's total land area. The population density on Java is estimated to be 788 people per square kilometre, compared to the national average of 90. In contrast, the population density of Kalimantan – one of the large Outer Islands – is only 15 people per square kilometre. The Outer Islands, with nearly 40 per cent of the population, have only around 5 per cent of their land in sedentary agriculture and only 20 per cent of the country's medium-sized and large-scale industry. Consequently, extensive agricultural development continues to be the main source of employment in the Outer Islands, as well as the spur to spontaneous and official migration of poor undercapitalized labour from Java and other Inner Islands.

With approximately 97 per cent of Indonesia's 114 million hectares of forests located in the Outer Islands, land use conflicts over remaining forest lands are inevitable. These are exacerbated by unsustainable management of timber production. Indonesia's production forest is

Table 5.1 Basic data

Island	Estimated 1987 population	People per km^2	Population growth (% p.a.)	Percentage land in sedentary agriculture	Percentage land* *a* in forest department boundaries	Percentage medium- and large-scale manufacturing
Inner Islands						
Java	104.2	788	1.7	43	22	80.0
Bali	2.8	503	1.3	–	22	2.7
Outer Islands						
Sumatra	35.1	74	3.1	8	65	11.0
Kalimantan	8.2	15	3.0	3	82	3.1
Sulawesi	12.0	63	2.2	8	68	2.6
Irian Jaya	1.4	3	2.9	1	99	–
Other	8.5	37	3.0	–	69	0.5
Total	172.2	90	2.1	8	75	100

*Includes reserves, protection, production and conversion forest. Note that these figures are based on the Ministry of Forestry's classification system, which assumes a total forest area of 144 million hectares.
Source: World Bank.

currently estimated at 55-65 million hectares, and is largely concentrated on the three largest Outer Islands containing 85 per cent of Indonesia's forested areas: Irian Jaya (34 per cent), Kalimantan (31 per cent) and Sumatra (20 per cent). Only 6.5 per cent of timber production is from Java and consists mainly of teak from old Dutch plantations. In contrast, that produced from the Outer Islands is tropical hardwood harvested from the primary rainforest. But recent analysis suggests that (a) only 35-40 million hectares of production forests are under 45 per cent slope and forested – which implies more than half the area would be environmentally destructive to log, and (b) much of the economically loggable areas has been harvested.[2] Thus, by failing to manage logging sustainably, the government of Indonesia (GOI) is further depleting its forest resources, and creating a situation where the industry must depend on more forest land being brought into production.

Although the major part of deforestation in Indonesia appears to be caused by shifting cultivation and planning agricultural conversion (see Table 5.2), the 'mining' of the production forests may pose the most serious threat to the economic viability of the tropical rainforests. For example, recent mapping suggests that Kalimantan, the most important timber producer, may have an economically harvestable area of 15 million hectares or less, rather than the previously believed 26 million hectares. By 1990 potential production in Kalimantan could be as low as 12 million hectares, and less than 10 million hectares in the year 2000.[3]

Yet timber production could, in principle, be made more efficient and sustainable. Whereas the major concern for Java is proper maintenance of the existing plantations and preservation of the watershed forest lands, for the Outer Islands implementation of an appropriate reforestation programme, sustainable management of the remaining natural stock and incentives for replanting on concessions are the major needs. This case study will therefore focus primarily on the policies of the GOI to manage the production forests, and the conflicts with other uses of forest lands.

Forests in the Indonesian economy
In the mid-1980s real GDP growth in Indonesia slowed considerably, probably falling in per capita terms over 1984-5, and only growing on average by 3.7 per cent per annum in 1986 and 1987. This has largely been due to the drop in world oil prices, which declined on average by

Table 5.2   Sources of deforestation, 1980–90 (ha)

Source of depletion	Annual	1980–6	1980–90
Shifting cultivation:			
Kalimantan	350,000	2,100,000	3,500,000
Irian Jaya	50,000	300,000	300,000
Other*	100,000	600,000	1,000,000
Subtotal	500,000	3,000,000	5,000,000
Development projects:			
Sponsored transmigration			
settlement	100,000	600,000	600,000
secondary development	–	–	300,000
Spontaneous migration	100,000	600,000	1,000,000
Estate crop development	20,000	80,000	200,000
Subtotal	220,000	1,280,000	2,100,000
Other			
Total logging†	(160,000)	(960,000)	(1,600,000)
Logging damage (no			
shifting cultivation)	80,000	480,000	800,000
Normal fire loss	60,000	360,000	600,000
Subtotal	140,000	840,000	1,400,000
Total	860,000	5,120,000	8,500,000
East Kalimantan Fire		3,000,000‡	675,000§

*Low estimates; the range is 100,000–300,000 ha yr^{-1}.
†Not included to avoid overlapping between losses due to logging and shifting cultivation – could be attributed to either category.
‡Primary and logged over forest, excluding area already under shifting cultivation.
§Assumes permanent conversion of 50 per cent of previously logged and burned areas.
Source: World Bank.

63 per cent over 1982–6 although the fall in other tradable commodity prices has also been significant. The result has been a current account deficit averaging around 4.6 per cent of GDP and a considerable depreciation in the real effective exchange rate.[4] Other factors contributing to slow growth include the deceleration of agricultural output growth, sluggish consumer demand and the decline in gross domestic capital formation. The latter declined by almost 10 per cent during 1983–5.

In this economic climate the development of timber production for exports has emerged as a major priority. Timber products extracted from Indonesia's forests are an essential and growing source of export earnings. In 1986 they earned over US $1.2 billion, which amounted to approx. 20 per cent of non-oil and 6.5 per cent of total exports. By 1987–8 sawn timber and plywood exports alone accounted for over 14 per cent of total merchandise exports (World Bank, 1988).

The forests of Indonesia serve numerous multi-functional purposes, however, with many contributions to economic development in addition to the value of the forests as a source of timber products. This is to a large extent acknowledged in Indonesia's forest classification system, which earmarks 30.3 million hectares of natural forest as protected biological reserves and an additional 18.75 million hectares as national parks of potential touristic value. In 1985–6 over 2.5 million people visited park and reservation forest areas in Indonesia, of which over 25,000 were foreign visitors.[5]

In addition, non-timber products from the natural forest, such as rattan, charcoal, cassiavera, copal, *tenqakawanq* (tree nut), resin, sandalwood, fruit, honey, meat and natural silk, not only sustain the livelihoods of forest dwellers and settlers, but also have significant export potential. Exports of non-timber forest products have already expanded from US $17 million in 1973 to $154 million in 1985, and in the latter year comprised 12 per cent of all forest product export earnings. In 1985 rattan exports alone earned US $80 million. With the current support to the labour-intensive rattan furniture industry, the value added export earnings from rattan furniture could be as high as US $270 million (Gillis, 1988; Ministry of Forestry, 1986; and World Bank, 1986a). Legal wildlife exports amounted to over US $9 million in 1985–6 (Ministry of Forestry, 1987, table 18). If properly developed Indonesia's non-timber forest products could have significant potential for supporting labour-intensive, small-scale industries which could greatly benefit rural people living in or adjacent to forest areas. As many of these products can be harvested with little damage to the forest, they are an important indication of the value of the tropical forest in its natural state.

However, perhaps the most important contribution of Indonesia's forests to economic development comes through its indirect and intangible benefits from watershed protection, soil stabilization, conservation of genetic resources, maintenance of wildlife habitats and climate stabilization. Thus the full economic contribution of the forests must include not only their productive value as timber resources, but also their value in supporting other economic activities dependent on their existence (e.g. husbandry of non-timber forest products and traditional shifting cultivation), other economic values (e.g. the option and existence values of preserving biological diversity, micro-climatic functions) and favourable cross-sectoral impacts on, in particular, neighbouring agricultural activity (e.g. maintenance of soil fertility and cohesion, hydrological cycles).[6] The sum total of these indirect and intangible benefits may in fact exceed the direct benefits from exploiting Indonesia's forests for timber and other forest products.

Finally, at a global level Indonesia's tropical forests may be valued for their function of absorbing carbon dioxide, thus counteracting any global warming resulting from the 'greenhouse effect'. Conversely, tropical deforestation in Indonesia may be adding significantly to this effect, as the clearing and burning of the world's tropical forests is thought to be an important and growing cause of the emission of CO_2 and other greenhouse trace gases into the atmosphere.[7]

The costs of deforestation

Table 5.2 indicates that the rate of deforestation in Indonesia is about 900,000 ha per year, or 850,000 ha per annum if the major Kalimantan fire of 1983 is excluded. The major sources of depletion appear to be from shifting cultivation (500,000 ha p.a.); from planned agricultural conversion (200,000–250,000 ha p.a.); and from logging and normal fire loss (140,000–150,000 ha p.a.). By far the greatest impact from planned agricultural conversion has come from sponsored transmigration, and increasingly spontaneous migration from the Inner to the Outer Islands; these figures appear in line with previous estimates, although lack of sufficient mapping and appropriate survey data severely hampers accurate measurement.[8] It is especially difficult to estimate the rate of depletion due to shifting cultivation.[9] One problem is that many diverse production systems come under the latter category. It is called 'shifting cultivation' because vegetation is cut and burned to release nutrients to the soil, plots are cultivated until fertility declines (usually within a few years), and are left fallow while new land is opened up.

A study by the World Resources Institute has calculated that the total costs of the depreciation of the forest stock in Indonesia due to deforestation, forest degradation and timber extraction amounted to around US $3.1 billion in 1982, or approx. 4 per cent of GDP (Repetto *et al.*, 1987). However, this estimate must be considered a lower bound, as it does not include the value of the forest stock in supporting other economic activities (e.g. husbandry of non-timber forest products, traditional and sustainable shifting cultivation by indigenous peoples, etc.); other economic values (e.g. the option and existence values of preserving biological diversity, micro-climatic functions, etc.); other economic values (e.g. the option and existence values of preserving biological diversity, micro-climatic functions, etc.); and favourable external impacts on, say, neighbouring agricultural activity (e.g. watershed protection, etc.).

Based on the estimates in Table 5.2, an approximate indicator of the economic cost of forest conversion can also be obtained. A hectare of primary forest yields a net present value of some US $2,500–3,000 in terms of timber output, and about US $500 if already logged. The present value of shifting cultivation yielding 2,000 kg of rice per hectare for one year with a fallow period of ten years is about US $250. If half the total new area of 500,000 ha going to shifting cultivation each year is from primary forest and half from selectively logged areas, it follows that the respective costs per hectare in terms of forgone forest rentals are US $2,250–2,750 for primary forest conversion, and $250 for selectively logged forest conversion. The total rental loss per annum is thus:

$$[250,000 \text{ ha* } (\$2,250\text{--}2,750 \text{ ha}^{-1})] + [250,000 \text{ ha* } (\$250 \text{ ha}^{-1})$$
$$= \text{US } \$625\text{--}750 \text{ million.}$$

With logging damage and fire accounting for additional costs of US $70 million, this would represent losses of around US $800 million annually. The inclusion of forgone minor forest would raise this cost as high as US $1 billion per year. In addition, the loss of timber on sites used for development projects could be to the order of US $40–$100 million. Although ordinarily it could be assumed that the latter costs would be offset by agricultural benefits of equal or greater value, the poor quality of the soils in converted forest lands has meant that many agricultural development projects on the Outer Islands have a poor success rate or have been plagued with low productivity.[10]

As will be discussed more fully in the next section, the particular policies adopted to encourage domestic wood processing have also been costly, and these costs need to be offset against the benefits to Indonesia of those policies. For example, it is estimated that during 1979–82, due to the inefficient processing operations resulting from these policies, over US $545 million in potential rents was lost to the Indonesian economy, or an average cost of US $136 million annually (Gillis, 1988).

Another measure of the costs to the economy of government policies to encourage switching from the export of raw logs to processed timber products (a policy designed to create employment in the processing industries) is the impact on export earnings. For example, as this switch in exports occurred at a time when forest product prices were falling sharply in real terms over 1981–4, there was a net loss in export revenues of US $2.9–$3.4 billion, or approx. US $725–$850 million per year. However, not only did Indonesia unnecessarily forgo export receipts by replacing logs with processed timber, but it also lost income by selling plywood below production cost. This amounted to US $956 million in 1981–4, or US $239 million annually (Fitzgerald, 1986).

In addition to the forgone benefits of deforestation, there are losses of the forest protection functions and in biodiversity. As noted above, it is not possible to estimate the value of these losses. The Malesian floristic area, which mainly lies within the Indonesian archipelago, contains the greatest diversity of species in the world. As to fauna, Indonesia has some 1,500 species of birds, 500 of mammals and 1,000 of reptiles and amphibians, while the marine and coastal environments of Indonesia hold some 7,000 fish species. The economic values of all these species is under-researched, both in terms of value to the Indonesian people and to the rest of the world. There are *use values*, as with genetic blueprints for plant-based medicines, genetic material for improved crop breeding, tourism and harvesting of wildlife and other minor forest products for both local consumption and export. There are values accruing mainly to the rest of the world in terms of *option and existence values*: values reflecting a willingness to pay to see species conserved for future use or for their intrinsic worth. Such values have potential major importance to Indonesia in terms of possible payments that the rest of the world might make to Indonesia to conserve forest lands.[11]

Table 5.3 summarizes those costs of deforestation in Indonesia for

Table 5.3   Annual costs of deforestation in Indonesia (US $m.)

		Estimate	Year of Estimate
Total resource degradation costs			
A	Resource accounting* (Repetto *et al.*, 1987)	3,100	1982
B	World Bank estimates (based on Table 5.2), of which	937–1,120	1987
	1 forest conversion (shifting cultivation) (development projects)	667–850 (627–750) (40–100)	1987
	2 logging damage/fire	70	1987
	3 loss of minor forest products (from both (1) and (2)	200	1987
Costs of production forest policies			
C	Loss of potential rent (Gillis, 1988)	136	1979–82
D	Inefficiency costs (Fitzgerald, 1986), of which	861–986	1981–4
	1 loss of export revenues	725–850	1981–4
	2 loss through selling plywood below cost	239	1981–4

*Includes estimate of forgone timber rents.

which at least rough estimates are available. Note that although Table 5.2 indicates that shifting cultivation is the major source of forest loss, the loss of timber from logging and the inefficiencies created by GOI policies for timber production have given rise to greater economic costs. Thus while it is desirable that Indonesia develops a coherent policy for controlling the destruction caused by unsustainable shifting cultivation, improving the efficiency and sustainability of timber production management would yield the greatest potential economic gains.

Factors influencing deforestation

To summarize, the major factors behind deforestation are the demand for land by shifting cultivators; conversion of forest lands by development projects, especially for sedentary agriculture, but also for estate crop production and increasingly for mining and other extractive activities; inappropriate logging practices; and government timber production policies. As we shall discuss below, the two latter factors are clearly related. In addition, the inability to police parks and protected areas and to provide adequate incentives to control illegal incursions is also a serious problem.

The demand for land

Given the current economic and demographic situation in Indonesia, increasing demands for land in the Outer Islands is inevitable. For example, between 1973 and 1983 dryland production in the Outer Islands increased by more than 50 per cent, expanding by at least 3.4 million hectares. If expansion continued at the same annual rate (3.6 per cent p.a.), the total area in production in the Outer Islands would be about 10.8 million hectares in 1989 and about 15.5 million hectares a decade later. Thus, in the 1990s, new land to be brought into agricultural production, including land for export estate crops, could average about 500,000 ha p.a. in the Outer Islands (Douglass, 1987).

A major factor behind the rapid extensification of agriculture on to converted forest lands is the poor productivity of the soils in the Outer Islands. As a result, outer island farmers require more land per family to earn the same income as in Java. For example, Sumatra as a whole requires 2.1 ha to produce the same value added as 1 ha on Java, Sulawesi requires 2.7 ha, Kalimantan 3.9, Maluku 10.7 and Irian Jaya 10.7 ha (*ibid.*, table 26 and pp. 55–7).

In fact under conditions of low fertility soils an abundance of land relative to labour and few institutional constraints, such as land registration and titling, shifting cultivation is a rational production system. Although there are approx. 12–13 million households in the Outer Islands, and the majority of those in agriculture rely on sedentary cultivation, at least 1 million families depend primarily on shifting cultivation and farm approx. 7.3 million hectares.[12] Many of these shifting cultivation systems, particularly developed by indigenous populations, can remain sustainable – unless population expands, which requires either the opening of new land or a reduction in rotation periods. The former increases deforestation, whereas the latter hampers forest regeneration and further reduces soil fertility.

However, shifting cultivation systems in the Outer Islands are extremely diverse and are used by a very broad spectrum of farmers encompassing all of Indonesia's ethnic and language groups. They include sedentary agriculturalists engaging in marginal shifting cultivation, spontaneous immigrants seeking land for permanent agriculture and indigenous peoples employed in more traditional *swidden* ('slash and burn') practices. At the same time, smallholder shifting cultivators grow most of Indonesia's pepper, coffee, coconuts, tobacco and rubber; for example, in 1982, 80 per cent of rubber production was grown by smallholders, most of them swidden cultivators (Dove, 1985).

Nevertheless, a major problem is arising from the incorporation of local people within forest lands. In some provinces a higher proportion of land within forest boundaries is under shifting cultivation than is found outside such boundaries. In such circumstances, the failure to recognize explicitly the *adat* (customary law) rights of cultivators within these boundaries and the resulting absence of secure tenure may give rise to an increase in shifting cultivation and thus forest destruction. At the same time, attempts to resettle swidden agriculturalists into sedentary agriculture have not been successful, and only 10,000 families have been resettled over 1972–82 (World Bank, 1986b). Most programmes lacked socially or technically appropriate packages to upgrade production systems. A more appropriate approach may be to aim at preventing encroachment into the forest by working more closely with the local people to understand their needs and the agro-ecological features of their farming systems, by developing contractual (reciprocal) commitment in which the local people voluntarily participate and by stabilizing the boundaries of smallholder land, even for land lying within current forest boundaries.

Both the official transmigration policy and spontaneous migration of households from the inner to the Outer Islands have been responsible for significant deforestation. The transmigration programme has been very expensive, costing an estimated US $9,000 per family in remote areas and additional expenditure on rehabilitating poor soils. In addition, the programme has attracted increasing criticism from environmental groups, both inside and outside Indonesia, for its 'wasteful' destruction of forests and other natural environments. The combination of these factors – the high cost of financing the programme, the lack of suitable sites and the increasing reluctance of donors to support the programme – has meant that transmigration was virtually halted in 1986. Nevertheless, since 1979 around 540,000 families have been resettled in the Outer Islands. By the end of the 1980s it is estimated that about 1 million ha of forested land will have been converted to agricultural land for transmigration.[13]

However, the ending of official transmigration has not stopped spontaneous migration to the Outer Islands. Past records suggest that for every family officially resettled, an additional family probably migrated to the Outer Islands spontaneously. This would suggest that spontaneous migration would increase the forest areas converted to agricultural production by another 100,000 ha p.a., which would mean an additional 1 million ha converted over the 1980s. However, recent studies suggest that there are little support and facilities for settling spontaneous migrants in the Outer Islands; consequently, they are more likely than sponsored transmigrants to depend on converting new areas of forests (World Bank, 1986b). Moreover, their unfamiliarity with Outer Island forest systems may lead them to develop less sustainable and more destructive shifting cultivation based production systems. Thus increased spontaneous migration to the Outer Islands may actually exacerbate rather than retard forest conversion.

Tree crop development on the Outer Islands is also contributing to deforestation. It is estimated that estate crop plantations would lead to the conversion of perhaps 40,000 ha p.a. of forested land during 1979–84. Due to the financial constraints facing the GOI, the rate may have slowed to 20,000 ha p.a. since 1986.[14] The establishment of palm oil estates, however, continues to be a major priority. In addition to benefiting from generous subsidies on fertilizers and other inputs, pricing policy interventions have been used to divert some palm oil production to the domestic market as a substitute for coconut oil. Thus the domestic selling price of palm kernel and oil has been consistently held well below the export price, and the retail price of palm oil is fixed lower than that of coconut oil to encourage substitution. Export restrictions, and in some years export taxes, have also been applied to ensure adequate domestic supplies. To meet this induced domestic demand and provide a surplus for export oil palm production has been rapidly expanded. Between 1979 and 1984 the area under oil palm grew at an annual rate of 9 per cent, total production rose at an average rate of about 12 per cent and domestic consumption by 28 per cent. In contrast, coconut oil production fell from a peak of 712,000 tonnes in 1980 to 508,000 tonnes in 1984, which is approximately the levels attained in the 1960s and 1970s (World Bank, 1986a).

The major assumption behind this policy is that forest lands on the Outer Islands can be relatively easily and inexpensively converted into palm oil estates. About 78 per cent of Indonesian palm oil production currently comes from northern Sumatra, and around 70 per cent of the total area planted is on state-owned plantations (*ibid.*). Recently, however, the GOI has actively encouraged a system of nucleus estates on the Outer Islands, where a government-owned estate company finances investment for smallholder oil palm planters which is to be repaid to the GOI after four to five years. Each smallholder plants approx. 2 ha with palm oil and a remaining hectare with food crops or home gardens. As recent increases in productivity have mainly arisen from trees on existing plantations reaching maturity, rapid expansion of the total area of production through the nucleus estates scheme is seen as essential to expanding future palm oil production. As noted above, however, the scheme has been afflicted by problems with over-fertilization, pest and disease attacks, and the poor quality of converted forest soils.

The total land allocation for oil, mining and other major development projects appears relatively small compared to the total land area of the Outer Islands. In general, most of the land allocated is for exploration purposes, and significant amounts of land are used only when minerals or petroleum is found. The overall impacts on deforestation are largely confined to relatively small areas. Where these extractive industries and their processing facilities are concentrated, however, has led to serious problems of pollution, which can be particularly damaging to coastal areas and forest zones. The recent and rapid expansion of goldmining activity in Kalimantan has led to excessive destruction of riverbanks and swamp areas in and near important protective and conservation forests.

Production forest management
Forestry products constitute the single most important non-oil export for Indonesia, and represent approx. 14 per cent of total

merchandise export earnings. The most significant policy change with regard to production has been the introduction of export takes on logs in 1978 to encourage domestic processing, which led to the 1980-3 phased ban on exports of logs. Since 1985 virtually all log production has been processed domestically and exported as sawn timber, plywood and veneer. This policy has been severely criticized for sacrificing valuable short-run earnings in order to subsidize an inefficient and too rapid expansion of processing capacity. Nevertheless, in 1985 plywood export industries employed over 597,000 workers and other wood export industries 64,000 workers. By 1995, under favourable export policies and conditions, this could expand to 991,000 and 91,000 workers respectively (World Bank, 1986a).

From a natural resource management perspective, the unknown question is whether value added processing will slow down the rate of timber extraction and thus conserve a valuable resource for future exploitation. Official statistics suggest that total log production peaked in 1979, before the ban on log exports, at around 2.53 million m³ p.a., but fell to around 15 m. m³ in 1986-7. World Bank statistics based on industry figures, however, indicate a peak log production level of 28.2 m. m³ (*ibid.*). Much of the decline in log production over this period can also be attributed to depressed world prices for all timber products, and therefore is not necessarily indicative of less exploitation due to the conversion to processing activities. None the less, with favourable export trends predicted, Indonesian log production is now solely constrained by the capacity of domestic processing industries. Existing installed capacity of the sawmill industry is 15.3 m. m³, and of the plywood industry 6 m. m³. Assuming a 54 per cent conversion rate for sawn logs, and a 43 per cent rate for plywood, this suggests a maximum annual demand for logs of 42 m. m³. Thus such a rapid expansion of processing capacity may not aid the conservation of Indonesia's valuable tropical timber.

Total GOI revenues from royalties, property and export taxes and reforestation fees (see below) accounted for about 20 per cent of total timber export earnings up to 1978.[15] As export taxes on raw logs were increased over 1978-82, this share rose to around 37 per cent. However, as the policy to promote domestic processing has meant that the proportion of logs in total timber exports has declined, and since 1985 there have been virtually no log exports due to the ban, and the ratio of all taxes to export earnings has sharply fallen.

Moreover, as with any natural resource, there is an economic rent, or stumpage value, relating to the standing stock of trees. This is the difference between the sale value of the timber and the costs of harvesting it. The rental is an approximate indicator of the maximum amount a forest concessionaire should be willing to pay for the concession; or alternatively, the maximum amount the government could take in tax without deterring the investor. In Indonesia a comparatively low proportion of the production forest rent is taken as government tax. In 1982, for example, the government share of the rental on logs was 55 per cent and on sawn timber 46 per cent. In addition, over 1979–82 the inefficiencies in log processing due to the too rapid expansion of ply and saw mills, coupled with the world recession, caused total available rents in the industry to drop by half; if these dissipated rents are included, the government share in rents over 1979–82 remained at approx. 33–35 per cent – a very poor rent capture.

As provincial governments receive 70 per cent of timber royalties and license fees, these regional governments are the main losers. In addition, as the costs of financing additions to nature reserves and parks are financed from the GOI forestry budget, the loss of potential revenues puts at risk these investments.

The failure adequately to capture rent means that Indonesia is being insufficiently compensated for the depletion of its timber base; this, in turn, has two effects:

- it encourages 'rent-seeking' behaviour – i.e. an acceleration in the rate of deforestation as concessionaires seek to secure their large share of high rentals;
- it implies a continuing emphasis by GOI policy on maximizing production as a means of increasing total revenue.

Such effects are also reinforced by timber royalties (and in the past export taxes) being assessed on the basis of timber removals rather than on the basis of the stock of merchantable stems in the stand. Combined with the Indonesian selective cutting policy (see below), this encourages logging operators to remove only the most valuable species and very large, marketable high-grade stems while ignoring less profitable, secondary species. Yet such 'high-grading' often leads to substantial damage to the stand and extensive forest intrusion and destruction. Furthermore, when royalties are based on logs taken from the forest rather than the current potential yield from mature trees in a given stand, operators have no incentive to harvest defective and oversized stems of commercial but lesser-known species. Even though the trees will have some commercial value once sawn, the concessionaires are discouraged by being charged full royalties on such trees.

Although some concessionaires are following the government's selective cutting guidelines, the incentives to replant the land either through enrichment planting under secondary forest or replanting clear-cut land are poor.[16] Although the selective cutting policy is based on a 35-year regeneration cycle, the lease on forest concessions is for only 20 years. The timber companies therefore have no incentive to ensure the long-term regeneration of the logged forest, instead their optimal commercial policy is to log the primary forest within the 20-year lease period, as market conditions and the costs of extracting from more remote areas allow. In some instances, concessions have been completely logged within 5–10 years. In some cases, where the selective cutting guidelines can be circumvented or where clear-cutting for conversion occurs, logging of the premature secondary forest is also optimal. Since over 80 per cent of these concessions are run by national enterprises or Indonesian controlled joint ventures, and since most major concessionaires now own and operate processing facilities, such a relatively short-term commitment to forest resources seems highly inappropriate.

The current reforestation fund policy has also failed to induce timber companies to replant on their concessions. The companies have been paying $4 per cubic metre of extracted timber into an Escrow account managed by the government. The companies are entitled to reclaim this money, once they have replanted their land. In practice, however, there is little incentive to do this. In 1980 the direct cost of replanting was estimated to be $500 ha^{-1}, yet if a company has produced 45 m^3 ha^{-1} from selective cutting, it would receive only $180 ha^{-1} back from the fund. Clear cutting would have to yield 125 m^3 ha^{-1} simply to cover the replanting costs, which do not include the indirect costs of infrastructure and O & M of the plantation area. With such relatively short-term leases, the concessionaires have very little motivation to reclaim their fund money and to invest from their own profits in long-term plantation operations.

Nevertheless, the reforestation fund is now estimated to be around

$183 million. Frustrated with the lack of replanting by the timber companies, the government is embarking on its own replanting schemes and is considering using $3 million from the fund to finance third-party reforestation. The objective is to expand the current area of timber estates from 2.2 million to 6.2 million hectares by the year 2000, capable of yielding 90 m. m³ p.a. of log production. Almost all planting, however, is with fast-maturing softwood species. Although undoubtedly such a policy would provide an important boost to Indonesia's pulp and paper industry, this makes little long-run economic sense as Indonesia's comparative advantage in export markets lies in its hardwood products. For example, Indonesia's hardwood plywood accounts for 70 per cent of the world market, and the country is now well-placed to capture increasing shares of the sawn wood and shaped wood market. In contrast, the world market for pulpwood is fairly elastic, as many species are potential substitutes, and Indonesia would have to compete with expanded capacity from the Soviet Union, Finland, Brazil and China.

Minor forest products
Rattan, Indonesia's most important non-wood forest product, supplies about 90 per cent of the world market, and currently earns export earnings of $80 million. The recent ban on raw rattan exports is intended to boost production, employment and exports for the labour-intensive rattan furniture industry. Concern has been expressed that this policy could lead to similar inefficiencies and economic welfare losses as the GOI's timber processing policy (World Bank, 1986a). The value added export earnings from rattan furniture could be as high as $270 million. Most economic activity surrounding minor forest products, particularly harvesting, is extremely informal. Very little is known about the size of this activity, its employment implications or its investment needs. From a forest resource management perspective, there is insufficient assessment of how this industry's use of the resource impinges on other activities in forest areas, including conversion to other uses. Even less is known about the economics of other important minor forest products.

Management of parks and protected areas
With over 700 declared or proposed protected areas, but with limited manpower and resources, Indonesia faces an uphill task in managing these areas. Given the remoteness of many Outer Island reserves,

their levels of management and protection are even less than those in the Inner Islands of Java and Bali. The need for boundary stabilization to stop encroachment and other illegal activities in conservation and protection forests is particularly acute. Part of the problem seems to stem from a poor or inaccurate definition of forest boundaries. In addition, many park officials have poor training, are not supported by funding and suffer from a lack of discipline and lack of reward for good work. Moreover, encroachment by local populations into protected areas is unlikely to be stopped unless an alternative means of supplying resources is made available. In some areas, the establishment of agro-forestry and harvesting activities in 'buffer zones' around protected areas has proved effective in reducing encroachment.[17]

However, even buffer zones may be ineffective in dealing with the problem of illegal logging activities. One effect of the complete ban on log exports has been to increase the level of these activities. Although no estimate of the amount of logs illegally exported exists, there is some evidence of substantial smuggling of logs from remote northern areas of eastern Kalimantan into the Malaysian provinces of Sabah and Sarawak. In addition, there exist thousands of small-scale independent processing mills – i.e. mills that are not tied to a particular logging company with a forest concession, which obtain their wood supply from 'unofficial' logging activities.

Policies for sustainable forest management
An essential priority is to improve the assessment of the trends of deforestation and land use patterns in the Outer Islands, to survey the remaining forest areas by classification (e.g. protection, production, conservation, etc.) and to develop more reliable descriptions of forest boundaries. Although a major remote sensing mapping effort is being undertaken by the GOI in conjunction with the UK Overseas Development Administration, it needs to be supplemented by ground surveys and census data. Of particular importance is providing better information on the pattern and trends in shifting cultivation; identifying and protecting critical ecosystems, natural areas and watersheds; and improving estimates of the rate of depletion of production forests.

For example, reliable estimates on how much of the standing stock of commercial timber remains are not available. Projections based on the current patterns of use are discouraging. Assuming that in the future the demand for logs will be at the current near-capacity level of 40m. m^3 p.a., and assuming the selective logging rate of 45 m^3 ha^{-1}, around 889,000 ha of forests will be logged each year. As a rough estimate, assume that half of the concession area of 53.4m. ha has already been logged. This suggests that in around 30 years all of the concession areas will be selectively logged once over. With a 35-year regeneration cycle, the secondary forests will not be ready for logging and, in any case, probably yield less timber. Thus without a serious commitment to renewing its hardwood timber stand through (preferably) enrichment planting, and with the current high-capacity demand for log production, Indonesia could eventually face severe depletion of its valuable hardwood production forests. If properly managed, these forests could instead yield continual export earnings over the long run.

As the future of Indonesia's production forests will continue to be determined by the logging activities of private concessionaires, which will remain difficult to monitor in the foreseeable future, policy measures should concentrate on incentives to encourage concessionaires to take an interest in the sustainable management of the concession forest and to ensure reasonable revenues for the GOI. For example, several modifications in the current 20-year concession lease have been suggested:

1. The lease could be extended to at least 35 years, to conform to the full regeneration period under selective cutting.
2. The concession could be awarded on a roll-over basis, whereby every 5 years the concession would be extended for 20–35 years, subject to satisfactory past performance.
3. Subject to GOI approval, a market in concession rights should be allowed to develop, which would give the concessionaire an interest in maintaining the value of its asset.

Even if the concessionaire is assured future harvest rights, as the timber is more valuable now than it will be at the future harvest, there is a strong financial incentive to re-harvest before the 35-year harvest cycle is finished. On the other hand, if stumpage fees (timber royalties) are assessed on the basis of the stock of merchantable stems in the stand and not on the basis of timber removals, the medium and smaller stems in the stands will appear less attractive to the concessionaire, who will prefer to wait for these undersized stems to reach maturity before harvesting them. In addition, concessionaires will have an incentive to harvest defective and oversized stems of commercial but lesser-known species; thus reducing 'high grading' of stands. Raising stumpage fees would also discourage logging forests with marginal commercial stands and limit overall extraction rates.

Although the establishment of plantations could help to slow down depletion of the natural forests and supply lower-quality timber to the domestic pulp and paper market, current reforestation efforts are a failure. In any case, as Indonesia has a comparative advantage in the production of natural hardwoods, outright conversion of natural forests to plantations should be discouraged. Instead concessionaires should be given technical support for proper species selection and appropriate site selection, which should be targeted to wastelands and deforested areas. In addition, enrichment planting of selectively cut stands and the development of methods of regenerating indigenous hardwoods (*dipterocarps*) should be made eligible for reforestation funds. As an incentive for concessionaires to manage their plantations, a 30-year lease for the reforested stands should be granted to the concessionaires; a proportion of their reforestation fee sufficient to generate an acceptable internal rate of return on reforestation should be rebated over this lease period; and the ban on the export of round logs from the plantations should be relaxed. Plantations serving pulp and paper mills will only be economical if they are located near the most efficient mills, to avoid the risk of these plantations failing if market conditions change after trees have matured.[18]

Recapturing the potential timber rent dissipated through the inefficient processing encouraged by government policies would require both improving the efficiency of the processing industries and by replacing the ban on log exports with a differentiated export tax system. As a large fraction of the high-valued (high-rent) timber is valued as an export, imposing a higher differential tax rate on exportable logs would not only encourage more efficient processing, but also increase government rent capture. Crucial to the success of this sytem would be eliminating the current practice of collecting taxes from the mill with the log input based upon mill output. Efficiency in processing could be further encouraged by eliminating any subsidies of capital investment in the industry. In addition, whereas rent capture might be improved by allowing a market in concession rights (see above), auctioning separately the rights to processing the harvest of the concession might increase processing efficiency. Thus with processing no longer tied to a concession, the more efficient processor would be able to bid for these rights.

Sustainable harvesting of Indonesia's production forests may also help reduce potential land use conflicts between timber harvesting, shifting cultivation, sedentary cultivation and other developments of forest lands. This would also allow the policy of setting aside forest land for conservation and protection – currently at around 45–50m. ha – to continue. The decision whether the remaining land should be used for timber production, shifting cultivation, minor forest product development, sedentary agriculture or any other development activity should then depend, in part, on the economic returns to the alternative land use systems, as well as the suitability of the land for forestry as opposed to agricultural and other types of economic development. As suggested by Ross (1984), a relatively simple but improved method of land classification could be based on determining the quantity and type of wood that a tract of forest land can supply through natural regeneration. Thus a high-valued dipterocarp forest of high-quality standing stock, with a high potential for regeneration and with good access for log disposal, should be preserved as production forest, whereas a low-valued secondary forest with low-quality standing stock and no possibility of regeneration regardless of access could be allocated to other purposes.

Such an approach may free sufficient land for the selective development of sedentary agriculture and even shifting cultivation. With regard to sedentary agriculture, greater investment needs to be targeted at improving the facilities and research and extension support for spontaneous migrants. Two additional problems remain for shifting cultivators: the need to improve low-productive and unsustainable systems with short-fallow rotations on poor soils, and the need to protect the rights of shifting cultivators where insecurity of tenure is leading to greater forest degradation. Whereas settlement within existing transmigration schemes or through new agricultural projects may be the answer for those spontaneous migrants who are practising shifting cultivation because they have no access to land, it is not an adequate solution for indigenous cultivators. Instead it may be more appropriate to work closely with the local people to understand their needs and the agro-ecological features of their farming systems, by developing contractual (reciprocal) commitments to minimize encroachments into the forest with local communities and by stabilizing the boundaries of smallholder land, even where they may cut or cross or lie within forest boundaries. Thus investments to upgrade the production systems of largely sedentary agriculturalists – on grasslands, swamplands and converted forest land – and of shifting cultivators, and to permit immigrants access to planned settlements, may do more to limit forest destruction than past programmes to relocate traditional shifting cultivators out of forest lands.

Estate crop development on the Outer Islands will also have to be better planned to ensure that conversion of natural forests is minimized. The current pricing policy for palm oil may achieve the short-run objective of expanding domestic supplies and exports, but it may be leading to an unnecessarily inefficient, and ultimately unsustainable, use of forest and other land in the Outer Islands. The price distortions are also discouraging the more sustainable production of coconut oil on non-forest lands in the Outer Islands. For example, appropriate farming systems based on coconut production may yield the greatest economic returns in the long run for the more acidic swampland areas found in many Outer Islands, and for the agro-forestry based systems suitable for erodible uplands and dryland cultivation (KEPAS, 1985, 1986).

The development of minor forest products needs to be encouraged, but the ban on rattan exports as a means to encouraging furniture production needs to be reviewed. Again, a differential export tax similar to that needed for log exports needs to be instigated. In general, analysis of the economic returns to all forest products is essential, as well as of their requirements in terms of forest preservation, in order to help determine the appropriate use of forest land.

Finally, if Indonesia is expected to keep a large proportion of its forest area as protection and conservation reserves, it will need generous support from the donor community. If the rest of the world is deriving use, existence and option values from these areas, it should contribute to their preservation and maintenance. A crucial area of funding is the improvement in the skills, resources and even payment of forestry personnel responsible for managing protected areas. Additional investment in the creation of 'buffer zones' or developments targeted at local people most affected by the designation of a protected area is required, as well as investments to enforce the control of illegal logging.

Notes

1. Unless otherwise stated, the material in this chapter is based on Barbier (1987).
2. World Bank estimates. However, the Ministry of Forestry of the government of Indonesia estimates forest area to cover 144m. ha, or 75 per cent of total land area (see Table 5.1). As this latter estimate includes large areas of 'conversion' forest and many areas that have long since been deforested, it is thought to be inaccurate. Nevertheless, Indonesia has twice as much land under forest cover (60 per cent) as the USA (32 per cent) – i.e. a country nearly five times as large. In addition, approximately 10 per cent of the world's tropical rainforest is situated in Indonesia.
3. World Bank estimates.
4. However, during 1987–8 the strong performance of non-oil exports (including timber products) cut the current account deficit to US $2.0 billion, or 3.1 per cent of GNF (see World Bank (1988), p. vi.
5. Ministry of Forestry (1987, tables 1 and 19). However, again note that the Ministry of Forestry's land classification system lists a total forest land area of 144m. ha, whereas more realistic figures suggest a total area of 114m. ha.
6. An *option value* is the valuation placed on something that is not in immediate use but which the *potential* user wishes to express as an *option* to use it at some later date. Option value can be construed as a sort of insurance payment against the uncertainty of irreversible development or conversion of an environmental resource. *Existence value* is perhaps more controversial as it is a valuation placed on a commodity for which the person expressing the preference has no current use, nor any potential use; simply knowing that the commodity is there is valued by the person. Most probably, existence values reflect concerns for the 'stewardship' of nature – i.e. they are values 'on behalf' of natural environments and their inhabitants. For further discussion see Krutilla and Fisher (1985) and Pearce (1987).
7. For more on the relationship between tropical deforestation and the 'greenhouse effect' see Barbier (1989).
8. For example, FAO (1981) estimated total deforestation in Indonesia to be around 600,000 ha per year.
9. For example, the World Bank estimate of 500,000 ha p.a. was arrived at by assuming that, in the absence of new technologies, the amount of new land brought into production by shifting cultivators each year should be roughly equal to the growth in the population. The population growth rate in rural Kalimantan of about 3 per cent per year was then applied to low and high estimates of the total area under shifting cultivation in Indonesia (approx. 14m. ha and 20m. ha respectively) to obtain a range of 450,000–650,000 ha of forest area lost to shifting cultivation annually, with 500,000 ha p.a. falling in the middle of this range.
10. For example, a German-financed project in eastern Kalimantan, in 1987, was spending an additional US $240 ha^{-1} (excluding extension costs) just on developing more appropriate cropping systems for transmigration sites on low-quality, converted forest lands. Similarly, many tree crop estates in the Outer Islands are being established without adequate research on the suitability of the soils of converted forest lands and on the problems caused by pest and disease attacks. Often over-fertilization is resorted to, with highly subsidized chemical

fertilizers, to overcome poor soil quality and boost short-term yields (Barbier, 1987).

11. For example, such a process has begun to emerge with respect to Costa Rican and Bolivian 'debt for nature swaps – i.e. debt purchase by groups concerned to preserve tropical forest. On the economic potential of this option see Hansen (1988).

12. World Bank estimates

13. World Bank estimates, and World Bank (1986b).

14. World Bank estimates.

15. The following discussion of taxation and government rent capture is based on Gillis (1988).

16. The following discussion on concession policy and reforestation incentives is based on Barbier (1987), Gillis (1988) and Sedjo (1987).

17. For example, the creation of a 'buffer zone' seems to have been effective in helping protect the Dumoga National Park: see Wind and Sumardja (1987).

18. For further discussion see Gillis (1988) and Sedjo (1987).

References

Barbier, E. B. (1987), 'Natural resource policy and economic framework', Annexe 1, in James Tarrant *et al.*, *Natural Resources and Environmental Management in Indonesia*, Jakarta: USAID, October.

Barbier, E. B. (1989), 'The global greenhouse effect: economic impacts and policy considerations', *Natural Resources Forum*, **13**, February.

Douglass, M. (1987), 'Changing patterns of access to agricultural land on Java and the Outer Islands', Department of Urban and Regional Planning, University of Hawaii, Honolulu, October.

Dove, M. R. (1985), 'The agroecological mythology of the Javanese and the political economy of Indonesia', *Indonesia*, **39**, 1–36.

Fitzgerald, B. (1986), *An Analysis of Indonesian Trade Policies: Countertrade, Downstream Processing, Import Restrictions and the Deletion Program*, CPD Discussion Paper 1986–22, World Bank, Washington, DC.

Food and Agricultural Organization (FAO) (1981), *Tropical Forest Research Assessment Project: Forest Resources of Tropical Asia*, Rowe: FAO/United Nations Environment Programme.

Gillis, M. (1988), 'Indonesia: public policies, resource management and the tropical forest', in M. Gillis and R. Repetto (eds), *Public Policy and the Misuse of Forest Resources*, Cambridge: Cambridge University Press.

Government of Indonesia (GOI) and International Institute for Environment and Development (IIED) (1985), *Forest Policies in Indonesia: The Sustainable Development of Forest Lands. Vol. 2, A Review of Issues*, Jakarta: GOI/IIED, November.

Hansen, S. (1988), *Debt for Nature Swaps: Overview and Discussion of Key Issues*, Environment Department Working Paper No. 1, World Bank, Washington, DC, February.

KEPAS (1985), *Tidal Swamp Agroecosystems of Southern Kalimantan*, Agency for Agricultural Research and Development, Jakarta.

KEPAS (1986), *Agro-ekosistem Daerah Kering di Nusa Tenggara Timur*, Agency for Agricultural Research and Development, Jakarta.

Krutilla, J. V. and Fisher, A. C. (1985), *The Economics of Natural Environments: Studies in the Valuation of Commodity and Amenity Resources* (2nd edn), Resources for the Future, Washington, DC.

Ministry of Forestry (1986), *Indonesian Exports of Forest Products*, Jakarta: Directorate of Marketing for Forest Products.

Ministry of Forestry (1987), *Forestry Indonesia 1985/86*, Jakarta: Ministry of Forestry, Jakarta.

Pearce, D. W. (1987), *Economic Values and the Natural Environment*. The 1987 Denman Lecture at the University of Cambridge, Cambridge: Granta Publications.

Repetto, R., Wells, M., Beer, C. and Rossini, F. (1987), *Natural Resource Accounting for Indonesia*, Washington, DC: World Resources Institute, May.

Ross. M. S. (1984), *Forestry and Land Use Policy in Indonesia*, Oxford: Oxford University Press.

Sedjo, R. (1987), 'Incentives and distortions in Indonesian forest policy', Resources for the Future, Washington DC, October.

Wind, J. and Sumardja, E. A. (1987), 'Dumoga – Indonesia World Bank Project for Irrigation and Watercatchment Protection', paper presented at IIED Conference on Sustainable Development, London, 28–30 April.

World Bank (1986a), *Indonesia – Policies and Prospects for Non-Oil Exports*, Washington, DC: World Bank, December.

World Bank (1986b), *Indonesia – Transmigration Sector Review*, Washington, DC: World Bank, October.

World Bank (1988), *Indonesia – Country Economic Report*, Washington, DC: World Bank, July.

6 Natural resources in the economy of the Sudan

Introduction

A traditional saying has it that 'when Allah made the Sudan, Allah laughed'. Certainly, the Sudan has had its share of political and economic misfortunes and Allah has been less than even-handed in respect of climatic variation. The Sudan is the largest country in Africa, extending 1,000 miles east to west, and 1,200 miles north to south (Figure 6.1). The north of the country is desert or desert-like, averaging less than 100 mm rainfall per annum, but this should not be taken to mean that people do not live there. There are active communities near to water, especially along the Nile. The far south is equatorial with high rainfall, up to 1,500 mm per year, and high humidity. The two basic forms of agriculture are subsistence crops and livestock; but the Sudan is also an exporter of food crops and livestock, together with its well-known cotton crops from the irrigated sectors south of Khartoum.

Agriculture generally provides the livelihood for the great majority of the Sudanese people (see Table 6.1). Given the climatic variation experienced in Sudan, both spatially and over time, there is a sensitive dependence on natural resources. Soil fertility is threatened by wind erosion, and given the dramatic force with which rains can come, by rainfall erosion as well. The general absence of artificial fertilizers means that the recycling of biomass residues and animal waste is essential to sustainable agriculture, yet both livestock and crop output is seriously reduced by periodic drought. Energy sources come primarily from fuelwood, but forests in the conventional sense exist only in the south and rapid deforestation supplies the ever-growing populations of Khartoum and Omdurman and other towns. The central areas are forested thinly, providing essential but fragile fuelwood sources.

The ecological conditions for agriculture and energy are thus fragile everywhere other than in the south. The potential of the south to 'export' resources to the north is severely limited by poor

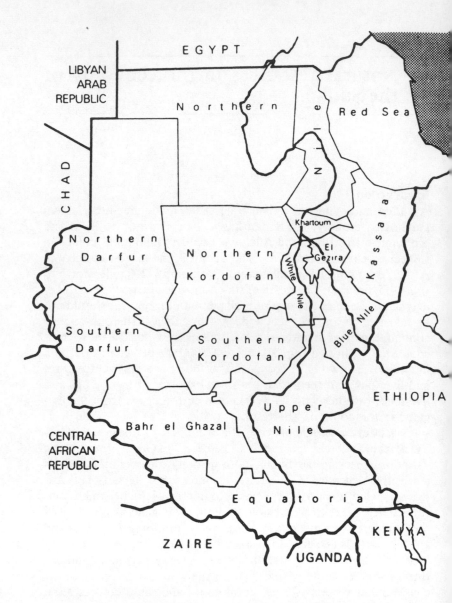

Figure 6.1   The Sudan

Table 6.1   Sudan population estimates, 1983 (millions)

Region	Urban	Rural	Nomads	Total
Northern	0.23	0.80	0.05	1.08
Eastern	0.64	1.01	0.56	2.21
Central	0.83	2.94	0.24	4.01
Kordofan	0.39	1.92	0.78	3.09
Darfur	0.32	2.31	0.47	3.09
Khartoum	1.34	0.37	0.09	1.81
Equatoria	0.18	1.23	–	1.41
Bahr El Ghazal	0.18	2.08	–	2.26
Upper Nile	0.05	1.55	–	1.60
Sudan	4.15	14.22	2.19	20.56

Source: Sudan Department of Statistics, Third Population Census

infrastructure, by rainfall which makes many roads and tracks unusable for much of the year and, above all, by civil war. Historically, the Sudan has been an arena for the clash of Islam in the north and Christianity (and a mixed paganism and Christianity) in the south. This conflict had been recognized even during the rule of Sudan by the Anglo-Egyptian condominium up to independence in 1956, but efforts to formalize the political distinctions came to nothing. After independence, efforts were made in the south to secede from the new nation, and a number of rebellions occurred. In 1983 civil war broke out and has continued. At the time of writing (early 1989), an agreement to end the war exists on paper, but has yet to be signed by all parties. The human cost of the war has been substantial. Many have starved, and many more have moved to the slums of Khartoum and Omdurman or across the borders to neighbouring countries. One estimate suggests that 250,000 people have moved north in the past few years (Jada, 1988).

Against this tragic backdrop of war issues of natural resource management may seem an irrelevance. It is certainly true that a lengthy period of political stability is the Sudan's greatest need if any semblance of sustainable development is to be achieved. Within an improved political context the Sudan has the capability to develop, provided that the natural resource base is protected and enhanced. Sudan offers perhaps the starkest possible example of a nation that needs to conserve and improve its natural capital stock for it to develop at all.

Natural resource degradation in the Sudan

Discovering just what is happening to the natural resource base in the Sudan is problematical. Many areas are poorly surveyed, and the war-torn situation in the south makes it impossible to know with any accuracy what is happening in that part of the country. Even overall population estimates, such as those given in Table 6.1, must be treated with extreme caution – in- and out-migration on a substantial scale have combined with marked internal population growth, mass starvation in 1984–5 and limited census data to make the situation uncertain.

Desertification

'Desertification' is a term widely used to describe degradation of land capability. Some writers regard it as (literally) the expansion of the true desert into areas previously capable of agricultural production, the alleged phenomenon of the Sahara Desert 'creeping south'. It is best to think of desertification as a *sustained reduction in the biological productivity of land* (Pearce, 1987).[1] This definition emphasizes permanent reductions in land capability, the cause of which may be man-induced or 'natural'. It may come about because of reduced soil capability (e.g. loss of nutrient) or loss of vegetation, especially perennial vegetation. The definition emphasizes too that it is the productivity of the land itself that matters, not reduced crop or livestock output because of a reduction in other inputs such as reduced labour effort.[2]

The Sudan was in fact the location for an early study which appears to have contributed to the idea of the southwards 'creep' of the Sahara Desert. Lamprey (1976) studied the incidence of vegetation and identified a 'desert boundary' just north of the 16° N latitude at Khartoum, sweeping down to 15° to the west of Khartoum, and with sand-dune 'plumes' extending south to Bara and, less dramatically, in one or two other places. Lamprey used a vegetation index based on earlier work by Harrison and Jackson (1958) in order to compare his identified boundary with that of the earlier study. The Harrison–Jackson boundary was north of the 16° latitude, for the most part, dipping below it only moderately about 500 km west of Khartoum. The southern movement of the boundary thus suggested the 'creeping desert', with rates of movement of about 5–6 km per year.

The Lamprey study has been severely criticized; in one of several important studies from Lund University, Sweden. Hellden (1984) makes several observations. First, the Harrison and Jackson 'boundary' was in fact not mapped at all, but was taken to be the 75 mm isoheyt (a rainfall contour). The Lamprey boundary was mapped but generally accords with the 100 mm isoheyt, so that the 'shift' in the boundary may have been nothing more than the delineation of two separate isoheyts, separated by 25 mm of rainfall. Secondly, Hellden could find no evidence of 'advancing desert' from Landsat imagery between 1972 and 1979 for one transect of the original Lamprey area. The 'desert boundary' (defined as the border between semi-desert bush/shrub and grassland) roughly coincided with the 100 mm isoheyt in the Hellden study, just as it did in the Lamprey study. That is, the boundary was fairly stable. Thirdly, the 'sand plume' found by Lamprey and extending south to Bara could not be identified by Hellden.[3] Hellden concluded: 'There was no creation of long lasting desert-like conditions during the 1962–1979 period in the area corresponding to the magnitude described by many authors and commonly accepted by the Sudanese Government and international aid organisations' (*ibid.*, p. 53).

In a further Lund study, this time of fuelwood in a subarea of that used by Hellden, K. Olsson (1985) found that: 'no woody species seemed to have been eradicated from the area, no ecological zones had shifted southwards and the boundaries between different vegetation associations appeared to be the same now (1981/2) as they were 80 years ago' (p. 171).

L. Olsson (1985) reports a study of biomass and albedo (the ratio of reflected light from the surface of the earth to incident light: the higher the level of vegetation, the lower is albedo since the vegetation absorbs the light); this was carried out for Landsat transects which overlap but lying further east than the Hellden and K. Olsson studies. He concludes that between 1973 and 1979, 'it has not been possible to find a consistent trend of a degrading landscape. The conditions vary with the climatic conditions' (*ibid.*, p. 147). In other words, the exact timing of the study period matters a great deal. Unless studies are repeated over long periods, or at least compare two years in which climatic conditions are the same, a false impression may be created; thus:

'reports on desertification have been very exaggerated and not based on a scientific approach. Most of the studies were based on a comparison of two occasions, one prior to the Sahelian drought and another during or shortly after it. Not surprisingly, the environmental conditions degraded from the first to the second situation' (*ibid.*, p. 147).

In yet more recent work from Lund University, located further east of the Hellden, K. Olsson and L. Olsson studies, Ahlcrona (1988) found that millet, sorghum and sesame yields fell between 1961 and 1986. The falls were well correlated with reduced rainfall, although fallow periods were found to be 'very short or entirely lacking' in 65 per cent of the villages studied. Reduced fallow is likely to result in declining crop yields as soils are given no time to recover. Interviews with local people suggested a shift in the balance of vegetation in favour of 'green desertification species' which are largely useless to man and livestock, due to both drought and man-made land degradation. No evidence at all was found for the shifting sand dunes phenomenon identified by other writers.

Ibrahim (1984) is a major source of views to the effect that land degradation has increased through man-made activities. His studies relate to northern Darfur, down to the border area with southern Darfur (in the west of Sudan). Ibrahim suggests an 'ecologically adapted agronomic dry boundary' – i.e. a boundary north of which agriculture should not be permitted if man-induced desertification is to be avoided. A southwards agronomic boundary is set by the rainfall pattern producing eight arid months per year, or 600–700 mm of rainfall p.a. A northwards limit, set by two semi-arid months per year, or roughly between the 100 and 200 mm isoheyts, is derived in order to show that the northern boundary of millet production lies above the southern boundary and below the northern one. That is, millet cultivation has extended northwards into areas that Ibrahim would regard as being ecologically unsuitable for agriculture. Whether the effect is meant to be *actual* desertification or simply the high *risk* of desertification in this area depends on which of Ibrahim's publications is consulted. Ibrahim compromises slightly by suggesting the northwards limit to cultivation should be 500–600 mm. Even then, the effect of such a limit, if it could ever be enforced, would be to remove cultivation from most of northern Kordofan and northern Darfur.

Ibrahim's evidence for *actual* desertification is based on the analysis of imagery for northern Darfur. Extensive areas of desertification are identified. Severely affected areas relate to rain-fed agriculture on old sand-dunes and over-grazing and tree clearance around settlements; moderately affected areas occur where there is rain-fed cultivation and over-grazing due to year-round grazing; desertification 'hazard' areas with seasonal grazing and tree clearing; and areas less exposed to desertification hazard. The types of desertification are fluvial soil erosion, reactivation of Qoz sand-dunes ('Qoz' relates to the soil type) and dune formation. Settlement areas with severe and moderate degradation round their perimeters are also identified.

Ibrahim's map of northern Darfur suggests that desertification actually does describe the basic condition of all areas north of approx. 12° latitude to approx. 15°. He estimates that 15 per cent of 'northern and central' Darfur is 'highly affected' by desertification; 30 per cent is 'moderately affected'; 35 per cent is 'highly exposed to desertification hazards'; and only 20 per cent is 'less exposed' to such hazards (*ibid.* p. 187). Unless there are good reasons to distinguish the situation in northern Darfur from that in northern Kordofan, this would imply that most of northern Kordofan would be similarly desertified or at risk, a result not consistent with the findings of Hellden, Olsson and Ahlcrona. Ibrahim's work also suggests that the main 'culprit' in terms of causes of desertification is the northwards push of millet production, the clearing of land around settlements for fuelwood and over-grazing around settlements. For her study area round Kosti, Ahlcrona found no evidence of changes in the size of village perimeters, no evidence of a northwards shift in millet cultivation and no transformation of sand-dunes. While it must be stressed that the areas of study are quite different, the contrast does seem odd (Figure 6.2 illustrates the areas covered by the different studies).

Olsson's strictures about comparing equivalent years have relevance to the more specific studies by Ibrahim. Comparing a single village in 1954 and 1968, Ibrahim had noted that there was millet production in the early year but there were sand-dunes in the later year. L. Olsson (1985) notes that nothing can actually be derived from such a comparison, unless events after rainfall were documented.

The other authors have also cast doubt on Ibrahim's methodology, particularly, in some cases, the use of unrepresentative, pair-

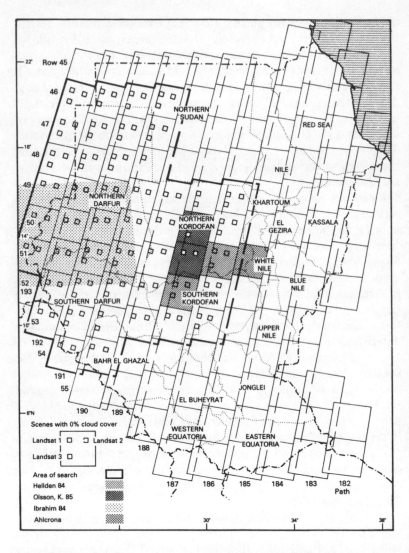

Study: Natural Resource Data Assessment Report, Borehamwood, HTS, for Environment Department, World Bank, Washington, DC, 1987.
Source: Huntings Technical Services, *Sudan Resource Management.*

Figure 6.2   Desertification studies in Sudan by landsat imagery

wise year comparisons. In so far as they observe desertification in the sense of reduced biological productivity, the Lund authors ascribe the reduced productivity to climatic changes (see below), not to man-made influences. However, there is evidence of qualitative changes in vegetation – i.e. changes in the type of vegetation – away from 'useful' to 'useless' species – which has been caused by man-induced land degradation (see esp. Ahlcrona, 1988). Another major theme of the Lund studies is the resilience of the land in the Sudan: despite prolonged and severe droughts in several years, much vegetation returns with the rains.

How, then, is the evidence on desertification to be interpreted? The studies by Hellden and the Olssons, and by Ahlcrona, all suggest no evidence of desertification as 'creeping desert' – areas permanently degraded or subject to mobile sand-dunes. Nor are they consistent with the popular picture of desertification as land degradation that spreads outwards in ever-increasing circles with settlements as the origin. All these studies are for areas in northern Kordofan and a limited part of southern Kordofan (the Olssons and Hellden) and the area round Kosti in White Nile Province (Ahlcrona). In contrast, Ibrahim's work purports to cover a much larger area, the whole of northern Darfur (less the extreme northern part), well to the west of the other studies (see Figure 6.2). It is difficult to explain so great a contrast by the choice of different areas, especially as the latitudes are similar. Clearly, there is a need for more extensive assessment of satellite imagery based on long-time series.

Crop yields and climate

If there is uncertainty about the underlying trends in the quality of productive land, perhaps *indirect* measures of desertification could be used. Since land quality is a major input into crop output, declining land quality should show up in declining crop yields per area. The obvious limiting factors to such an analysis are that declining land productivity could be due to: (a) reductions in labour inputs, especially labour which is attracted into other areas or forced out of traditional cultivation areas; (b) reductions in 'natural' inputs such as rainfall; and (c) extensification of farming into areas which are naturally less biologically productive.

Difficulties concerning data make it impossible to be certain what the long-run trend of land productivity is in terms of crops. Figure 6.1 illustrates movements in output per *feddan* (approx. 1 acre or

0.42 ha) for millet, sorghum and sesame for several provinces in the Sudan. The general trend in land productivity is downwards, while the area cultivated is clearly upwards. The picture is fairly systematic: output has been sustained only because of increases in the area cultivated. In the absence of any information on the nature of the new land put under millet production, it is impossible to tell whether the new land is 'naturally' less productive (as Ricardian theory would predict) or overall land productivity is declining, or whether there is a combination of factors. Ahlcrona (1988) presents some evidence to suggest that fallow periods have been reduced, compared to a period ten years ago, but while the majority of interview answers indicated zero fallows, interviewees indicated that they were generally also zero ten years previously. L. Olsson (1985) indicated that in the intensively cultivated sandy soils of northern Kordofan nutrient status of the soil down to a depth of 30 cm had been depleted. Declining crop yields could thus be consistent with this decline in soil nutrient quality, but *further* crop yield reductions would be unlikely in face of soil erosion. Basically low existing yields reflected the minimally low soil nutrient status and could be expected to remain at that minimum in the absence of longer fallows or the application of fertilizers.

An overall decline in land productivity is also consistent with 'natural' factors such as climate change. Ahlcrona (1988) reports correlation coefficients (r^2) of 0.56 between rainfall and crop yields in 1961–86 in White Nile, Blue Nile and Gezira provinces, suggesting that other factors are present in terms of a full explanation of crop yield variation. Ahlcrona concludes that: 'the decline in crop yields cannot be ascribed mainly to man-made land degradation as argued for example by Ibrahim' (*ibid.*, p. 39).

Forest cover

Little is known about the woody biomass cover of Sudan, especially in the south. Accurate assessments of the areas of woodlands, plantations and forests await a detailed forest inventory.[4] Such estimates as are available are shown in Table 6.2, but caution needs to be exercised in adopting the figures. If the figures were broadly of the right magnitude, however, they indicate that some 60 per cent of potential wood resources are in the south (Equatoria, Bahr El Gazal, Upper Nile) and 40 per cent in the north. Converting the hectarage in Table 6.2 to wood resources is hazardous, but the figures are

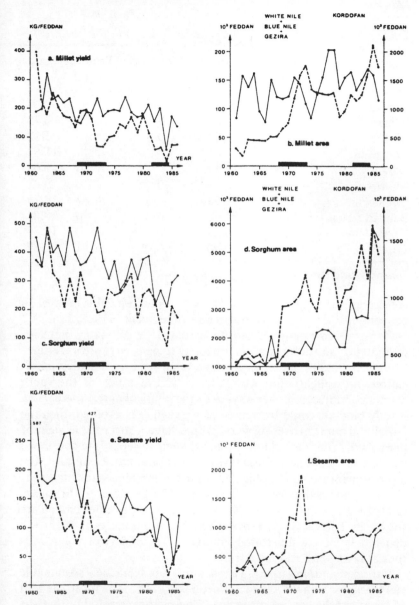

Note: Crop statistics for the White Nile, Blue Nile and Gezira Provinces (solid line) and for the northern and southern Kordofan provinces (broken line). The Sahelian drought (1969–73) and the recent drought (1982–4) are indicated; 1 feddan = 0.42 ha.   *Source:* Ahlcrona (1988).

Figure 6.3   Land productivity and area cultivated

Table 6.2   Estimated woody biomass in Sudan (million hectares)

Region	Savannah grassland	Savannah woodland	Plantation	Tropical forest	Total
Northern	0	0	0	0	0
Eastern	0	2.75	0	0	2.75
Central	0	5.09	0.03	0	5.12
Kordofan	0	11.63	0	0	11.63
Darfur	0	17.69	0	0	17.69
Khartoum	0	0	0.01	0	0.01
Equatoria	5.33	11.83	0.01	1.62	18.79
Bahr El Gazal	0.46	17.62	0	0	18.08
Upper Nile	15.51	4.29	0	0	19.80
Total	21.30	70.90	0.05	1.62	93.87

Source: World Bank.

consistent with a growing stock of some 2.8 billion cubic metres, 30 per cent of this being in the north and 70 per cent in the south.[5]

Given the uncertainty about the actual stock of woody biomass, estimates of any deforestation are likely to be even more uncertain. Moreover, taking Sudan as a whole is misleading if policy implications are sought since woodland stocks in much of the south cannot be subject to policy in view of the political unrest there. If *all* woody biomass could be treated as an available resource, then the 2.8 billion cubic metres of wood would have a sustainable yield of perhaps 90m. m^3 per annum; that is, 90m. m^3 could be consumed yearly while holding the natural forest capital stock constant, the basic principle of sustainable development introduced in Chapter 1. Consumption estimates are uncertain, adding further to the uncertainty of the analysis. World Bank estimates of possible demand are shown in Table 6.3. The overwhelming dominance of fuelwood demand is clearly illustrated compared to other wood demands (poles, sawnwood and industrial wood).

If the demands in Table 6.3 are actually met from local sustainable yield, and by 'mining' the local forest stock, then the future pattern of wood stocks can be projected. The picture is roughly that the eastern and central and Kordofan regions will totally exhaust their stocks by the end of the century. Khartoum and Northern regions begin with zero stocks. The south regions, on the other hand, would

Table 6.3   Wood Demand, 1983–2000 (10^6 cubic metres)

	1983	2000
North	35.3	52.8
South	10.6	15.4
Total	45.9	68.2
% fuelwood:	93	93

roughly maintain their existing stocks, as would Darfur. Recall that movement of wood from 'surplus' to 'deficit' areas is difficult in Sudan because of the absence of roads and because of the factors of climate and political unrest. Overall, the projections would suggest a rate of depletion of Sudan's woody biomass of some 0.8 per cent p.a. But the regional picture reveals the 'energy crisis' in Sudan since, for the north generally, the rate of decrease is 5.5 per cent p.a., and for Kordofan it is over 25 per cent p.a.

Obviously, given the considerable problems with data, with uncertainty about population figures and household wood demand, such figures are only illustrative. But they do reveal the nature of the wood crisis in Sudan: it is concentrated in the north, where 75 per cent of the Sudanese people live (see Table 6.1).

The role of natural resources in the economy
In terms of Figure 1.3 (see p. 18), Sudan fits the stage of economic development illustrated by the ray OC. Indeed, Sudan is located near and probably below the point k_n, the minimum viable natural capital stock. The dependence on natural resources is readily illustrated: agriculture accounted for 31 per cent of GDP in 1985–6 and supports some 85 per cent of the people; 85 per cent of all Sudan's exports are natural resource based. The breakdown is shown in Table 6.4. Because of climatic variation there are substantial cycles in the importance of individual crops and of livestock in the export totals. None the less, it is clear that Sudan relies critically upon its soil quality, on grazing land and on the gum arabic tree for its export performance. Cotton remains the most important export crop, accounting for 42 per cent of all exports in 1986–7. Yet even here the role of natural resources is vital. Cotton is primarily an irrigated crop relying on the Nile waters for its main resource input. Yields per

Table 6.4   Natural resource-based exports (LS million, current prices)

	1974–5	1984–5	1986–7
Cotton	55.6	417.8	473.4
Gum Arabic	14.6	77.8	250.0
Sesame	19.2	80.8	76.4
Groundnuts	28.7	21.7	6.1
Food Grains	4.4	1.5	100.6
Livestock	7.5	153.5	19.8
Other Agriculture	10.9	57.7	n.a.
Total exports	149.8	833.9	1125.3

Source: Government of Sudan.

land area have fluctuated significantly over the years, but doubled between 1975–6 and 1984–5.

The value of trees to the economy can be indicated in several ways. Consider the role of charcoal, for example, which is bought and sold in Sudan towns in well-developed markets. Recent years have seen marked increases in prices. Taking mid-1986 Khartoum prices and very crude estimates of probable consumption in Sudan as a whole, the value of charcoal consumption in 1986 was of the order of LS 1.6 billion, or about 7.7 per cent of GNP in that year.[6]

The special role of gum arabic
Trees in Sudan have a value much wider than that of producing charcoal. *Acacia senegal* is a thorny leguminous tree, producing pentameous flowers and brownish, oblong seed pods. *A. Senegal* is distributed widely in the Sahelian–Sudanian zone, from the Red Sea in the east to Senegal in the west. In particular, it is to be found in Mauritania, Senegal, Mali, Nigeria, Chad, parts of Ethiopia, Somalia and Sudan. It is known by many different local names, but in Sudan Arabic it is known as the hashab. If the hashab tree is injured or scarred in some way, the wound is subject to *gummosis* – it produces a gum, often in quantities out of all proportion to the need to seal and protect the wound. Somewhat surprisingly, the exact nature of the gummosis is not understood. Of some significance is the fact that hashab grows further north than other gum-producing trees, its northern limit roughly coinciding with the 150 mm isoheyt and its southern limit with the 860 mm isoheyt.

Another gum-producing acacia is *A. seyal* which produces a gum known locally in Sudan as *talha*. But talha is typically regarded as being inferior to hashab.

The gum exuded by *A. senegal* has a very large number of uses. These are discussed shortly; but *A. senegal* itself is extraordinarily diverse in its other functions.

Its deep tap root and the lateral expansiveness of the remaining root system, with up to 40 per cent of the total tree biomass being underground, make it highly valued for its soil stabilizing functions, including where appropriate containing sand-dunes, acting as a buffer against wind erosion and decreasing water runoff. It is this feature, in particular, which has led many commentators to suggest that *A. senegal* acts as a 'buffer' against desertification. For this to be correct, it is not necessary to characterize desertification as a north–south 'creeping desert' phenomenon. Removal of hashab trees in a vicinity increases risks of wind erosion and is likely to lower water retention rates.

It fixes atmospheric nitrogen and encourages grassy growth (graminaceous cover) in the immediate vicinity, assisting pasture growth. Leaf and pod decomposition help supply proteins to the surrounding soil. For this reason, hashab trees are widely seen as an integral part of any programme to rehabilitate or augment silvo-pastoral systems. This is relevant to sedentary farming in the E Sahel–Sudan zone and to some nomadic systems in the West. The effect of nitrogen fixation on intercropped and rotated cereals and root crops is disputed, but there is some evidence that yields are higher in rotations based on *A. senegal*.

Some authorities regard the tree as essential to the microclimate through various bio-geochemical cycles based, in particular, on the encouragement of grasses in the vicinity of the trees.

A. senegal is a favoured source of fodder for cattle, but is browsed by sheep, goats and camels as well, which also eat the pods.

Gum production is a convenient source of seasonal employment and income, gum being collected in November at the start of the dry season and in March–April before the onset of the rainy season. This seasonality is particularly important in locations where off-farm income opportunities are limited. Gum harvested by nomads from untended trees can also be a useful supplementary income source.

A. senegal is a source of fuelwood. Gum production takes place with trees aged 4–15 years, so that older trees are unlikely to yield significant quantities and become suitable for fuelwood.

Hashab trees are also very tolerant of temperature and rainfall variation, making them invaluable as a tree that can be grown towards northern limits of cultivation in the Sahel and hence encouraging 'buffer zones' against desertification.

The gum exuded from *A. senegal* and *A. seyal* is a polysaccharide, which is highly soluble in water, is a good emulsifier and has low viscosity. It is non-toxic, non-polluting and is odourless and flavourless. As a result, it is widely sought after in confectionery production where its properties of anti-crystallization, providing a protective film, adhesive and thickener are of considerable importance. In beverage manufacture it is important as an emulsifier and suspensoid and is widely used for flavouring and wine stabilization. In the pharmaceuticals sector all the previous attributes are of value. In lithography and photography it is used to provide protective films, and in insecticides/pesticides it is an emulsifier, protective film, suspensoid and adhesive.

The main competition for gum arabic comes from the various types of starch and modified starch and these have already secured major shares of the confectionery, beverages and flavourings markets. In pharmaceuticals gum arabic can be replaced by dextrins, cellulose esters and other synthetic polymers. After the drought of 1972–5, the substitutes made major gains in the market as gum arabic supplies fell. In the USA alone a demand level of over 12,000 tonnes p.a. fell to 2,700 tonnes in 1975, and Japanese demand virtually halved in the same period. Substitution is feasible in most uses, but there is a premium on the use of high-quality hashab in offset lithography processes. Demand is also likely to be inelastic in uses which rely on the zero-calorie characteristic of gum arabic.

The general and ready availability of substitutes with varying degrees of price and quality competitiveness clearly influences the decision about supply price. Most gum arabic comes from Sudan and the price is fixed by the Gum Arabic Company which is the sole exporter of gum. The GAC is highly sensitive to the use of substitutes and sets the world price accordingly. There is some evidence on the price elasticity of demand (i.e. the responsiveness of demand to price). Bateson and El-Tohami (1986) suggest that price elasticity is about unity at a price level of some $1,900 per tonne – i.e. around this price, a 1 per cent price fall would result in a 1 per cent increase in

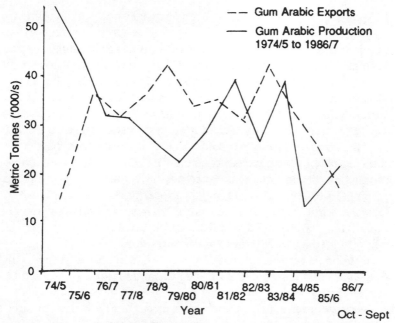

Source: Gum Arabic Corporation.

Figure 6.4 Gum arabic production and exports

induced demand. This result could be taken to imply that the gum
arabic market is less price-sensitive than the above discussion of
substitutes would imply. But the additional problem is the reliability
of supply. The GAC has attempted to regulate supply through
holding buffer stocks, but even these have not been able to withstand
the major impact on supply of the 1984–5 drought. Moreover, the
elasticity estimates above predate the drought and may therefore not
be applicable to the situation in the late 1980s. Identifying the
maximum price at which consumers will retain loyalty to gum arabic
is thus a complex issue.

Most gum arabic comes from Sudan. Sudan's production and
exports are shown in Figure 6.4. The considerable variability in
supply will be noted, as will the extent to which the Gum Arabic
Company has been able to 'iron out' production cycles using buffer
stocks.

A great deal of attention has been focused on the pricing of gum arabic from the producer's point of view. First, there is evidence that supply elasticities – i.e. the response of suppliers to a change in price – is high. Bateson and El Tohami (1986) report elasticities on price of 0.87–0.93, i.e. a 10 per cent price rise will lead to about a 9 per cent increase in supply. Moreover, about a third of the response is in the current year – i.e. price rises lead to increased tapping and collection. The remaining two-thirds of the supply response is 'lagged', relating to price changes in the previous year. If correct, such elasticities show that one of the fastest and surest ways of increasing gum arabic production (hence both farmer incomes and Sudan foreign exchange earnings) is to find ways of raising producer prices, the prices paid to farmers, without jeopardizing world markets by inducing substitutes from starches. An ancillary result is that by operating on market-based incentives there may be less need to engage in significant public investment: essentially, farmers can be left to engage in financially and environmentally beneficial activities in response to market forces.

There are several qualifications to this finding. First, the elasticities relate to the pre 1984–5 drought period and it is still not clear how supply responsiveness has changed since then. Secondly, the supply elasticies reported effectively relate to the existing stock of trees because the main supply response so far has been to tap existing stocks that have remained untapped. They tell us very little about the tree planting response to price increases. But it is more planting that is needed if, in addition to short-run income increases, we are interested in the longer-run, more permanent income opportunities, and in expanding the environmental benefits arising from *A. senegal* planting. Thirdly, planting decisions will be heavily affected by the very poverty to which desertification contributes. The poorer farm communities become, the less and less likely they are to consider benefits that accrue the year after next or even next season. In terms of economic language, their personal discount rates are very high because of the poverty in which they find themselves. But if discount rates are high they are not likely to plant hashab trees which yield gum only after a gestation period of 5 years or so. By not planting them, they contribute further to environmental degradation and hence to longer-term poverty. This 'environmental–poverty trap' is the single most important reason for *not* leaving anti-desertification

Table 6.5   Producer and export prices of gum arabic

	FOB ($)*	FOB Price (LS)†	Prod. price (LS)	Prod. price/ FOB price (%)	Prod. ('000 tonnes)	Export
1984/5	1,600	3,216	1,558	48	11.3	24.2
1985/6	1,900	5,168	2,801	54	18.0	19.3
1986/7	5,000	14,400	8,458	59	30.0	16.0
1987/8	3,495	15,278	11,130	71	(35.0	20.0)

*$ = US dollar;
LS = Sudanese pound.
†*Source:* Gum Arabic Company.

decisions to the market, although such an observation in no way reduces the importance of 'getting prices right'.

Dramatic increases in price were made in 1985–6, partly in an effort to raise the rewards to farmers in light of large-scale damage to the stock of trees in the 1984–5 drought. In the event, prices were raised beyond the world market's willingness to absorb increased costs, and significant stocks remained unsold (perhaps 14,000 tonnes being unsold in 1986–7). In 1987–8 the price has been lowered in an effort to regain some of the market.

Table 6.5 shows the broad relationship between export price and the prices received by farmers. Notice that the previous price rises were used to increase the producer share of the export price from around 48 per cent in 1984–5 to 59 per cent in 1986–7. Despite the lowering of the export price in 1987–8 the producer share is likely to rise further to 71 per cent. This is possible because of the devaluation of the Sudanese pound.

It is evident that price is a potentially powerful weapon in securing increased supplies of gum arabic from existing stock. By raising producer incomes such a measure alone will have beneficial effects by helping to break the environment–poverty cycle, as noted above. Other policies, such as improved handling, transport and storage to raise quality, will also assist.

Table 6.5 also suggests a further mechanism for increasing producer response, namely reducing further the share of the FOB price taken by non-producers. In this respect, many commentators have focused on the monopoly power of the Gum Arabic Company itself, but other candidates should include the government through its taxes and local merchants. Merchants, in particular, take a significant share of the final export price, perhaps 13–16 per cent (Pearce, 1987, p. 60). Merchants adopt the 'sheil' system of loans to farmers. This is basically a form of sharecropping in which farmers mortgage part of their crop to the merchants in exchange for other goods. The implicit rates of interest are reported to be extremely high, perhaps of the order of 50–75 per cent per annum (*ibid.*, p. 32). Such high rates reflect a number of factors: (a) the absence of other sources of credit to farmers; (b) the lack of personal resource tenure among farmers, so that collateral has to be sought in the crops themselves, and (c) genuine high-risk of crop failure. These observations suggest that a concerted effort to supply rural credit, perhaps through co-operative schemes, would assist in breaking the environment–poverty linkage.

Investing in gum arabic

For the reasons given above, it is unlikely that much more than a token planting of gum arabic is likely to take place in response to market forces. None the less, there are reports of replanting efforts, especially in light of better rainfall in 1987–8. It is important to overcome the obstacles to replanting. The basic gains to be obtained are:

- farm income will increase from gum sales, and increase in a sustainable fashion because the trees will have a continuous yield for about 10 years;
- Sudan will secure foreign exchange;
- the Sudan government will obtain tax revenues;
- environmental benefits will ensue, including a contribution to overall anti-desertification policy.

How far these effects can be generalized beyond Sudan to other Sahelian countries is open to serious question, especially as more generalized production could well threaten an already fragile world market. But for Sudan, at least, and perhaps for one or two other Sahelian countries, gum arabic shows how environmental quality and economic development can be wholly consistent social objectives.

Table 6.6   Livestock population, 1976 (million)

Sheep	11.358
Cattle	12.056
Camels	2.414
Goats	9.804

The livestock issue

Overgrazing is widely cited as a major cause of environmental degradation in Sudan. As noted above, the extent of rangeland degradation is in fact poorly researched, so that it is unclear whether overgrazing can be said to exist on any systematic scale. Moreover, the meaning of the term 'overgrazing' is itself obscure in much of the literature. It is frequently used to refer to populations of livestock in excess of the *carrying capacity* of rangeland. In the economic sense, however, it seems preferable to refer to overgrazing as any level of animal population in excess of that which *optimizes* net social benefits from livestock.

Whichever definition is adopted, there are formidable problems of estimating overstocking of animals in Sudan because of the absence of reliable inventories of livestock. A census in 1976 suggested the levels shown in Table 6.6. These estimates are, in all probability, understatements of true numbers, partly because of the difficulties of carrying out accurate censuses and partly because of the incentive to understate numbers.

Ibrahim (1984, pp. 128–30) has suggested some crude estimates of overstocking, in terms of measures of livestock population in excess of carrying capacity for northern Darfur. His procedure is as follows. The amount of grazing land that actually can be used for livestock is put at 85,000 km². The number of animals in the 1976 census is doubled (contrary to the official projections which assumed very little growth) and converted to livestock units (LSUs) to give 2.44 million LSUs. Each hectare of land is assumed to produce 1000 kg of plant biomass yearly, and each LSU requires 4562 kg of biomass. Thus the carrying capacity is:

$$(8,500,000 \times 1,000 \text{ kg})/4,562 = 1.86 \text{ million LSUs}$$

compared to Ibrahim's guess of 2.44 million LSUs in existence. This gives an overstocking rate of 31 per cent for northern Darfur. The obvious problem with this calculation is that the doubling of the 1976 livestock figures is arbitrary.

Widely quoted estimates of overstocking suggest that the excess of livestock, measured in livestock units (LSUs), is some 5 million LSUs (27 million LSUs compared to a carrying capacity of 22.1 million LSUs) for Sudan as a whole. This implies an overstocking rate of some 22 per cent. However, as we have noted, the estimate of actual stock is suspect. The official projections of the 1976 census would suggest the following figures for 1985:

sheep	14.92 million
goats	12.71 million
camels	2.92 million
cattle	17.38 million

which, using Ibrahim's LSU conversion factors (sheep and goats at 0.12, camels at 1.00 and cattle at 0.75), gives a total LSU of 19.24.

While the exact numbers of livestock, and their growth over time, are not known with accuracy, the general trends suggest that not only have livestock numbers increased with population, but they have actually increased very much faster, implying significant increases in per capita holdings. In the south of the two regions cattle are the main nomadic livestock; in the north it is camels. Sheep and goats tend to be held in the vicinity of villages, in small herds for daily pasturing and browsing, and larger ones for more extended excursions outside the village. While population growth itself explains some of the livestock increase, for example, through the need to expand stock to meet milk demand and, to a lesser extent, meat consumption, most of the increase is due to increased per capita holdings and this, in turn, requires explanation.

The motives for holding livestock are varied. Animals provide a stock of wealth both in themselves and which can always be converted to cash income, if needed, and given a sequence of good rainfall years, it can also be fairly easily expanded. In turn, for some owners, cash needs are relatively low, encouraging only limited offtake of stock. The animals are also a store of food. Threats to this joint store of wealth and food come from drought, land scarcity and political events. But all can, in principle, be overcome by moving the stock to alternative grazing areas. This will be especially true for nomadic tribes, less true for transhumant pastoralists, and obviously still less true for sedentary livestock owners. 'Supply side' factors have combined with these underlying motives to keep the animal population high, notably improved animal health through the supply of veterinary services.

These combined factors tend to encourage long-term stock increases, but are not sufficient to explain why stock size fails to adjust to deteriorated rangeland conditions. What appears to happen is that expectations of poor rangeland quality and fodder availability encourage the maintenance of existing stock levels, with adjustments being confined to compensating for natural loss. Such behaviour raises the stock level above the effective carrying capacity of the land, but can be explained as an insurance against the uncertainty generated by resource depletion. If livestock is virtually the only form of wealth, and money is not directly substitutable for it beyond a certain level, and also if resource depletion threatens food supplies, then it is rational to hold on to the wealth and food supply when both are threatened. Stock size and off-take are both increased only when there is some assurance about the pasture, the availability of crop residues and low price sorghum surpluses.

The effect of all these factors is to generate a 'ratchet' movement in livestock population. Outside of severe droughts, stocks are held approximately constant in bad years and are expanded in good years. Similarly, off-take is likely to drop in bad years as existing wealth is consolidated, and expand in good years, though by not as much as the increase in stock. The resulting pressures all favour expansion.

How far such a model of livestock ownership behaviour explains the trends in Sudan is uncertain since testing the model is complicated by the unreliability of livestock population data. But the main features seem clear and go some way to explaining the apparent non-response of livestock off-take to prices. What price reaction there is is more to input prices – i.e. sorghum as feedstock. If this is a reasonably correct characterization of the processes at work, it will be evident that policies to encourage increased off-take and the containment of stock size will have to be directed at the basic motivations of stockholders. If so, any 'livestock policy' faces formidable problems, and this is the general experience in African countries. Policy has somehow to succeed in demonstrating the carrying capacity constraint, and that the policy of 'holding on' in the expectation of better years to come actually has long-term resource depletion consequences. In practical terms, it means excluding some livestock owners from defined areas. This can only be done by establishing well-defined land rights and at an obvious cost to the excluded populations. They, in turn, must be accommodated neither by encouraging settlement – as has taken place in a number of areas – or by rangeland improvement in the common property areas.

Policy factors impairing natural resource quality
Government policy itself is frequently a major factor in reducing the stock and quality of natural capital. Five policy areas, in particular, are relevant to Sudan: land tenure and resource rights; agricultural policy and prices; energy policy relating to charcoal; credit; and institutional problems.

Land tenure
The traditional form of control over land use under the Anglo-Egyptian condominium (1899–1956) was exercised by the Native Administration through the medium of the *nazir, omda* and *sheikh* in the context of tribal homelands (*dar*). The exact nature of these customary rules and regulations is complex and varies across the regions. Actual ownership of land has largely been vested in the government. The 1899 Title to Lands Ordinance gave absolute title to land to anyone who cultivated it continuously for five years. The Settlement and Registration Act 1925 contained the provisions relating to the registration of private land. The Unregistered Land Act 1970 declared that all land not registered before the commencement of the Act was to be deemed government property and to have been registered as such. During the condominium period customary and Islamic law were allowed to determine land use through the medium of the Native Administrations. With the 1970 Act, the government could still allocate land use rights, or usufruct rights (the right to use land belonging to someone else). However, the allocation process became uncertain and even more complex with the Local Government Act 1971, which abolished the upper echelons of the Native Administrations.

The Native Administrations were replaced by district and rural councils. The extent to which the councils came into conflict with tribal administration has varied. Notable differences appeared in respect of redefinitions of village borders, with councils being unwilling to encroach on government land (Hammer, 1987). By and large, however, the tribal administration has continued to be powerful in terms of land use. Where it continues to prevail, it allocates land to cultivators and their usufruct rights. Cultivation is reasonably secure in terms of rights, although crop residues can and are communally grazed unless land is fenced. Gum arabic trees on fallow land remain the property of the cultivator but the land itself can be reallocated and fallow lost if there is sufficient pressure to cultivate it.

In 1984 the Civil Transactions Act was implemented, reflecting the Islamicization of law in Sudan (Shari'a). This law governs the possession, ownership and rights relating to land (Gordon, 1985). It declares that land registered as being under freehold ownership on or after 6 April 1970 be deemed the ownership of usufruct only; that is, the 1970 Act's intention of placing all land in government ownership, other than that registered as in private ownership prior to 1970, is confirmed. Usufruct rights (*manfa'a*) – the right to use land belonging to someone else – can still be allocated. Moreover, and extremely important, usufruct rights to rural 'waste' land can be acquired by cultivating it. The allocation process is to reside with committees at regional and central level, and the guidelines on allocation contain explicit reference to resource conservation and drainage, among other things. Water rights are also defined, and central and regional authorities are given control over grazing and tree cutting. As to crops, the Act places the right to the crops with the owner of the land, not the cultivator, although separate provisions appear to be made for usufruct holders and those with defined leases.

The Civil Transactions Act is under revision to enable a better definition of usufruct rights and hence improve the potential for security in land. In turn, security of usufruct rights is essential if farmers are to invest in the land and, as noted above, if the incentives to overstock animals are to be reduced. The current situation is a confusing one, and the government of Sudan has declared its intent to adopt policies on land allocation and leasing aspects to establish the economic and socially optimal size of holdings. The mechanism for this could be conditional long-term leases and the granting of titles related to collateral security, together with incentives to develop and maintain agricultural land and its productivity.

Agricultural policy and prices

A major factor influencing agricultural production in the two regions is the income obtained by farmers for their crops. This, in turn, involves the producer price and the cost of production. Measures to reduce the latter include the introduction of hybrid crops in an effort to increase yields. On prices, what matters, in particular, is the export price and the proportion of that price accruing to farmers. One would typically expect an increased producer price to bring forth increased supplies, and there is widespread evidence to support this view. But the effect on natural resources is ambiguous. Higher domestic prices may encourage continuous cropping of single crops. On fragile soils, such as those in much of Kordofan and Darfur, such monoculture tends to exhaust soil nutrients and encourage weed infestation. Relative crop prices also influence the type of crops sown, and the introduction of agriculture to marginal lands. Indiscriminate clearing of land for such crops tends to reduce biological productivity on the adjacent lands because of wind and water erosion. Expanded groundnut cultivation has been criticized on this basis. Clearly, then, a pricing policy that encourages increased product supply and which at least maintains resource productivity is not straightforward, and careful analysis of relative and absolute prices and their effects is required. Finally, any pricing policy unrelated to improved land security is obviously going to be of limited value.

Table 6.7 shows the ratio of domestic producer prices to world prices for sorghum, groundnuts and sesame 1984–6. It will be observed that domestic prices are currently well above their border equivalents. Jansen (1986) shows that a devaluation to £S4 sterling to $1 would bring domestic prices virtually into line with border prices. But as well as the issue of an overvalued exchange rate, there exist other factors affecting the domestic–world price ratio.

Sorghum   Sorghum prices are domestically supported, so that removal of the support will tend to push domestic prices down and reduce the ratios shown in Table 6.7. Sorghum was subject to an export ban from December 1983 to 1986 in order to conserve supplies for the domestic population. Between 1981 and 1983 sorghum exports ran at over 300,000 tonnes per year, or $70–$90 million per year, out of a production of some 2 million tonnes per year. Most of these exports were to Saudi Arabia, which favoured Sudanese imports with a subsidy until 1981 when the predium was removed in favour of a

Table 6.7   Ratios of domestic crop price to world prices
       (at £S2.5 = $1)

	1984–5	1985–6	1986–7
Sorghum:			
rahad	2.79	1.27	1.06
mechanized (Gedaref)	2.36	1.54	1.30
Groundnuts:			
rahad	0.17	0.46	1.53
traditional (Darfur)	1.46	0.68	1.62
Sesame:			
mechanized (Gedaref)	0.74	0.84	1.33
Gum arabic	1.04	0.52	1.44

Source: Computed from data in Jansen (1986).

bilateral agreement fixing the Sudan export price to Saudi Arabia. Although the export ban severed links with previous customers, making restoration of previous export levels very difficult, removal of the bank has resulted in significant exports.

Groundnuts   Groundnut exports in the mid-1970s totalled some 250,000 tonnes per anum (around $100 million) out of a production of around 400,000 tonnes, but these have fallen to only 15,000 tonnes in 1984–5, worth under $7 million. Groundnut oil exports have declined from approx. 39,000 tonnes in 1978–9 to approx. 19,000 tonnes in 1984–5; production has declined to approx. 217,000 tonnes in 1985–6. Table 6.7 shows that domestic prices are some 60 per cent above border prices, with scope for significant gains from exchange rate adjustments. The high domestic–world price ratio has encouraged diversion to home sales and the crushing of groundnuts of export quality.

Sesame   Table 6.7 suggests that the ratio of domestic to export prices for sesame has risen in the very recent period. Sesame exports currently run at about 50,000 tonnes, about half the level achieved in 1977–8, and worth around $39 million. Production is none the less around the level it was in the mid-1970s, some 210,000 tonnes. The major problem with improving sesame production and exports lies in the difficulty of 'timing' sesame harvesting before shattering occurs. Again, however, the impact of oilseed pricing on natural resource degradation is uncertain. Oilseeds have low productivity, so that higher prices will tend to encourage extensive cultivation rather than any increases in yields on existing land, resulting in vegetation clearance and potential involvement in resource degradation.

Mechanized agriculture   Mechanized agriculture warrants separate attention because of the particular environmental problems that it gives rise to. There are perhaps 4.2 million feddans of demarcated (authorized) mechanized farming, 4.6 million feddans of undemarcated area and a further 2.4 million feddans allocated to large companies, making 11.2 million feddans in all. Some 8.5 million feddans were cultivated in 1985–6, and under cultivation is now almost entirely in private hands, state farms having been sold off. Demarcated schemes are those approved by the Ministry of Agriculture via the Mechanized Farming Corporation (MFC) and the General Administration of Agricultural Investment (GAAI). Schemes over 2,000 feddans are controlled by GAAI directly without reference to MFC. Thus one company farms 1 million feddans, another 500,000 and two more each have some 200,000–250,000 feddans, all in Blue Nile Province. Undemarcated schemes are particularly damaging to natural resources since no controls are exercised over them and they have expanded into ecologically fragile areas.

Demarcated mechanized farming land is leased for 25 years at a nominal rental of £S1 per feddan, primarily because of the desire to attract farmers to the land by offsetting their high clearance costs. None the less, at this price the demand for land steadily outweighs the available land for release. One of the resulting problems is that the price attracts 'rent seekers' whose primary concern is short-term profit rather than a sustainable agricultural livelihood. Recommended rotations of 50 per cent sorghum, 25 per cent sesame and 25 per cent fallow are systematically ignored in favour of sorghum monoculture. This tends to be reinforced by the difficulty of harvesting sesame due to the 'shattering' problem. In the Dilling area, for example, the 1985–6 cultivation was 625,000 feddans of sorghum and 26,000 feddans of sesame, a ratio of 24:1 instead of 2:1. Like most crops, sorghum is soil degrading if it is cultivated continuously, giving rise to infestation by the weed *striga*.

The resulting environmental degradation in mechanized farming areas is well known. Leasing conditions which stipulate, for example, that 15 per cent of land be left for shelterbelts are ignored. Sub-

surface soils are subject to 'hard-panning', arguably due to continuous constant-depth disc ploughing, and absentee owners pay little
attention to resource degradation because of the ability to abandon
farms after short-term gains of 8–9 years are achieved in favour of
developments in new areas. Land secured from local authorities
carries with it no requirements relating to trees or shelterbelts.

Clearly, pricing policy as it relates to land rental is only a
contributory factor to the environmental problems generated by
mechanized farming. The wider issue concerns the controls that can
realistically be expected to be exercized over the tenants of such land,
together with the need to appreciate the financial plight of local and
regional government which allocates undemarcated land in an effort
to secure revenues.

Urban demand for charcoal
The demand for wood products in 1983 was perhaps some 46 million
cubic metres of wood. Out of this, woodfuel comprised the overwhelming proportion at 43m. m^3. That total was, in turn, comprised
of:

> fuelwood: 15.8m m^3
> charcoal: 27.1m m^3

Out of that charcoal total, Khartoum Province accounts for 22m.
m^3. Without conservation measures, charcoal demand may grow to
45m. m^3 by the year 2000, with particularly drastic consequences for
southern Kordofan which supplies some of the demand in Khartoum. Just one of the consequences is the loss of 22m. ha of
savannah woodland with an animal fodder equivalent of 10m.
tonnes of dry matter. In value terms, this is worth some $1,000
million. In human terms, perhaps 250,000 people will be displaced
by the loss.

It is abundantly clear, then, that solving the problems of resource
degradation in western Sudan involves not just action to raise
ecological productivity in those areas, but also measures to constrain
the demand for charcoal in urban areas and especially Khartoum.
Demand conservation measures are very attractive in both economic
and environmental terms. A World Bank study suggests that some
29 per cent of woodfuel could be saved by 2000 through conservation
measures: 17 per cent in fuelwood and 34 per cent in charcoal.

As far as charcoal is concerned, this comes about through improved charcoal stoves and through improved charcoal production by more efficient kilns.

The difficulties facing such a policy are formidable. Control over the charcoal industry, for example, is limited because the Forest Administration, which is responsible for giving permits for removal on land designated for mechanized farming, has extremely limited resources for checking the location of production activities (Earl, 1984). Illegal production also occurs outside the designated areas. The diffusion of more efficient stoves is never easy. Thus any conservation programme has to be supported by institutional strengthening and a careful pricing policy. A stumpage fee (i.e. a tax on removed trees) could also be introduced on land presently undemarcated. World Bank (1986) suggests that a fee of £S1 sterling per cubic metre would generate perhaps £S2 million per annum in government revenue.

Credit
Very little of the available bank credit in Sudan reaches small farmers. Instead farmers are forced to rely on the *sheil* system, or informal loans made by merchants in the form of cash, seed, food or other goods against a share of the farmer's crops. *De facto* interest rates are reported to be in the region of 50–75 per cent p.a. In part, this is a result of non-availability of bank funds, but in the main it arises because banks are unwilling to lend against high risks when more secure, and larger, investments can be made, including speculating on grain prices. At the macroeconomic level, the bias reflects the attention given to urban outlets for funds and big farmers, and the neglect of the traditional rural sector.

A feature of the high risk in lending to small farmers is their lack of well-defined rights to their land and the trees and crops that are on it. There is widespread evidence that lack of tenure rights is the single largest obstacle to securing credit. Therefore, to some extent, it might be expected that the foundations for improved credit will be laid down as these rights are better defined. But much more than this is needed. In this respect, a drive towards rural co-operatives which can reduce risks by pooling resources could assist. Some existing credit channels, such as the Agricultural Bank of Sudan (ABS), already combine loans with the provisions of machinery and extension services. Provided there is evidence that this is a least-cost provision of credit (*a priori*, one would expect this because of the economies of information), this is a useful model to retain. The ABS itself lends only a minute proportion of its funds to small farmers, however, and improvement of this situation is currently under investigation.

Institutional weakness

Whatever policies relating to incentives and output encouragement are pursued, they will have no effect unless there are effective institutions responsible for relaying information to producers and processing their responses. Yet in the Sudan local, regional and central government is weak simply because of lack of resources, lack of training and lack of communications networks. Thus outside the areas served by the various 'development projects', extension services are usually not available at all, or available only in name. If extension workers exist, they invariably have no mechanism for travelling to the areas they serve. Yet flows of information relating, for example, to modified rotation practices, are essential if the arid area farms are to reduce their vulnerability to climatic variation and price vagaries.

What is true of extension services is also true of government agencies at regional and central level. Knowledge of the resource base in western Sudan is severely deficient because of the inadequate means to map and quantify them and to update information. The protection of resources is also nominal because of the lack of equipped manpower to supply, for example, forest range services. Yet in all this one absolutely vital factor must be understood. At all levels, from village to ministry, there exists a vast fund of knowledge and understanding about the natural resource problem in Sudan. It is tapped frequently by consultants and donor agencies, often with little reward to those with the real expertise. Institutional strengthening thus involves more than supplying more equipment, better buildings and more manpower. It also involves a reconsideration of the incentive structure for this vital, longer-term work within government.

Conclusions on policy measures for resource augmentation

Clearly, the range of policy issues relating to natural resources is extensive. The previous brief overview suggests various ways in which resource issues can be tackled, at least containing the decline in the natural capital stock, perhaps augmenting it. Action on prices and exchange rates (variable incentives) is important in order that households and farm units can respond to the correct economic signals rather than ones which contribute to non-sustainable resource use. But ensuring socially optimal behaviour responses also requires that individuals are *enabled* to respond, and the clearest mechanisms for ensuring this lie in granting individuals a stake in their natural environment. In turn, this means modifying land tenure and resource rights and ensuring local participation and involvement in resource decisions. Flows of information are also critical as enabling devices, and this therefore implies improved communication, more education aimed at locally diffused information, strengthening of the agencies of government and the general raising of environmental issues to those of highest priority in national planning.

Notes

1. The conclusions about desertification and its extent differ in this chapter compared to Pearce (1987), due to the integration of the Lund University studies which were not generally used in the earlier work.
2. This definition is broadly consistent with that given in Nelson (1988), but Nelson confines its use to 'arid, semi-arid and dry sub-humid areas', whereas there appears to be no *necessary* reason to restrict its application. Equally, Nelson includes in the definition that man must be, partly at least, the *cause* of desertification. Again, there seems no compelling reason for this to be so. For an overview of the many definitions of desertification in the literature, see Glantz and Orlovsky (1986).
3. A landsat image in our possession and obtained from the US Geological Survey does, however, indicate sand encroachment in the area of Lamprey's mobile dunes.
4. At the time of writing, such an inventory is planned, using Landsat imagery and surveys.
5. Stocks of wood will not translate one-to-one into hectarage due to different growing rates according to rainfall. Hence the percentage of the stock in the south is higher than the south's share of wood-covered land.
6. Again, extreme caution in using such figures is required. The calculation is as follows. In 1986 charcoal reached LS 20 per sack in Khartoum (approx. 37 kg). Thus the price was LS 540 per tonne. Estimates of charcoal consumption vary widely, but here a figure of 3 million tonnes p.a. is adopted to give a value of approx. LS 1,620 million.

References

Ahlcrona, E. (1988), *The Impact of Climate and Man on Land Transformation in Central Sudan*, Geografiska Institutioner Publication 103, Lund: Lund University Press.

Bateson, W. and El Tohami, A. (1986), 'Gum arabic sector model for Sudan',

Planning and Agricultural Economics Administration, Ministry of Agriculture and Natural Resources, Khartoum.

Earl, D. (1984), *Sudan Renewable Energy Project: Report on Charcoal Production*, Khartoum: Energy Research Council and US AID.

Glantz, M. and Orlovsky, N. (1986), 'Desertification: anatomy of a complex environmental process', in K. Dahlberg and J. Bennett (eds), *Natural Resources and People: Conceptual Issues in Interdisciplinary Research*, Boulder, Colo: Westview Press, 321–40.

Gordon, C. (1985), *Land Law in the Sudan: A Legislative Analysis*, Rainfed SubSector Task Force of the Government of Sudan, Khartoum.

Hammer, T. (1987), 'Fuelwood crisis causing unfortunate land use', *Norsk Geografisk Tidsskrift*, **33**, 32–40.

Harrison, H. and Jackson, D. (1958), 'Ecological classification of the vegetation of Sudan', *Forest Bulletin No. 2*, Ministry of Agriculture, Khartoum.

Hellden, U. (1984), *Drought Impact Monitoring: A Remote Sensing Study of Desertification in Kordofan, Sudan*, Report No. 61, Naturgeografiska Institution, Lund University, Lund.

Ibrahim, F. (1984), *Ecological Imbalance in the Republic of the Sudan. With Special Reference to Desertification in Darfur*, Bayreuth: Druckhaus Bayreuth Verlagsgesellschaft.

Jada, M. (1988), 'The four enemies', in A. Ahmed *et al.* (eds), *War Wounds: Development Costs of Conflict in Southern Sudan*, London: Panos Institute.

Jansen, D. (1986), *Economic and Financial Analysis of Sudan's Major Crops*, Development Technologies Inc., Larkspur, California.

Lamprey, H. (1976), *Survey of Desertification in Kordofan Province*, United Nations Environmental Programme, Nairobi.

Nelson, R. (1988), *Dryland Management: The 'Desertification' Problem*, Environment Department Working Paper No. 8, World Bank, Washington, DC.

Olsson, K. (1985), 'Remote sensing for fuelwood resources and land degradation studies in Kordofan, the Sudan', doctoral dissertation, Geografiska Institution, University of Lund, Lund.

Olsson, L. (1985), *An Integrated Study of Desertification*, Geografiska Institution, University of Lund, Lund.

Pearce, D. W. (1987), *Natural Resource Management in the Western Sudan*, Government of Sudan and World Bank, Washington, DC.

World Bank (1986), *Sudan: Forestry Sector Review*, Washington, DC: World Bank.

7 Sustainable development in Botswana

Introduction

Botswana is a landlocked country with borders shared with Zimbabwe, South Africa, Namibia and Zambia (see Figure 7.1). The land area is approx. 580,000 km^2, but most of its population of 1.2 million live in the eastern margin drained by the Limpopo River. In the north-west is the Okavango delta, an inland swamp arising from the River Okavango which drains inland from Angola; this swamp is one of the most remarkable wildlife areas anywhere in the world. The remaining two-thirds of Botswana is occupied by the sands of the Kalahari Desert where surface water is present only after the rains, and then only in 'pans' (shallow depressions). Rainfall is variable and generally comes in short, intensive bursts; from 1982 to 1986 there was a major drought.

By African standards, Botswana is relatively wealthy. On the World Bank classification it ranks as a lower middle-income country with a per capita income in 1986 of $840, the equivalent of that of Jamaica. The major part of this economic success is owed to mining of diamonds, copper-nickel and coal. Botswana also has a significant livestock sector based on cattle. The environmental challenges in Botswana are several: the overgrazing of cattle on fragile soils has led to land degradation; cattle conflict with wildlife in terms of competition for land and through the effects of veterinary fences on migratory animals; and accessible water is scarce, causing pressure on groundwater and a focus on the Okavango delta as a potential source for diverted water. Although rich in wildlife, including the inhospitable Kalahari regions, Botswana has deliberately not pursued a policy of developing its wildlife resource. Tourism is moderate in comparison to the diversity and stock of wildlife and in comparison to the generally well-developed communication system.

The 1981 census indicated the population data shown in Table 7.1. The total population of under 1 million people is broadly split, 80 per cent in the rural areas and 20 per cent in urban areas, but this is expected to change to 75 and 25 per cent respectively in the early

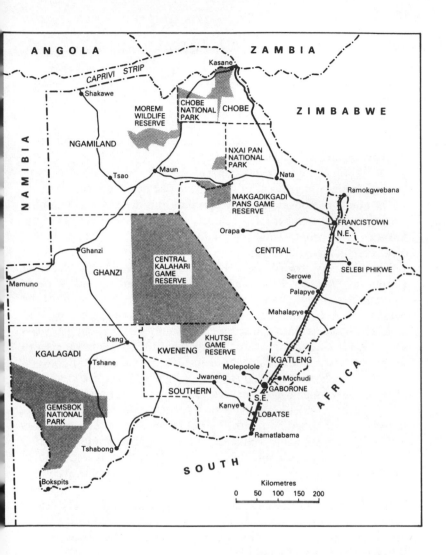

Figure 7.1   Republic of Botswana

Table 7.1 *Botswana: Population ('000s)*

	1971	1981	1991
Urban	63.5	166.3	341.1
Rural	510.5	774.8	1006.4
Total	574.1	941.0	1347.6

Source: Central Statistical Office.

1990s. Population growth, in general, is fast at 3.6 per cent p.a.
The ethnic composition of the population is difficult to determine accurately. The number of 'bushmen' is unknown, these being the Basarwa (San) people, who first inhabited what is now Botswana, and could comprise anything from 2–25 per cent of the population (Cooke, 1988), with very few of them still occupying the lifestyle made so famous by Van der Post (1958), most being assimilated in other communities. The Bamangwato account for about 40 per cent of the population, being one of the cattle-herding Tswana peoples who invaded Botswana from Zimbabwe and South Africa about 300 years ago. Other Tswana peoples are the Bakwena and the Bangwaketse. In 1891 the British Cape Colony Protectorate was extended to Botswana and tribal lands were assigned to eight recognized Tswana tribes, three of them (the Bamangwato, the Bakwena and the Bangwaketse) occupying the best agricultural land in what are now Central District, Kweneng District and Southern District respectively. Still other tribes moved in from the south and some from the north, producing a rich ethnic variety of population which, none the less, has created political tension. In general, the Tswana elite have remained in political control of Botswana and various efforts have been, and are being, made to distribute national benefits in a more widespread manner. The ethnic composition, and particularly the Tswana dependence on cattle, is important for an understanding of the relationship between the Botswana environment and the economy.

The state of the environment
Water
Water is a major constraint on Botswana's development. The five years after 1981 were characterized by below-average rainfall. The major users of water are currently irrigation and livestock, about 35 per cent of total consumption each, with mining and urban demand

Table 7.2   Water demand in Botswana, 1987 (10^6 cubic metres per annum)

Urban	21
Major villages	5
Rural villages	2.5 – 4.5
Mines and energy	17
Livestock	45 – 50
Irrigation	30 – 40
Total	120.5–137.5

Source: Background papers to draft Botswana National Conservation Strategy.

accounting for perhaps a further 12 per cent each. Total demand was some 120–140m. m³ in 1987. An approximate breakdown of demand is given in Table 7.2.

Growth in demand is expected to be substantial. Total domestic demand is expected to increase by a factor of 5 by 2007, while demand for livestock and mining uses will grow only slowly. The other sector that might grow dramatically is the irrigation sector, depending on national policies towards food security. Some estimates suggest a tenfold increase in demand by 2007, making irrigation responsible for 60 per cent of projected demand. But how far a policy of expanded irrigation is feasible is uncertain.

How far existing consumption rates exceed the sustainable yield of water from rivers and groundwater,[1] reached by boreholes, is not known. But the major growth in demand for water has been in the south-east where water resources, as far as they are known, are in potential deficit. There is a regional imbalance between supply and demand not only for geographical reasons – highest demand occurring where surface water is in short supply – but also because some catchment areas lie outside Botswana. The implications are either that groundwater sources, the extent of which is not known accurately, need to be developed or that some form of surface water diversion is needed. Groundwater sources primarily supply the livestock sector, industry and the urban sector. Surface water primarily supplies irrigation and wildlife.

Water shortages have shown up most in terms of precluded development – i.e. land developments have not occurred because of the absence of identified water supply. The livestock sector has also

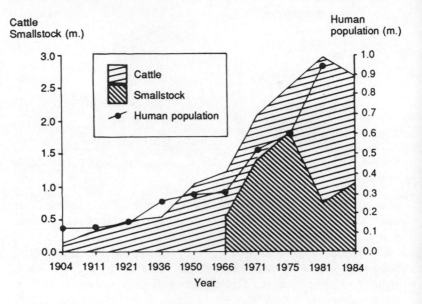

*Figure 7.2   Cattle and smallstock numbers in Botswana (× 1000)
(Arntzen and Veenendaal, 1986)*

suffered because of the difficulty of finding new boreholes.[2] Urban demand has been rationed at times of rainfall deficit.

Land degradation
Livestock numbers have grown rapidly in Botswana. Figure 7.2 shows that the growth has generally been related to population change, with some more erratic variation in numbers of smallstock (e.g. goats). Overgrazing in the sense of animal numbers in excess of the range's carrying capacity appears to be common. Arntzen (1986) assembles available data to show that overstocking occurs throughout Botswana. The main holders of cattle are the relatively wealthier households: 8 per cent of farmers held 45 per cent of cattle stock in 1984; and 30 per cent of cattle holders held 4 per cent of the stock (Arntzen, 1986). There is little systematic investigation of the cattle-range quality linkage, but most commentators agree that much of

range degradation arises from excess livestock numbers (Cooke, 1985; Ringrose, 1986). Thus bush encroachment – the loss of palatable perennial grasses in favour of less palatable species and woody biomass – appears to emanate from centres of cattle concentration. Soil erosion can ensue as the protective functions of the grassy cover are lost, although evidence on soil erosion in Botswana is very limited.

Interpretation of Landsat imagery by Ringrose (quoted in Arntzen, 1986) suggests fairly extensive land degradation. She finds severe degradation around some villages, degradation in western Botswana and around the Okavango delta, and elsewhere. However, the relative contributions of climate and man-made factors appears to be unknown. Time-series analysis is generally not available, but in a further paper, Ringrose (1986) found marked increases in the area of exposed soils in the area round Gaborone in south–east Botswana between 1982 and 1984. The changes were particularly notable in the communal grazing areas close to Gaborone and in the settled areas of the eastern Kalahari. Moreover, actively growing vegetation declined in the Kalahari and agricultural lands to the east.

There is some evidence that crop production is contributing to soil erosion in some areas, but again adequate time-series analysis of the possible linkages between choice of crops and soil quality is lacking.

Loss of woody biomass

There is no systematic inventory available to determine wood stocks in Botswana. One study (Environmental Resources Ltd, 1985) of eight regions in eastern Botswana suggested that fuelwood supply was only just keeping pace with demand in the south–east region and that demand would outstrip supply by the end of the 1980s. Elsewhere few regions faced prospective risk of major shortage, but some of the major towns other than Gaborone (the capital of Botswana) already experience some shortages. In fact the situation is worse than is revealed by an analysis of fuelwood demand alone, since other wood demands (e.g. poles for building) can more than double demand based on fuelwood needs only. The study suggested that fuelwood demand would increasingly involve a switch to less preferred species, a rise in fuelwood prices, spontaneous conservation measures (reduced cooking, use of animal dung for fuel) and for the richer households a switch to petroleum products.

Wildlife
Botswana is immensely rich in wildlife resources. The 1981–6 drought affected populations significantly, but extensive populations of the larger animals – buffalo, antelope, elephant, hippopotamus, giraffe, etc. – remain, and Botswana has a virtually unparalleled population of birds and smaller wildlife. Controversy surrounds the extent to which cattle fences have interfered with migration patterns and contributed to mortality. Williamson (1987) has analysed the effects of the Kuke fence built in 1958 and running west–east to the south of the Okavango delta. At the time of the fence construction, migrating wildebeest died because the fence blocked their migration path, or forced them into the Lake Xau area in large numbers where many died. Williamson estimates the deaths at 'hundreds of thousands of wildebeest alone, plus nobody knows how many deaths of other species' (*ibid.*, p. 26). Others have disputed the extent of the losses.

The main impression left from this brief review of Botswana's environment is a familiar one – lack of information makes it difficult to assess both the existing stock of natural capital and its rate of change over time. There is sufficient evidence, however, to suggest that Botswana's major problem is a threatening water shortage. A wood supply problem seems of less concern. Range degradation does appear to be occurring and, regardless of the relative contributions of overstocking and climatic variability to the problem, it seems clear that some form of improved range management is required. For wildlife, the problem lies with direct competition with cattle for land, an issue that is likely to be best resolved by a more positive approach to the sustainable management of wildlife for economic benefit. The rest of this chapter develops these themes.

The economic contribution of natural resources
Table 7.3 shows the relative contributions of different sectors to the GDP of Botswana. The sectoral composition of GDP indicates Botswana's high level of dependence on natural resource-based activities. In 1984–5, the beginning of the current plan period, mining and agriculture together accounted for 54.5 per cent of GDP, 92.3 per cent of exports and approx. 90 per cent of all employment, formal and informal. Significantly, however, within the natural resource-based sectors there are extraordinary differences in the performance of the exhaustible and renewable resource-based

*Table 7.3   Real GDP, by sector: 1980–1 to 1985–6
          (at constant 1979–80 prices) (million pula)*

	1980–1	1981–2	1982–3	1983–4	1984–5	1985–6
Agriculture	75.0	71.8	60.1	50.9	48.0	48.0
Mining and quarrying	260.6	222.1	393.3	533.4	560.6	673.2
Manufacturing	37.0	45.8	42.4	44.0	46.0	45.0
Electricity and water	15.3	15.9	15.7	19.5	19.6	20.7
Construction	32.0	37.2	26.2	38.7	32.3	30.3
Wholesale and retail trade	163.8	150.7	162.1	182.2	204.4	223.4
Transport and communications	14.8	18.1	23.8	23.1	25.2	26.1
Financial institutions	49.7	55.6	58.9	65.2	67.9	74.0
General government	104.7	113.9	122.9	136.5	156.2	165.7
Household, social and commercial services	25.6	29.2	35.0	34.9	34.9	35.5
Dummy sector	−16.7	−17.0	−19.9	−22.4	−24.2	−26.3
GDP	761.8	743.3	920.5	1106.0	1170.9	1315.6

Notes: The 1984–5 and 1985–6 figures are preliminary, the latter determined by industrial activities only. The dummy sector is a correction for imputed bank service charges. In 1985–6 1 pula = approx. 0.53 US dollars.
Source: Botswana CSO, *Statistical Bulletin*, 1987.

sectors. Where real mining GDP grew at an average annual rate of 21 per cent between 1980–1 and 1984–5, real agricultural GDP fell over the same period at an annual average rate of just under 11 per cent.

The high level of dependence on natural resources is sufficient to justify a resource conservation policy. Moreover, the dominance of mining is not expected to continue, which means that the balance of the economy has to switch either into some form of manufacturing or expansion of services or of agriculture, or some combination of these. This *diversification* of the economy is consistent with the principle of sustainable development since reliance on a single activity subjects the economy to exogenous risks (e.g. world price variations). This, in turn, suggests that agriculture has to be rehabilitated and that other resource-based activities need to be developed.

Table 7.4 shows some crude estimates of the contribution of various natural resources to the economy of Botswana. The table suggests that activities not typically accounted for in the GDP

Table 7.4 *Economic contributions derived from the natural resources of Botswana**

Resource	Gross output (million pula)	Value added (million pula)	Employment (rounded)
Rangeland:			
Mainly livestock			
commercial	76.7	54.5	14,300
freehold	17.7	0.4	
Veld products			
commercial†	4.4	n.a.	2,640
subsistance	50.0	n.a.	n.a.
Wildlife/tourism			
photographic			
safari	13.4		
hunting safari	2.6	2.9	2,020
wildlife			
farming	0.1		
trade/processing	0.9		
subsistence	7.5–11.5	6.2	5,020
Fisheries:			
commercial	4.7	n.a.	900
subsistence	2.6	n.a.	5,000–11,000
Forestry:			
commercial	n.a.	n.a.	n.a.
traditional	10.3	n.a.	n.a.
Wood fuels:			
urban	13.0	n.a.	n.a.
rural	16.6	n.a.	n.a.

*The estimates displayed are derived from a wide variety of sources. They relate solely to the annual flow of benefits – i.e. changes in the capital value of the resource are *not* included. Furthermore, the figures do not all refer to the same year. Thus the figures need to be regarded as *preliminary*, indicative estimates.

†These include mokola palm, mopane worm, grapple, phane, silk cocoons, thatching grass.

‡In addition, the tourism-related craft industries provide at least 3,500 jobs.

Source: Perrings *et al.* (1988).

estimates might be worth 100 million pula p.a., or perhaps 7–8 per cent of GDP. The *potential* is clearly significantly greater.

Resource degradation and management policy
In the remainder of this chapter we look at the resource sectors in light of the factors giving rise to resource degradation or the risk of degradation, and the policies that might be adopted to combat resource loss.

The mining sector
Over 9,000 people are employed in Botswana's mining sector, about 7 per cent of all formal sector employment.[3] Although currently mining contributes approx. 40 per cent of GDP, and half of government revenues, its contribution is expected to decline in the future. The economic issue is how to utilize the 'rents' that have been created from this mineral wealth for the development of the rest of the economy along a sustainable path. Botswana has typically pursued a policy of rapid extraction of its mineral wealth, which is justified by the low expectations of future real price increases.[4] Diamond extraction is coupled with a policy of storing the output. This can be justified by the fact that storage costs are low, extraction costs are a small fraction of the diamond price and fixed costs of extraction are a high proportion of total costs. Additionally, continual extraction maintains employment in the industry, and this can be thought of as a 'positive externality' by the industry which further justifies the extraction profile.

Any environmental degradation associated with mining would offset this presumption that rapid exploitation is justified. Essentially, any environmental costs should be added to the costs of extraction to determine the real social cost of extraction. The higher the environmental cost, the higher is the real cost of extraction, and this should modify the policy of rapid extraction. There is air pollution from Botswana's mining activities, and emissions at one mine, Selibe-Phikwe, do appear to exceed government standards. There may also be some contamination of groundwater sources used to meet the mining sector's water demands. Overall, however, it seems unlikely that resource conservation objectives should alter the pattern of exploitation of Botswana's minerals unless clearer evidence of associated environmental degradation comes to light.

Livestock
Botswana's livestock increased dramatically up to the 1980s, receiving a setback only between 1982 and 1985 when drought reduced the

cattle herd from approx. 3 million to 2.5 million. Cattle have a high cultural importance in Botswana. Briefly, to be a 'real Motswana' (an individual of Botswana), one must own some cattle. The extent to which an individual's opinions are respected varies directly with cattle ownership. A complex system exists whereby cattle are loaned between individuals (*mafisa*), partly based on the need to distribute cattle so as to minimize risks of raiding and partly to insure against pests and drought. Thus the larger the herd that is owned, the more secure an owner may feel against the risk of disease and drought, and the more he can assist smaller herd owners by lending cattle under the *mafisa* system to help with reconstituting herds affected by drought. Cattle play a major role in *rites de passage* – i.e. they have a ceremonial role at birth, marriage, achieving adulthood, etc. In rural areas there are few alternative opportunities for employment but many cattle are owned by absentee owners in towns. As population expands, so does the cattle population.

Livestock ownership is directly encouraged by government policies which provide fiscal incentives to overstock. Many inputs are subsidized, as with veterinary fences and veterinary services in general. Extension and research services are provided by the government, as are slaughterhouse facilities. A critical incentive is the ability to write off losses in agriculture against income from other activities, so that there is no incentive to manage herds to maximize pre-tax gains. The pricing system has also encouraged overstocking. During the earlier years of the 1981–6 drought the Botswana Meat Commission chose to pay the highest possible price to sellers to secure short-term gains, encouraging overstocking rather than understocking. Moreover, prices tend to be lowest at the onset of the dry season, providing no incentive to sell at that point, despite the fact that it would avoid cattle making demands on the rangeland environment at its most susceptible time. The EEC market gives preferential treatment to Botswana beef under the Lomé Convention, further encouraging increased herd size.

Criticism of Botswana in terms of policies encouraging environmental degradation have centred on the livestock sector, and especially the alleged help given to the expansion of the sector by international aid and lending agencies. Early efforts to redistribute the cattle stock included the First Livestock Development Project, approved by the World Bank and co-financed by Sweden in 1972. This aimed to shift the expansion of commercial ranching to the western lands to remove overgrazing pressure in the east. The project failed because of the difficulties of monitoring activity in these remote areas; because what benefits there were did not reach the intended population of the west and the north; and because of the unwillingness of ranchers to pursue the management policies that were an integral part of the project.

In 1975 the government in Botswana introduced the Tribal Grazing Lands Policy. To understand that policy it is necessary to have some grasp of land tenure in Botswana; the three basic types of tenure are illustrated in Figure 7.3. Approximately 32 per cent of land is state land, including reserves and national parks; just 3 per cent of the land is freehold land, privately owned; and 65 per cent of the land is tribal land. Originally, under the Protectorate, control of tribal land was exercised by the tribal chiefs. The Tribal Lands Act 1968 transferred control to District Land Boards, the aim being to ensure a better and fairer allocation of land use. The Boards were to determine an appropriate land use and allocate use rights to individuals, while the ownership remained communal. At the same time, the development of boreholes established a new kind of *de facto* right in remoter areas – he who drilled the borehole and paid for it controlled the water and hence, effectively, the land within a day's walking distance of it.

The Tribal Grazing Lands Policy (TGLP) was aimed at controlling overgrazing in the tribal lands. It set up fenced leasehold ranches on the lands (see Figure 7.2), designed to absorb the large herds. The aim was to leave the rest of the tribal lands available to smaller ranchers who would continue communal grazing, and a further proportion was to be left as 'reserve' areas in preparation for wildlife management schemes. Thus tribal lands were to be split as large commercial leasehold ranches, smaller commercial units, tribal communal grazing and potential wildlife management areas. The District Land Boards were to be responsible for deciding land use plans, now supported by representatives of central ministries in light of doubts about the Land Boards' effectiveness. But the Land Boards faced opposition from tribal groups, used to the more traditional allocation of use rights through their own institutions, and distrusting the Boards because of some of the decisions already made.

The TGLP also fell foul of the 'dual rights' problem. Batswana

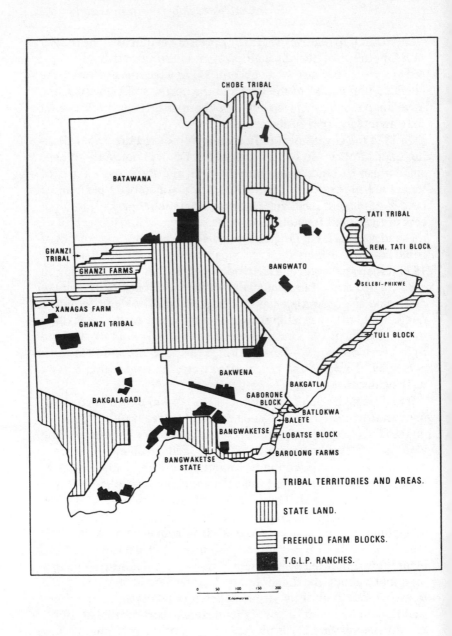

CHOBE TRIBAL

BATAWANA

TATI TRIBAL

REM. TATI BLOCK

GHANZI
TRIBAL →

GHANZI FARMS

BANGWATO

SELEBI-PHIKWE

XANAGAS FARM

GHANZI TRIBAL

TULI BLOCK

BAKWENA

BAKGATLA

GABORONE
BLOCK

BAKGALAGADI

BATLOKWA
BALETE

BANGWAKETSE

LOBATSE BLOCK

BANGWAKETSE
STATE

BAROLONG FARMS

TRIBAL TERRITORIES AND AREAS.

STATE LAND.

FREEHOLD FARM BLOCKS.

T.G.L.P. RANCHES.

0   50   100   150   200
Kilometres

Figure 7.3   Land tenure in Botswana

deciding to go in for the commercial (leasehold) ranching did not give up their traditional tribal rights to the communal land. They could thus degrade their leasehold land and then move their cattle on to common land and wait for the overgrazed land to restore itself. Additionally, through the *mafisa* system the ranchers would allow other cattle owned by family and kinsmen on to their land, furthering the degradation process.

In 1977 The Second Livestock Development Project was started, aimed at implementing the TGLP. The aim was to encourage the development of the commercial leasehold ranches and to protect the interests of the small farmer left on the communal lands. In the event, the policy failed for several reasons. First, the take-up of TGLP ranches was small and large herd owners still refused to adopt modern management practices. Secondly, the dual rights issue was not tackled. Thirdly, while small farmers were encouraged to move to allegedly virgin lands occupied by wildlife and, perhaps, by bushmen, less of these lands were suitable for cattle than was thought hitherto. In addition, development costs were much higher than expected.

The debate over the appropriate policies to pursue continued into the 1980s. The World Bank focused attention of the fiscal incentives to overgrazing, while the Botswana government tended to stress measures to protect the communal grazing areas, including the modification or abolition of dual rights. In 1985 a Land Management and Livestock Project was launched. This focused on the preparation of land use plans consistent with the carrying capacity of the rangelands, gives credits for ranch development, has funding for livestock extension services and seeks to strengthen central institutions' planning capacity. It strengthens the Land Boards. It also called for a price incentive study, which was eventually released in 1987 (McGowan International, 1987). But as the report itself notes, its terms of reference were changed by the government to exclude discussion of taxation allowances. At the time of writing, this aspect of the work still has to be completed.

The livestock sector thus remains controversial, especially so because the alleged environmental costs of international aid to Botswana were highlighted in a publication, *Bankrolling Disasters*, produced by environmental organizations in 1986. The essence of the criticism was that commercial ranching is not suited to the tribal lands, that wildlife was being 'squeezed out' by the expansion of cattle lands, wildlife migrations were impaired by fences, and the benefits of the livestock development projects accrued mainly to the wealthy. While some of the criticisms rest on fairly extensive misinformation about the nature of the component parts of the development projects, the general focus on overgrazing is actually shared by all parties. The dispute is about what to do. It seems clear that only a policy which effectively addresses the use and land tenure rights of cattle owners, and which deals with the incentives to overstock, can succeed.

Undoubtedly, there is conflict between wildlife and cattle and this raises the issue of the extent to which wildlife management can substitute for cattle ranching. Various estimates exist to show that some forms of wildlife ranching can yield economic rates of return above those achieved by cattle ranching, but assuming no fiscal incentives for cattle ranching such as exist at the moment. That, together with other rural development concepts, defines the proposed Botswana National Conservation Strategy, sponsored by the International Union for the Conservation of Nature and still being completed at the time of writing (early 1989).

Arable farming
Perrings *et al.* (1988) note the major difference between the productivity of arable farms. Traditional farms tend to be on communal land, whereas commercial farms are on leasehold or freehold farms. The land tenure argument previously outlined would suggest that we might expect output per hectare to be higher on commercial than on traditional farms, and this is indeed the case. However, incentives to conserve land in which there are distinct rights are only one factor in a complex of reasons for this differential productivity. Commercial land also tends to be located in areas of better rainfall. Virtually all irrigated land is freehold. Moreover, poor farmers tend to engage in risk-averse strategies (akin to the loss aversion phenomenon noted in Chapter 1), so that output tends to be maintained at low but reliable levels compared to the higher output levels obtainable with a more 'adventurous' profit-maximizing strategy. The differential productivity also reflects the lack of more advanced technologies in communal areas, where 'advanced' can include the use of animal draught power.

Towards sustainable development

How, then, does this brief overview of issues assist in identifying a sustainable development path for Botswana? A number of issues have emerged, as follows.

1. Future economic development in Botswana needs to be more broadly based. Progress in the past has been largely based on the mining sector, with the agricultural sector being allowed to decline. Past development has also paid little or no attention to the economic potential of the rich wildlife and natural habitat resources of Botswana.
2. The existing structure of price and income incentives in the agricultural sectors – arable and livestock – tends to encourage resource degradation. Such incentives include tax write-offs and subsidies to livestock and the existing arrangement with the EEC with respect to elevated beef prices. Resource conservation considerations suggest a lowering of these administered prices and a reduction in the subsidies and tax allowances. Grain prices, on the other hand, tend to be linked to subsidized prices in South Africa, making for disincentives to produce grain. Farm input subsidies (e.g. in the form of land clearance allowances) have probably made environmental conditions worse.
3. The existing structure of land tenure acts as a 'disabling' incentive. Overgrazing is encouraged in communal lands, and the existence of dual grazing rights, whereby landowners can still graze communal land, both encourages a non-caring attitude to the commercial land and adds to the pressure on communal land.
4. Laws and regulatory capacity in place are not used. The Land Boards in Botswana have the power to control the allocation of grazing lands, arable land and water rights. Lack of progress in securing an allocation system which conserves the natural capital of the land is partly explained by the sheer political difficulty of modifying property rights in a country where cattle have more than economic significance. But if *communities* could be given rights of exclusion over defined areas of grazing land, then the principle of communal tenure can be preserved while avoiding the worst excesses of open access resource use. Indeed the aim should be to establish common property in its true sense, as a form of defined communal ownership, and prevent *de facto* open access use whereby anyone can lay claim to grazing rights. Such a policy

would have to include the abolition of dual grazing rights. Some evidence of a shift of attitude, in this respect, already exists, as with exclusive assignment of water rights to syndicates of farmers.

5. Under-utilized resources should be 'developed' so as to be both conserved and managed for a sustainable yield. This suggests the development of some of the rural products, especially tourism.

Overall, a judicious mixture of (a) removing environmental destabilizing incentives, (b) introducing enabling incentives based on resource rights and (c) focusing modest financial resources on the development of certain rural industries would assist in the sustainability of Botswana's economy.

Notes
1. Surface water is rainfall held in surface catchment areas. Groundwater is underground water held in aquefers, and subject to natural rates of recharge. Clearly, both sources can be used non-sustainably if extraction rates exceed flow and recharge rates.
2. An aquefer can serve several different boreholes, so that simply sinking extra boreholes in a given area is not a solution to the scarcity problems. Indeed the issue is exacerbated by causing conflict between users. In Botswana boreholes must be at least 8 km apart, to reflect this fact, and to maintain the grazing area around boreholes.
3. A further 20,000 are recruited for work in South Africa's mines.
4. The rationality of rapid extraction in this context lies with Hotelling's rule for optimal extraction of a finite resource. If expected real price increases are higher than prevailing interest rates, it is better to leave the resource 'in the ground' to collect capital appreciation. However, if price expectations are below the interest rate, it pays to extract the resource rapidly and invest the proceeds at the ruling interest rate.

References
Abel, N., Flint, M., Hunter, N., Chandler, D. and Maka, G. (1987), *Cattle Keeping, Ecological Change and Communal Management in Ngwaketse*, Integrated Farming Pilot Project, Gaborone.
Arntzen, J. and Veenendaal, E. M. (1986), *A Profile of Environment and Development in Botswana*, Institute for Environmental Studies, Free University of Amsterdam, Amsterdam.
Cooke, C. (1988), 'Botswana land management and livestock: a case study', paper presented at Africa Region Environmental Seminar, Annapolis, Maryland, 18–20 May.
Cooke, H. J. (1985), 'The Kalahari today: a case of conflict over resource use', *Geographical Journal*, 151.
Environmental Resources Ltd (1985), *A Study of Energy Utilisation and Requirements in the Rural Sector of Botswana*, London; Overseas Development Administration.

McGowan International (1987), *National Land Management and Livestock Project: Incentives/Disincentives Study*, Gaborone: McGowan International.

Perrings, C., Pearce, D. W., Opschoor, H., Arntzen, J. and Gilbert, A. (1988), *Economics for Sustainable Development: Botswana – a Case Study*, Ministry of Finance and Development Planning and Ministry of Local Government and Lands, Gaborone.

Ringrose, S. (1986), 'Desertification in Botswana: progress towards a viable monitoring system', *Desertification Control Bulletin*, No. 13.

Van Der Post, L. (1958), *The Lost World of the Kalahari*, Harmondsworth: Penguin.

Williamson, D. (1987), *An Environmental Analysis of Botswana*, IUCN, Conservation Monitoring Centre, Cambridge.

8 Natural resources and economic development in Nepal

Introduction

Nepal is a landlocked country extending 800 km from east to west in the central Himalayas, sharing a border with India to the south and Tibet to the north. The land area of 141,181 km^2 covers some of the most varied terrain to be found within one country. Broadly speaking, there are three geographically distinct regions. To the south, and as part of the Gangetic Plain, is the plains region commonly referred to as the Tarai, with elevations below 300 m and a tropical climate. Northwards from the plains, is the hilly region, lying between 300–3,000 m, which has a climate that is subtropical to warm temperate. Finally, the northern frontiers of the country consist of the mountain region, lying above 3,000 m and including the main Himalayan range, its high spurs and the trans-Himalayan areas; the climate varies from the temperate to the arctic, with pronounced aridity north of the main Himalayan range. A map of the country is given in Figure 8.1. and an elevation profile in Figure 8.2. In relative terms, 12 per cent of the country's land area consists of the plains region, about 60 per cent in the hills region and the remaining 18 per cent in the mountains. These mountains consist of a succession of ranges running east to west across the country and separating and confining various depression areas that form the main settlement zones. Lateral communication between these zones has always been, and still is, difficult.

The way of life in each of the three regions naturally varies. The plains are fertile lowlands and support, in addition to a growing subsistence agricultural population, most of the modern development activities. Their share of the country's population increased from 38 per cent in 1971 to 44 per cent in 1981 (Table 8.1). The hills have traditionally been the zone of settlement for the Nepalese population but land pressures and resource degradation in that region have resulted in considerable outmigration, so that their share of the population has fallen from 49 per cent in 1971 to 44 per cent in

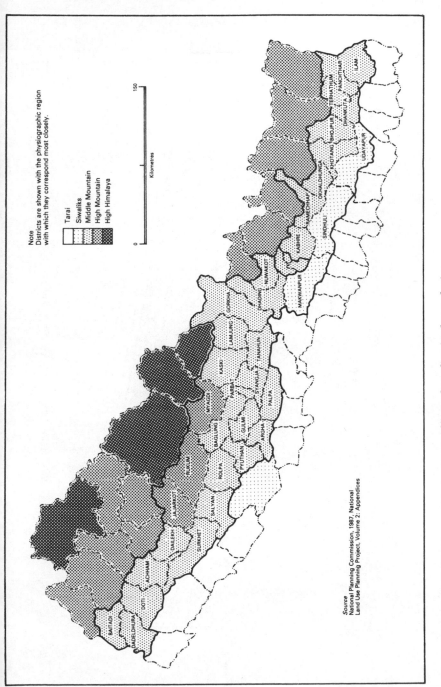

Note
Districts are shown with the physiographic region with which they correspond most closely.

Tarai
Siwaliks
Middle Mountain
High Mountain
High Himalaya

0   Kilometres   150

Source
National Planning Commission, 1987, National Land Use Planning Project, Volume 2: Appendices

Figure 8.1   Nepal: physiographic regions adjusted to district boundaries

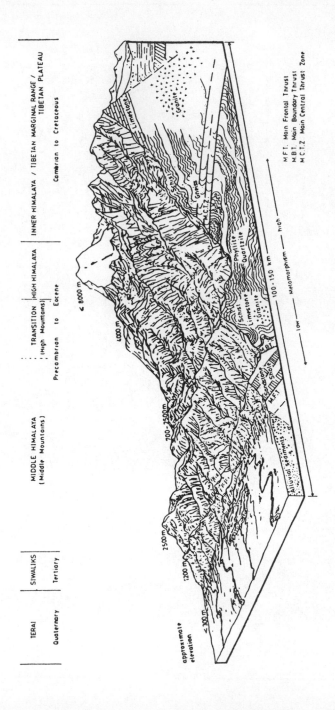

Figure 8.2 Physiographic regions: Nepal Himalaya (Ramsay, 1986)

Table 8.1 Population increase and density in Nepal

	Population		Increase		Growth	Density
	1971	1981	absolute	percent	rate	(persons per km²)
Mountain	955,930	1,070,570	114,590	12.0	1.14	21.7
Hilly	5,071,357	5,875,179	804,622	15.9	1.48	109.7
Kathmandu Valley	607,377	766,345	158,968	26.2	2.35	852.2
Inner Tarai	908,884	1,279,081	370,197	40.7	3.48	87.6
Tarsi	1,012,385	2,018,479	50.3	4.16	295.0	
Nepal	11,555,983	15,022,839	3,466,856	30.0	2.66	102.1

Source: Gurung (1986).

1981. The mountains are areas of sparse settlement, where livelihood has been based on pastoralism and seasonable trade. Their population share has also declined by approx. 1 per cent, as the table indicates. In economic terms, Nepal is a poor country. In the World Bank rankings it appears among the poorest of the low-income countries, with per capita GNP of $150 in 1986. In that year only Ethiopia had a lower per capita GNP figure. This poverty is reflected not only in the income figures, but also in other indicators of the standard of living and the quality of life. Life expectancy at birth is 47 years, compared to 61 for all the low-income countries taken together. Daily calorie consumption is around 2,000 calories per capita, which is 14 per cent below the average for the low-income-country group. Energy consumption at less than 200 kg of oil equivalent per person is also one of the lowest in the world.

The natural resource base of Nepal
Nepal's natural resources consist of its cultivable land resources, forest resources, soil and water resources and its natural areas, which are of great scenic and biological value. Apart from the latter, in which there is a tremendous interest from the international community, the other resources are critical to the livelihood of the mass of the people of the country, and likely to remain so for the foreseeable future. Hence it is necessary, in formulating any plans for the sustainable development of the country, to understand what is happening to these key components of the national patrimony.

Cultivable land resources
Table 8.2 gives the amounts of different types of land per capita for each of the regions. There is about the same amount of farmland per person in each of the zones, excluding the relatively urabanized Kathmandu Valley. These figures reveal a population of 4–5 persons per hectare of farmland, with the greatest density being found in the hilly region of the country. Although there are no earlier surveys with which this data can be compared, there is conflicting evidence from secondary sources on the question of whether agricultural land pressure has been increasing over the recent past. The Land Resources Mapping Project (LRMP, 1986) reported little change in the agricultural area in the hills between 1965 and 1979, although there were substantial population increases over that period.

Table 8.2   Land per capita, by type, 1978–79 (ha)

	Mountains	Hills	Kathmandu	Tarai
Farmland (gross)	0.22	0.20	0.06	0.24
Non-cultivated inclusions	0.12	0.11	0.02	0.03
Grassland	0.91	0.09	0.00	0.01
Forest	1.02	0.45	0.04	0.27
Shrubland	0.18	0.07	0.01	0.01
Other	1.72	0.07	0.01	0.03
Total	4.17	0.99	0.13	0.59

Source: Adapted from Wallace (1988), using LRMP and CBS data; ERL (1988).

Another survey by the Agricultural Projects Research Centre (APROSC, 1986) indicated an increase of 2 per cent p.a. in the hills between 1972 and 1982. If the latter is correct, there has been no increase in land pressure, as population (net of migration) has been growing at 1.5 per cent p.a. in that region (see Table 8.1).

Whatever view one takes of the past trends, there is general agreement that substantial further increases in cultivated land area are not feasible in the hills and mountain regions of the country. There is some scope for such increases in the Tarai, especially in the west, but even this is limited. Hence if the supply of food is to be maintained (let alone increased) for a growing population, there must be significant increases in agricultural yields. On the basis of recent trends, the prospects of achieving that are bleak. Although consistent data are lacking, the prevailing view is that agricultural yields have been stagnant, principally because of the lack of availability of plant nutrients, given the intensity of cropping and the past expansion of cropped area. Most nutrients applied to the soil consist of compost and manure, with the use of fertilizers being very low outside the Kathmandu Valley. An estimate by ERL (1988) of nutrient application in the hills region of Nepal calculates that about 35 nutrient kilograms are applied per hectare, on average. This figure is lower than the nutrient value of fertilizer applied in most Asian countries; for example, applications are around 51 kg in Bangladesh and 71 kg in Sri Lanka.

The productivity of the croplands is also adversely affected by the loss of soil and nutrients as a result of unsustainable farming practices. One cause is the high cropping intensity relative to the availability of water, and another is the cultivation of marginal lands on steeper slopes with poor terracing. However, the impact of the latter on overall productivity is debatable as soil from the higher terraces is frequently transferred to lower paddy lands, which tend to be well-banded, level terraces. But the total impact of soil loss, and the reasons for it, are much more complex in the case of Nepal. These are discussed more fully below, but the point should be noted that soil erosion through unsustainable cropping practices is only a very small contributor to the overall rate of soil movement observed in the country.

Forest and soil resources
It is a commonly held view that Nepal's forest resources are dwindling fast and that soil erosion from the hills and mountains is the result. Without trees to hold back the monsoon rains, it is argued, the soils are washed away into the rivers of India and Bangladesh, thereby raising their level and causing the kinds of post-monsoon floods recently experienced in Bangladesh; for example, the *Sunday Times* has reported: 'At the present rate of cutting, the Himalayas will be bald in 25 years, topsoil will have disappeared, and the climatic effects threaten to turn the fertile plain into a new Sahel – the drought-stricken region of central Africa' (11 September 1988). This view expresses the kind of easy and false generalization that is all too common in a subject where the truth is complicated and, more importantly, often unknown. If the evidence on deforestation is examined closely, the picture is much more complex. Only two surveys exist on which one can make a comparison between forest areas and forest cover at different points of time in Nepal: one is an air photographic survey undertaken in 1964, and another was undertaken in 1978–9 (the Land Resources Mapping Project). The Water and Energy Commission Secretariat (WECS) compared the results of these different surveys, taking account of differences of technique, methodology, coverage, etc. and came up with the conclusions summarized in Table 8.3. Following on from this, the Master Plan for the Forestry Sector (MPFS) projected the rates of change of forest area given in Table 8.4. These show that the rates of change of forest land in the hills (these come under 'middle mountains' in the tables) and mountains have been very low and, in some cases, statistically insignificant. Where forest land has been lost is in

Table 8.3   Changes in forest area: Nepal 1964–1979

	1964–5 ('000 ha)	1978–9 ('000 ha)	Area change	Percentage change	Annual percentage change
Middle/high mountains	3,950	4,000	50	0	0.1*
Siwaliks	1,740	1,475	− 265	− 15	− 1.2
Tarai	780	590	− 190	− 24	− 2.0
Nepal	6,460	6,080	− 380	− 5	− 0.4

*Not statistically significant in the original survey.
Source: WECS (1986).

Table 8.4   Changes in forest area: Nepal, 1979–85

	Percentage change (1979–85)	Annual percentage change
High Mountains	0.0	0.0
Middle mountains	− 1.9	− 0.3
Siwalks	− 0.8	− 0.1
Tarai	− 24.1	− 3.9
Nepal	− 3.4	− 0.5

Source: MPFS (1988).

the Tarai and its associated foothills, the Siwaliks. Wallace (1988) sums up the findings as follows:

> Except for the Tarai, forest area is pretty much what it was 25 – or even 100 – years ago. The forest has been lost in valleys and areas where access to inputs and outside employment makes conversion profitable (1988, p. 7).

What *has* been changing is the quality of the forest, as measured by its crown cover. This comparison is given in Table 8.5, which shows that the percentage of forest with crown cover greater than 70 per cent has fallen in the middle and high mountains from 40 per cent in 1964–5 to 13 per cent in 1978–9. Since all land classified as forest is capable of supporting a full crown cover, it can be concluded that

Table 8.5   *Percentage of forest area in forest density categories:*
Nepal, 1964–5 and 1978–9

Mean		Percentage crown cover			Total
		10–40% 25%	40–70% 55%	70–100% 85%	
Middle/high	1964–5	18	42	40	100
mountains	1978–9	35	52	13	100
Siwaliks	1964–5	17	42	41	100
	1978–9	11	77	12	100
Tarai	1964–5	16	40	44	100
	1987–9	7	56	37	100

Source: WECS (1986).

areas with less than 70 per cent crown cover are over-used and depleted. Within the country, there are major differences between regions and zones. In the hilly region dense forest is rarer than in the mountains, with the central and eastern zones having virtually no dense forest at all.

Forest areas provide fuelwood, timber, fodder and compost for the agricultural populations they support, and as they become degraded, the available long-term supplies of these commodities decline. However, as we shall show the present availability of these materials has not reached critical proportions, particularly in the environmentally sensitive hilly regions. What is more immediate, and more sensitive, as already discussed, is the impact of the degradation on the environment through soil erosion and hydrology effects. On soil erosion it is widely accepted that in the Himalayas, being an unstable fast-rising mountain range, there is a great deal of mass wasting that is naturally induced.[1] A careful review of the evidence on erosion from different types of land by Ramsay (1986) concluded that erosion was unlikely to be serious on forest land with even a small amount of cover. Where it was likely to be serious was where the land had been converted to grassland, and where it was heavily overgrazed. In that case, the rate of soil loss, resulting from uncontrolled de-vegetation and severe gullying, was several times higher than for any forest (see Table 8.6).

Increased forest degradation is likely to reduce water infiltration rates and cause increasing run-off. Again, the evidence on this

Table 8.6   Surface erosion rates reported from run-off plot studies

Land use	Erosion rate (tonnes)
Various forest, to grazing	7.8–36.8 ha yr^{-1}
Severely degraded, heavily grazed forest on intensively gullied badlands	200 ha yr^{-1}
Fenced/unfenced grazing	9.4–34.7 ha yr^{-1}
Protected pasture mixed with forest overgrazed land*	1.01–9.85 ha yr^{-1}/ per 4-month period
Dense forest	0.43 ha yr^{-1}/per 5-month period

*Same fenced pasture as Mulder study.
Source: Ramsey (1986); ERL (1988).

supports the view that, even on sparsely forested sites, soil infiltration is sufficient to prevent significant run-off for most of the monsoon. It is only on overgrazed compacted soils that run-off is a major problem (Gilmour, King and Fisher, 1987). Certainly, the evidence for the kind of catastrophic scenario outlined in the *Sunday Times* is lacking. In a reply to that article, published in the *Independent*, Hamilton from the east–west centre is quoted as saying:

> Even if the entire river basin had been forested, there would have been floods. The forests are beautifully functioning ecosystems. They must, in places, be totally protected and, in others, wisely managed. But they will not prevent floods and sedimentation on the lower reaches of major rivers. (17 September 1988)

Water resources
Water supplies for the majority of the population are directly determined by the rainfall patterns. Only 19 per cent of the rural and 23 per cent of the total population have access to piped water. Irrigation is also predominantly rain-fed. Estimates by Macdonalds (1988) indicate that only about 15 per cent of the gross cultivated area is potentially irrigable, and of that about 64 per cent has already been developed.

The combination of soil loss and demands on the water resources has resulted in a deterioration of conditions in 18 of the 43 main watersheds of the country (Shrestha *et al.* 1983). Although it is accepted that natural factors are largely responsible for what has been happening in these areas, the protection of the watersheds is crucial to the future of Nepal, and the government with the assistance of donor agencies is embarked on a number of projects which involve the stabilization of streambanks, gully control terrace improvements and the protection and rehabilitation of grasslands.

Natural areas

The mountains of Nepal provide some of the most spectacular scenery in the world, which attracts large numbers of trekkers and visitors each year. The country's economic needs dictate that tourism, a major source of foreign earnings for the country, be developed and increased as much as possible. Indeed this has been happening, and the number of visitors to Nepal has increased from fewer than 10,000 in 1960 to more than 250,000 in 1988. Government plans have a target of 1,000,000 visitors by the year 2000. The direct impact of this on the natural resource base of the country is to increase demands for fuelwood and, more insidiously, to destroy the wilderness, natural beauty and isolation that attracted the visitors in the first place. On the other hand, the cash that is generated by tourism could be used to protect these very features of the landscape and thereby ensure a sustainable use of this most valuable resource. At the present moment, there are some worrying signs. For example, increasing litter[2] in the main parks where access is possible and a strong belief among those responsible for the management of the country's dozen or so conservation areas that, if the access routes were improved to make them even remotely efficient in Western terms, parks such as Sagarmatha would be damaged beyond recognition.

In addition to its natural scenic beauty, the country is rich in flora and fauna that reflects its unique range of variation in humidity, altitude and soil type. As far as food and fodder plants are concerned, this has been well documented by Stainton (1972). The protection of these resources is undertaken as part of the national conservation effort, of which the creation of the national parks and conservation areas was the beginning.

Factors determining the demand for resources

Most of the demand for resources in the environmentally sensitive hills and mountains comes from an agricultural population that is

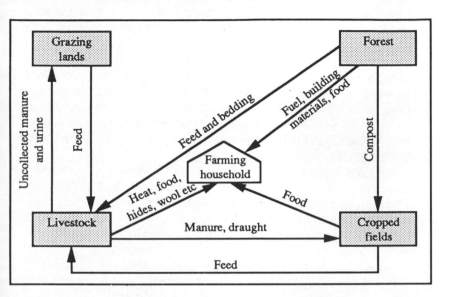

Figure 8.3   Agriculture, forestry and livestock interrelationship (LRMP, 1986)

operating, to a large extent, on the margins of subsistence. The linkages between the resource base and the activities of the farming household are depicted in Figure 8.3. Note the key role for the forest in providing compost for crops, fodder for livestock and fuel and timber for the household. In view of this, and the lack of any feasible substitutes on a large enough scale, it is generally accepted that the expansion of agriculture at the expense of forest land would be unsustainable. The level of agricultural production that this sytem supports is fairly uniformly low. The Department of Food and Agricultural Marketing Services (DFAMS) estimates that annual per capita foodgrain consumption is around 120 kg in the hills and 144 kg in the mountains. To meet a target Basic Needs food consumption of 2,340 calories per day would require over 200 kg of foodgrains annually. A similar remark holds for the consumption of energy for heating, lighting and cooking.

The greatest part of the household's time is spent in subsistence agriculture. The extent of off-farm employment varies considerably from region to region, but the average for the hills region has been estimated at approx. 15 per cent of the household's total time (DFAMS, 1986). Opportunities for this arise from a small but diverse and growing cottage industry base, or from tourism or forestry-based activities. Such work, along with a small part of the farming activities and remittances from migrant family members, generate cash income. Again, looking at data for the hills, this varies between 37 and 52 per cent of a landowning household's total income (cash plus kind), according to a recent survey by Rasta Bank, quoted in ERL (1988).

Most agricultural households are owner-cultivator farmers, who therefore have a strong incentive to manage the land sustainably. There are a number of tenancies still, and a distinction is made between formal and informal tenancies. In principle, one might think that tenants, particularly informal ones, would be less likely to take a long-term view of productivity. However, an Integrated Development Systems study (1986) investigated the relationship between tenurial conditions and productivity and was unable to come up with conclusive results. Hence the pattern of farmland ownership is not generally regarded as a cause of poor farming practices.

This contrasts sharply with the position regarding forest and grasslands. The former were nationalized in 1957 but government ownership only existed in name. In many places community property rights continued to be practised, but in a number of others traditional rights were abandoned and replaced by an effectively open access use of the resource (Mobley, 1987). Hence today the redefinition of these rights in socially and operationally effective groups is a major issue in forest management. As far as grasslands are concerned, the situation also appears to be varied. According to Panday (1982), much grassland is owned by the government but in fact is treated as open-access property. Some is communally or privately owned, but the extent of such ownership and management is not documented. However, the severe pressure on grasslands, which is very evident in the country, is almost certainly the result of an open-access exploitation of this resource. There is anecdotal evidence to indicate dramatic increases in yields on grasslands that have been protected and where rotational grazing systems have been employed.

So the overall picture is predominantly one of an agricultural society operating at very low levels of output, using traditional methods which involve a balance between cropland, forest and grassland. At the same time, there are some opportunities for earning a cash income. These arise from some farm-related activities (particularly livestock rearing), from a range of cottage industries, from tourism and from migration of some family members to urban areas in Nepal or abroad. The incentive to maintain sustainable use is there for the privately owned farmland but less so for the forest and grassland, much of which is treated as an open-access resource.

Coping strategies by the people and government
Whatever is concluded about the rate and extent of natural resource degradation in Nepal, no study of the problem can be effective without an understanding of human responses, both at the individual and the collective levels, to the changing environment. It is only by examining these responses that one can evaluate future prospects and formulate suitable policy measures to achieve sustainable development in the country.

At the micro level, one would expect households to respond to resource scarcities and shortages, *should they be perceived*. The evidence on the perception of resource scarcity is mixed. Clearly, there has been some awareness of a rising cost of feeding and maintaining livestock because there has been a shift away from cattle to buffalo and smaller ruminants. Villagers in some areas have also altered livestock management practices by stall feeding or rotational grazing. In total, cattle and buffalo populations are not increasing as fast as human populations, but the numbers of goats and sheep are so doing. Also farmers have begun to substitute chemical fertilizer for manure and leaf litter. This process is very much limited by the limited availability of fertilizer in the hill and mountain regions (outside of the Kathmandu Valley) and, as stated earlier, present levels of fertilizer application in these areas is very low; but it is increasing. According to ERL (1988), fertilizer use in the hills has been growing at over 20 per cent each year over the recent past.

As far as fuelwood is concerned, the picture is less encouraging. Scarcity of this commodity in the rural areas would typically show up in increased collection times. Although there is some evidence that time spent on fuelwood collection is rising in some areas, this is not a widespread or generally observed phenomenon. Evidence to indicate that fuelwood shortages are not conceived of as a problem is partly provided by the low adoption rate for fuel-efficient stoves in the hill and mountain regions. Although there are many reasons for the poor adoption of these stoves (USAID, 1988), undoubtedly one main reason is that users do not sufficiently value the savings in fuel. In the Tarai, and in urban areas where fuel shortages are more severe, acceptance rates for the stoves have generally been higher. Where fuelwood costs are rising, the response has also been to increase private growing of trees (Wyatt-Smith, 1982; Mahat, 1985). However, as was pointed out in Chapter 2, scarcity of fuelwood often is not transmitted to the users until it is too late; the mining of forest resources can continue for some considerable time before shortages of supplies are felt.

Although changes in farming practices are an important response to a declining resource base, the most important and effective response at the micro level would be a change in the human population pressure on that base. Such pressure can be reduced by a declining birth rate or by outmigration, or both. The birth rate has shown no appreciable fall in the recent past, and if one compares the natural rates of increase in the different regions of the country, there is very little difference between them. Certainly, there is nothing to indicate that the areas subject to the greatest natural resource pressure have lower rates of natural increase in population. However, migration is and has long been a major response to resource shortages in the hills and mountains. As the data in Table 8.1 shows, there has been, since 1971, a substantial net migration out of the hills and mountains and into the Tarai and the Kathmandu Valley. Work by Gurung (forthcoming) indicates that outmigration accounts for over one-third of the hills and nearly half the mountains' natural population increase. Much of the hill outmigration is international, principally to India. The patterns of migration are complex and not fully understood, but it is accepted that the major reason for migrating is the shortage of land, food and employment. Of these, the lack of adequate land is the most important. Whether migrating on a seasonal basis or for longer periods, the migrants often maintain a continuing link with their village or community of origin. They remit cash and goods and return to participate in the community for varying lengths of time. In general, this process is thought to be beneficial to the protection of the resource base, partly because it directly reduces the pressure on that base and partly because it provides a source of cash wealth for the household that permits it to acquire goods, such as fertilizer and kerosene, which should reduce the demand for their natural substitutes. A similar effect is believed to be created by increasing income opportunities through off-farm employment, but it is important to point out that no systematic study exists which relates the demand for natural resources to the household's wealth, cash income and other key variables. This is one of the serious gaps in the available knowledge on the linkages between the resource systems and the economic systems and is something that has been consistently observed in all the case studies looked at in this book.

So far the responses looked at have been at the micro level – i.e. by the individual or household. Action is also taken, however, at the macro level – i.e. by the village community as a whole, or by various levels of government. In Nepal there has been an enormous effort on the part of the government, with the assistance of agencies from many donor countries, to try to tackle the environmental problems of the country. A complete review of this would require a lot more space than is available here. However, a broad description of the main areas where the government and the aid agencies have been active, and where there are environmental implications, can be organized as follows:

- population and migration control;
- natural resource management and conservation;
- research, training and information dissemination;
- fiscal incentives via prices, taxes, etc.;
- tourism development;
- transport and hydropower development;

Population pressure is clearly something that needs to be tackled at the state level in Nepal; and official family planning programmes exist to disseminate information and to make services accessible to the population. In terms of spreading information, the programmes have been successful but the usage rates for contraception methods are still very low, and it is generally accepted that they are not increasing fast enough to affect significantly population growth for the next generation. Hence for the areas that are environmentally at risk – the hills and mountains, in particular – the burden of reducing human pressure on the resource base must lie with migration. Here the government has tried (with limited success) to channel and control the movement of people into the Tarai, where large tracts were cleared for settlement as a result of the malaria eradication programmes of the late 1950s and early 1960s. However, the scope for further migration into this area for agricultural settlement is fast dwindling and so this cannot be viewed as a major solution to the problem. Undoubtedly, urbanization will take some of the pressure off the land, and although it creates its own environmental problems, it should open up more policy options for a government that wants to protect the ecologically valuable forest and water resources of the country. The rate of urbanization is expected to continue rapidly, with the urban population rising from 6.8 per cent of the total in 1981 to 16.3 per cent by the year 2000.

Natural resource management and conservation are rightly seen as important areas of government policy. For forestry, there is the much-vaunted community forestry programme which allocates areas of degraded and semi-degraded forest land to 'panchayats', or local government bodies, for management, controlled exploitation and reforestation. The programme has been extensively commented upon and the general conclusions seem to be that it has not achieved as much active community involvement as would be desirable. Most important, however, the scale of the problem is much bigger than the efforts being made to deal with it. By 1986 community forestry and other plantation projects (chiefly private leaseholds and national schemes) had brought 61,000 ha under management in the hills. This is around 5-6 per cent of the forest area of that region. Under current trends, about 15 per cent will be managed by 2009, and that is too little. Although success in overall terms has been limited, some individual programmes have achieved very encouraging results. Notable among these is the Nepal-Australia forestry project, located in two districts east of Kathmandu.

To protect the watersheds of the country the Department of Soil Conservation and Watershed Management was established in 1974. Its activities have focused mainly on constructing checkdams, stabilizing streambanks and slopes, gully control, terrace improvements and the protection of grasslands. The difficulties faced by the agency arise, to a large extent, because of problems in co-ordinating with other agencies which also have responsibility for land management; improved grassland management is one policy area that has suffered as a result. To date, management efforts have had only a small impact on the actual state of the watersheds of the country.

The need for conservation of areas of special interest and ecological value has been recognized by the government. Conservation plans are being drawn up for the Annapurna area, as well as new areas that are being opened up for trekkers and other visitors. In the past it has been the lack of adequate planning capability that has, understandably, discouraged the government from opening up new areas for trekking and tourism in many of the country's national parks and reserves. It should be noted, however, that such plans need to take account of major infrastructure projects, such as roads and hydroelectric dams and, again, the government appears to recognize this in its current attitude to conservation strategy.

To encourage better resource management practices requires substantial extension services that are conspicuously lacking in the hill and mountain regions of Nepal. Hence the benefits of knowledge gained in the country's research farms and centres are not fully disseminated. Equally important, the researchers often do not appear to understand the problems facing the farming families located in the more remote regions. An improved two-way flow of knowledge and information is clearly required.

In many countries fiscal incentives are of great importance in managing natural resources, but in Nepal their scope is limited by the fact that few key users of the resources are sufficiently part of the monetary economy to be able to respond to these incentives. One policy that the government has employed has been a subsidy on fertilizer for farmers. The intention, in part, was to relieve pressure on fodder resources by substituting for dung and on cropland resources by raising yields. However, it has been shown that even without a subsidy, the use of fertilizer was economically viable (Nelson, 1986). Its limited use was then more related to unavailability or to lack of financial resources, or both. Some people have argued that to encourage the use of fertilizer in the hills it would be better to give a transport subsidy, so that it would pay to move it to the more remote areas. But this has not been attempted. Other areas of fiscal intervention by the government that could be relevant are output support prices, subsidized food distribution and subsidized credit. Both subsidized output prices and subsidized food distribution have had little impact in the hills and mountains. The high costs of transport effectively isolate these areas in market terms, so that their products would only benefit from support prices if the government also paid a transport subsidy. This has been proposed by Scherer (1985) but it is generally thought not to be implementable; its impact on the demand for resources is also unclear. Subsidized credit could be beneficial to farmers in developing their agricultural systems and could be used to encourage those developments that were likely to reduce the pressure on the resource base. Again, one needs to remember that the whole process is dependent on a monetary economy, and although such transactions are increasing, they have a long way to go.

Some of the issues of tourism have been touched upon in earlier remarks on the economy and on government conservation policy. The government is pursuing a policy of increasing tourism in the country at a rapid rate but it recognizes the dangers to the ecologically fragile areas of uncontrolled use by visitors. Hence the management plans for the parks are of considerable importance. In terms of uses of natural resources, it is mainly the use of fuelwood in the hills and mountains that is critical. A policy requiring trekking parties to carry their own kerosene has been instituted and is partly effective. But the same restrictions do not apply to tea-houses for trekkers. There is some evidence to suggest that the latter is substituting for the former, thus reducing the impact of the no fuelwood policy. Although tourism has both negative and positive effects on the environment, the interest in the country and the problems that it creates is a force for the good and, moreover, one that can be channelled in its development interests. For example, visitors could well be encouraged to pay a 'conservation levy' if it was made clear that it was earmarked for that purpose. The resulting resources – if properly applied – could be of great benefit to the process of sustainable development.

The main government investments that have a direct impact on the resource base of the country are its investment in roads and in hydropower plants. Apart from the connections between the Kathmandu Valley and Pokhara, the roads run mainly east to west in the Tarai; spurs into the valleys generally do not extend far. The principal environmental impact that has to be watched for with roads, in this terrain, is the danger of accelerated erosion (Schaffner, 1987). This has been a problem in a number of cases. It can be prevented by careful design and adequate expense, but the government is not always willing to accept this. Roads also increase access to remote areas which can change the local socio-economic systems. The overall effects of this are mixed and no general conclusions can be drawn (*ibid.*). Similar issues arise with regard to hydro plants.

The access roads are often the only roads in the areas concerned (e.g. the Arun access road opening up the Arun Valley). So far Nepal's major hydro developments have not resulted in major adverse environmental impacts of the kind witnessed in India; and the proposed schemes at Arun and Karnali appear to be subject to very careful environmental impact analysis. In addition to the major hydro plants, there are a number of mini hydro projects supplying power to small, often isolated, communities. They are used mainly for lighting and do not substitute for fuelwood.

Prospects for the future

On the basis of the data available, projections of future demands and supplies of food, fuelwood and fodder have been made under three scenarios, assuming: a continuation of expected trends, an optimistic set of future developments and a pessimistic set of such developments (ERL, 1988). The optimistic case allows, on the demand side, for a higher rate of migration from the areas under resource pressure; a reduced rate of growth of livestock; a substitution of other fuels for fuelwood; and an increase in overall efficiency in the use of fuelwood. On the supply side, it assumes an increase in the rate at which forest area is brought under management and control; an increase in the yields of fuelwood and fodder from managed areas; and a faster improvement in agricultural yields. The pessimistic scenarios assume the opposite for each of the demand and supply factors listed above and the expected trends case assumes something in between, based on an extrapolation of current trends.

The results of carrying out the analysis for the hills area to the year 2010 show that:

(a) food deficits are only avoided under optimistic assumptions;
(b) fodder deficits occur in most areas but can be improved quickly under the optimistic assumptions;
(c) fuelwood deficits are likely to become more serious under all scenarios and there is less room for improvement;
(d) on the demand side, the dominant factor is population growth, although there is some scope for savings from reduced fodder demand and the use of improved stoves;
(e) on the supply side, the dominant factor is the rate at which forest can be brought under management and the potential for improving agricultural yields.

The value of such an exercise is not in forecasting what will actually happen, but rather in showing what changes are needed in current trends if the resource problems are to be overcome. On that basis, the above analysis has shown that in the case of Nepal the required increases in forest management, outmigration from hills and mountains, fuel use efficiency and reduced fodder demand are substantial if a crisis in the hill and mountain regions is to be avoided. However, what is still not clear is how these increases are to be achieved. A great deal still needs to be done to formulate the appropriate policies and to find the resources to carry them through. In this chapter some of the issues involved in doing this have been discussed. The will is certainly there, both on the part of the government of Nepal and the international community. Whether a way can be found remains to be seen.

Notes

1. Although this is undoubtedly true, it is interesting to note that Nepal's rates of soil loss on average are lower than those of countries such as Ecuador and Madagascar. In Nepal the upper end of the range for terraces is 100 tonnes ha yr^{-1} which compares with figures of 250–560 tonnes ha yr^{-1}, in Ecuador and Madagascar (IIED and WRI, 1987).
2. A recent survey of Nepal in the *National Geographic* magazine, November 1988, quoted bemused Sherpas as deciding that the sheets of discarded toilet tissue to be found on the main tourist trails must be the white man's prayer flags.

References

APROSC (1986), *Perspective Land Use Plan (1985–2005)*, Agricultural Projects Services Centre, Kathmandu.

DFAMS (1986), *Report on Food Production and Water Use at the Farm Level, 1985*, Department of Food and Agricultural Marketing Services, Ministry of Agriculture, Kathmandu.

ERL (1988), *Natural Resource Management for Sustainable Development: A Study of Feasible Policies, Institutions and Investment Activities in Nepal with Special Emphasis on the Hills*, London: Environmental Resources Ltd.

Gilmour, D. A., King, G. C. and Fisher R. J. (1987), *Management of Forests for Local Use in the Hills of Nepal: Changing Forest Management Paradigms*, NAFP Discussion Paper, Kathmandu.

Gurung, H. (1986), *Nepal: Environment and Development*, Kathmandu: UNEP.

Gurung, H. (forthcoming), *Regional Patterns of Migration in Nepal*, Papers of the East–West Centre, Honolulu.

IIED and WRI (1987) *World Resources 1987*, New York: Basic Books.

Integrated Development Systems (1986), *The Land Tenure System in Nepal*, Kathmandu: IDS.

LRMP (1986), *Land Resources Mapping Project, Summary Report*, Kathmandu: Kenting Earth Sciences Ltd.

Macdonald and Partners (1988), *Assistance in the Establishment of Design Criteria and Manual for Irrigation Projects in Nepal*, Sir M. Macdonald and Partners, Inception Report, Cambridge UNDP/World Bank.

Mahat, T. B. S. (1985), 'Human impact of forests in the middle hills of Nepal', unpublished PhD thesis, Australian National University.

MPFS (1988), *Master Plan for the Forestry Sector of Nepal*, Jaakko Poyry Oy, Madecor (Consultants), HMGN/Asian Development Bank/FINNIDA, Ministry of Forests and Soil Conservation, Kathmandu.

Nelson, G. C. (1986), *Agricultural Price Policy in Nepal*, Asian Development Bank, Manila.

Panday, K. K. (1982), *Fodder Trees and Tree Fodder in Nepal*, Swiss Development Corporation, Swiss Federal Institute of Forestry Research, Birmensdorf, Switzerland.

Ramsay, W. J. (1986), 'Erosion problems in the Nepal Himalayan Overview', in S. C. Joshi (ed.), *Nepal Himalaya: Geo-Ecological Perspectives*, Himalayan Research Group, Naini Tal, India, pp. 359–95.

Schaffner, U. (1987), *Road Construction in the Nepal Himalayas: the Experience from the Lamosangu-Jiri Road Project*, ICIMOD Occasional Paper No. 8, Kathmandu.

Scherer, A. (1985), *Considerations about the Foodgrain Distribution Policy in Nepal*, UNDP/FAO Project NEP/80/008, Food and Agricultural Organisation, Kathmandu.

Shrestha, B. *et al.* (1983), *Watershed Conditions of the Districts of Nepal*, Department of Soil Conservation and Water Management, Kathmandu.

Stainton, J. D. (1972), *Forests of Nepal*, London: John Murray.

USAID (1988), *Assessment of Cookstove Programs in Nepal*. Kathmandu: USAID.

Wallace, M. B. (1988), *Forest Degradation in Nepal: Institutional Context and Policy Alternative*, Winrock Research Report series, No. 6, HMG-USAID-GTZ-IDRC-FORD-WINROCK Project, Kathmandu.

WECS (1986), *Land Use in Nepal, A Summary of the Land Resources Mapping Project Results*, Water and Energy Commission Secretariat, Kathmandu.

Wyatt-Smith, J. (1982), *The Agricultural System in the Hills of Nepal, the Ratio of Agricultural to Forest Land and the Problem of Animal Fodder*, Agricultural Projects Services Centre, Kathmandu.

9 Sustainable management of Amazonia

Introduction

In the Amazon region of South America[1] current economic policies, incentives and investment strategies are blamed for widespread deforestation and the degradation of the region's tropical forests.[2] Much of the region's forest appears to be disappearing at an alarming rate. This is leading to further ecological disruptions through changes in soil quality and erosion, water runoff, rainfall patterns and local climate. There may also be important consequences for the biosphere if excessive Amazonian deforestation continues: forests act as absorbers of carbon dioxide. Forest removal by burning for clearance contributes directly to CO_2 and other greenhouse gases build-up by adding to emissions, and indirectly by reducing the CO_2 'sink' on the earth's surface. To understand the reasons for these concerns, it is necessary to appreciate the complexity and vastness of the Amazonian ecosystem.[3]

The Amazon River Basin is approx. 5.8 million km^2 in area. It is horseshoe-shaped and lies along the 6,500 km Amazon River and its tributaries. Roughly 70 per cent of this surface area is covered by tropical forest, which extends into six South American countries – Brazil, Colombia, Peru, Venezuela, Ecuador and Bolivia. The Amazonian forest represents a significant proportion of the world's tropical forests; for example, Brazil – which contains around 67 per cent of the Amazonian tropical forest – accounts for one-third of the global tropical moist forest (Pearce and Myers, 1989; Salati and Vose, 1984; Vidart, 1981).

The vast Amazonian ecosystem can actually be classified into three distinct types: the *terra firme* (solid or dry ground) of the tropical forest proper; the *varzea* (swampy areas and floodlands) along the riverbanks flooded during rainy season and rich in nutrients; the *iqapos* (submerged areas) that are basically aquatic ecosystems fed by the various 'black', 'white' and 'clear' water rivers. Together, its tropical forest and river system make Amazonia the wettest region of its size in the world, containing two-thirds of the earth's surface fresh water. Although the Amazon River system discharges one-fifth of all the river water that flows into the world's oceans and seas, more than half of the region's moisture remains within the ecosystem (Myers, 1984). This is due to the high rates of rainfall and equally high rates of solar evaporation and tropical forest evapo-transpiration. Thus the Amazon River Basin is virtually self-sufficient in material cycling and energy balance except for continuous inflows of solar radiation and a major influx of atmospheric water from the Northern Hemisphere trade winds.

In the past, the vastness of the Amazonian forests has allowed a 'balance' between the use of forest resources for economic activity and sufficient preservation to ensure ecological stability and sustainability. For example, traditional forest dwellers have for centuries developed sustainable productive systems that minimize deforestation and degradation. Their economic activities have included hunting, fishing, growing of crops, food gathering and the use of trees to produce homes and canoes. Important cultural mechanisms have been employed to prevent this livelihood being threatened by overpopulation. In Brazil the forest-dwelling Indian population was estimated to be as high as 6–9 million people in 1500, compared to less than 200,000 in the early 1980s (Caufield, 1982; Posey, 1985).

Similarly, traditional shifting cultivation, which involves clearing a small area of forest, burning some of the felled vegetation and leaving the remainder to decompose and gradually leach nutrients to the soil, can be a sustainable and self-contained system that minimizes deforestation. As long as population density remains at two or three people per square kilometre and land is left fallow for at least 10 years, then farmers need only to clear the secondary forest that has grown on the fallow land. Often the secondary forest is seeded with fruit or timber trees that make it valuable even when lying fallow. Thus many of these traditional systems have tremendous potential not only for meeting subsistence needs, but also generating marketable surpluses of valuable crops (Caufield, 1982; Fearnside, 1986a; Hall, 1987; Padoch *et al.*, 1985). The *varzeas*, or alluvial foodplains, could also be sustainably developed, provided that clearance of natural ground cover, swamp drainage and use of agrochemicals were carefully controlled. Similarly, both non-timber and timber forest products could contribute to a number of important modern industries with minimum deforestation and environmental disruption, provided that trees of the forest are properly harvested to eliminate unnecessary extraction and damage. The biological diversity of Amazonia would surely also continue to be an important source of genetic diversity.

In sum, Amazonia has traditionally existed and could continue to exist as a highly diverse and stable ecosystem capable of yielding essential environmental services and supporting a number of important economic activities. Exploitation of forest resources could increase even further, provided that deforestation and environmental degradation is minimized. However, overwhelming evidence suggests that current patterns of exploitation are not sustainable. Distortions created by economic policies are unnecessarily accelerating Amazonian deforestation, which could irrevocably disrupt the ecological balance of many parts, if not the whole, region. On a human timescale, the loss of such a highly developed ecosystem is tantamount to the loss of an irreplaceable asset; even if favourable conditions allow for it, the regeneration of an integrated tropical ecosystem approaching the complexity and diversity of Amazonia would take tens if not hundreds of thousands of years.

Deforestation in Amazonia
It is difficult to obtain estimates of deforestation for all of the Amazon region. Table 9.1 reports estimates of forest clearance in Brazil's Legal Amazon to 1988. The figures, based on Landsat imagery, show that very little clearance has taken place by 1975, perhaps 0.6 per cent of the total area. But between 1975 and 1985 a further 11 per cent or so was cleared to bring the total cleared area to 12 per cent by 1988. Table 9.1 also shows that the regional distribution of deforestation varies widely – around a quarter of the Mato Grosso and Rondonia areas have been cleared, compared to about 1 per cent in Roraima and Amapa. Intense clearing has followed the Belem–Brasilia highway and the Cuiaba–Porto Velho highway. Figure 9.1 indicates these areas and their relationship to the entire Amazon region.

The economic contribution of Amazonia
The recent 'opening up' of Amazonian areas to extensive economic exploitation through cattle ranching, colonial settlement, timber production and major development projects has been highly destructive to the region's tropical forests. Yet the benefits, in terms

Table 9.1 Landsat surveys of forest clearing in the Brazilian Amazon

State or territory	Area of State or territory km²	Area cleared (km²)				Percentage of state or territory classified as clear			
		by 1975	by 1978	by 1980	by 1988	by 1975	by 1978	by 1980	by 1988
Amapa	140,276	152.5	170.5	183.7	571.5	0.1	0.1	0.1	0.4
Para	1,248,042	8,654.0	22,445.3	33,913.8	120,000.0	0.7	0.8	2.7	9.6
Roraina	230,104	55.0	143.8	273.1	3,270.0	0.0	0.1	0.1	1.4
Maranhao	257,451	2,940.8	7,334.0	10,671.1	50,670.0	1.1	2.8	4.1	19.7
Goias	285,793	3,507.3	10,288.5	11,458.5	33,120.0	1.2	3.6	4.0	11.6
Acre	152,589	1,165.5	2,464.5	4,626.8	19,500.0	0.8	1.6	3.0	12.8
Rondonia	243,044	1,216.5	4,184.5	7,579.3	58,000.0	0.3	1.7	3.1	23.7
Mato Grosso	881,001	10,124.3	28,355.0	53,299.3	208,000.0	1.1	3.2	6.1	23.6
Amazonas	1,567,125	779.5	1,785.8	3,102.2	105,790.0	0.1	0.1	0.2	6.8
Legal Amazon (total)	5,005,425	28,595.3	77,171.8	125,107.8	598,921.5	0.6	1.5	2.5	12.0

Source: Mahar (1988).

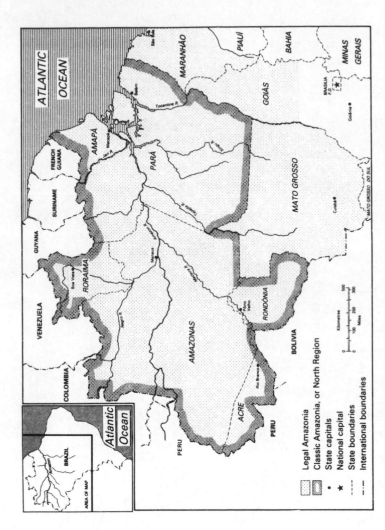

Figure 9.1   Amazonian Region

either of increased national economic growth or of providing sustainable livelihoods for growing populations, seem to be far from dramatic. For example, the Brazilian Amazon contributes only 5 per cent to the country's GNP, and the region's forests account for only 10 per cent of the national output of industrial timber. And despite extensive settlement, the Brazilian Amazon still contains only about 5 per cent of the country's 147 million people (Pearce and Myers, 1989).

Although the Amazon's share in national roundwood production doubled between 1975 and 1980 and the number of its sawmills increased from 194 in 1965 to 1639 by 1982, the forest sector is more vital for the regional than for the national economy.[4] Most of Brazil's timber exports consist of mahogany, which is being heavily logged in Rondonia and south of Santaren. Given that only a few species of trees are commercially exploited, and that the population density of any particular species is extremely low, vast areas of tropical forest must be covered in order to make logging feasible. There are other species of wood that either currently serve or could serve as substitutes for mahogany include virola, pau marfim, jacareuba and jatoba or jutal. However, because supplies of mahogany adequate for current demands exist, there is little immediate incentive commercially to exploit other tree species (Dowling, 1981).

Amazonia yields economic values other than those generated through either timber production or conversion of forest land to other uses. In particular, the preservation of key ecological functions is vital to sustainable agricultural development in the region, and the sustainability of the livelihoods of indigenous shifting cultivators. In addition, the Amazonian forests have indirect production values through non-timber and wood-based products industries, and the biological diversity of the region may have significant option value.

For example, although the *varzeas* cover only 2 per cent of Amazonia, with proper flood control, small farmer production of irrigated rice, tree crops, food crops and jute, as well as water buffalo and fish, could be substantially improved without damaging the environment. Assuming a generous allocation of 10 ha per farmer, the floodplains could support up to 1 million farming households, or more than 5 million people (Barrow, 1981; Hall, 1987; Pearce and Myers, 1989).

Minor forest products from Amazonia are contributing, and

could substantially contribute further, to a number of important modern industries. The phyto-chemicals derived from some forest products may prove to be ideal renewable substitutes as the price of petroleum-based synthetics increases. Although 400 of Amazonia's identified tree species are known to have commercial value, only 50 of them are being exploited, and usually on an extensive scale without regard to environmental destruction. In addition, because of the complex and highly specialized species interdependence, some forest products cannot be exploited unless the plants are allowed to remain fully integrated in their natural tropical environment.[5]

A preserved tropical forest ecosystem is also a source of genetic material for agriculture, industry, medicine and science. Although the world's tropical moist forests contain approx. 40–50 per cent of the earth's estimated 5–10 million species, only 1 per cent has been subjected to intensive screening for their potential benefits to humanity. The Amazon is believed to contain at least 30,000 plant species – three times as much as in all of temperate South America. In medicine, some species have already been identified as possible sources of drugs to combat cancer, heart disorders, high blood pressure and other illnesses, and as safe contraceptives and fertility compounds. New industrial uses of forest genetic materials are being discovered, such as the development of new hybrids for boosting crop productivity and/or increasing resistance to pests (Barbier, 1989, ch. 6; Pearce and Myers, 1989).

However, many of these indirect production, protection and option values are in direct conflict with the use of the forest for timber harvesting or for conversion to alternative use.[6] If the latter activities are making inefficient, or inherently unsustainable, use of Amazonian forest resources, optimal management of the Amazonian ecosystem requires that those resources should not be logged or converted.

Wider economic values are involved in the issues of developing or conserving Amazonia. Land use change effects local and global climate. Forest destruction is contributing a significant proportion of carbon release and other trace gases to the atmosphere, contributing to global warming – the 'greenhouse effect'.[7] If so, one of the social costs of deforestation is the economic damage done through global warming, including health hazards, sea-level rise, disruptions to patterns of agricultural production, and so on. Many of these costs occur in countries outside Amazonia, so that Amazonian forest destruction imposes a *trans-boundary externality* on the other nations.

A second feature of the wider economic value of Amazonia is that the preservation of natural forest yields a benefit to those who derive aesthetic, scientific and 'existence values' from the forest. An existence value occurs when welfare is derived from knowing that an environmental asset simply exists, quite independently of any *use* it may have. Quite clearly, much of the international concern about the Amazon is based on 'existence' value, the feeling that a unique asset should be preserved.

Combining these two wider economic values, we see that deforestation (a) imposes a direct cost on other nations (as well as on the deforesting countries) in the form of damage which has to be tolerated or which has to be ameliorated at a cost, and (b) involves a loss of preservation values felt widely within and outside Amazonia.[8] These are components of the economic value of Amazonia.

Proximate causes of Amazonian deforestation
The pattern of deforestation in Amazonia is highly concentrated and the process takes place in two stages: roadbuilding, new settlements and the expansion of cattle ranching to secure speculative claims come first, then clearing within these areas increases, once they are established (Fearnside, 1986b). For example, forest areas undergoing major conversion at rapid rates include parts of Colombia's lowland rainforests, especially along the Caqueta and Putumayo Rivers, and parts of Brazil's eastern and southern sectors of Amazonian lowland rainforests, notably in Para, Mato Grasso and Rondonia. Both are due to cattle-raising colonist settlement and forest farming. There are additional areas of Amazonia undergoing moderate conversion at intermediate rates, such as much of Ecuador's Amazonian lowland and upland rainforest. Here the causes are colonist settlement, forest farming, some planned agriculture and oil exploration. Much of Peru's Amazonian lowland and upland rainforest is being converted by colonist settlement, forest farming and some planned agriculture. Other parts of Brazil's Amazonian lowland rainforests, notably in Amapa, Acre and sections along the Trans-American Highway system, the *varzea* floodplains and the Tapajas River area, have been converted by colonist settlement, forest farming, cattle raising and timber exploitation. Only after settlement has been well established with surveyed plots and boun-

daries, as in the older official settlement areas in Rondonia, does the rate of forest clearing show any sign of slowing.[9] Cattle ranching assisted by generous official subsidies is probably the greatest single factor behind this increasingly rapid deforestation. Much of the output is geared for export. Estimates of the contribution of pasture formation to the total forest altered area range from 38 to 73 per cent (Browder, 1985; Caufield, 1982; FAO, 1982; Myers, 1984). Maher (1988) estimates that forest conversion for pasture took place at the rate of 8,000–10,000 km² per annum in the 1970s, most of it in the form of large landholdings each in excess of 1,000 ha. As population growth in the Brazilian Amazon has been increasing by 6.13 per cent p.a. – compared to a national rate of 2.78 per cent – small farmer settlements are considered the second major cause of deforestation. Small farmers are thought to have been directly and indirectly responsible by 1983 for about 11 per cent of the Brazilian Amazon's deforestation (Repetto, 1988, pp. 74–5). Non-Brazilian regions of Amazonia are also suffering high deforestation rates as a consequence of small farmer settlement; in Peru it has been estimated that each year some 3,000 new settlers destroy 20,000 ha of natural forest (Vidart, 1981). Clearance due to annual cropping, mainly by small farmers, probably increased by 2,000 km² in the 1970s, usually followed by reversion to secondary growth or converted to pasture when abandoned (Mahar, 1988).

It is difficult to estimate how much deforestation is caused by logging activities. However, extensive damage to the forest in order to exploit a limited number of trees is likely to continue. Further potential timber earnings are also frequently wasted when forest land is cleared for agriculture, ranching, roadbuilding, mining, hydroelectric schemes and other large-scale operations without any attempt to salvage commercially valuable trees. Logging tends to be a by-product of agricultural clearance. Selective clearance of a few trees is followed by clearance for agriculture.

The economic costs of deforestation

The user costs of Amazonian deforestation – in the form of the loss of potentially exploitable commercial tree species, dissipation of potential rents from inefficient timber harvesting and the loss of minor forest products – may be substantial.[10] However, as Amazonian deforestation represents a significant increase in environmental degradation and ecological instability in the region, the resulting external costs might be even more important. General environmental quality losses occurring as a result of Amazonian deforestation would include:

1. the loss of the potentially useful genetic material of unique Amazonian species;
2. the decline of unique natural habitats and ecosystems that are the source of cultural, aesthetic and recreational benefits;[11]
3. disruption of the culture and livelihoods and decline in the population of traditional forest-dwellers;[12]
4. the spread of endemic diseases and pests;[13]
5. loss of productivity and other economic damage due to water runoff, soil degradation and erosion accompanying deforestation. This often undermines the productivity of shifting cultivation, commercial cropping and ranching operations,[14] for example, after converted pasture is worked for two or three years, rainfall leaches nutrients from the thin surface soil; soil runoff leads to siltation of waterways and increased flooding, which affects cultivation and fishing in the floodplains;[15]
6. in the long run deforestation may cause major disturbances in the climate of Amazonia and its neighbouring regions, this arises from the permanent loss of water from the region's hydrological cycle as deforestation spreads;[16] as the Amazonian system relies on the extra energy input of frequent rainfall to recycle vital nutrients, even a relatively small decline in precipitation could disrupt nutrient cycles and energy flows and cause surface temperature fluctuations;[17]
7. a net loss of water in Amazonia could reduce precipitation in the Chaco Paraguayo and in central Brazil, shifting the climate towards increased continentality and affecting agriculture in south-central Brazil and other South American regions, for example, increased continentality may either extend the winter period or induce lower winter temperatures, resulting in the loss of valuable export earnings from sugar, oranges, soybeans and coffee production, and causing major setbacks to Brazil's import-saving biomass fuel programme;[18]
8. as noted above, deforestation in Amazonia may also contribute to the global climatic changes associated with the 'greenhouse effect'; approx. 115 trillion tonnes of carbon are retained in the forest matter of Amazonia, converting all of this forest biomass

to pasture or annual crops would mean a net increase of 8 per cent in the CO_2 content of the atmosphere; given that atmospheric CO_2 has increased by only 16 per cent since the last century, yet may have already caused some global warming, the additional contribution from Amazonian deforestation may be highly significant; moreover, destroying the Amazonian forests also releases other important greenhouse 'trace gases' (e.g. methane, nitrous oxide, CFCs, etc.) into the atmosphere.[19]

Underlying causes of Amazonian deforestation
If the current pattern of economic development in Amazonia is leading to environmental costs, as well as to increased social conflicts among smallholder squatters, larger commercial farmers, ranchers and other developers and indigenous peoples, then economic policies need to take into account these costs. Certainly, in the case of the Brazilian Amazon, these costs have been ignored in the development strategy:

> During the past 20 years official development strategy for the region has been, except for a brief interlude in the early 1970s, almost exclusively directed at the expansion of corporate forestry, agricultural and, more recently, mining interests virtually irrespective of any negative social and environmental side-effects . . . Thus, the increased level of state intervention in Amazonia has served to attract cheap labour to the region (to prepare the rainforest for agricultural use by later incoming livestock and other farmers, as well as to supply temporary wage labour on estates) without allowing substantial small-scale ownership to take hold in a 'preemptive' process of settlement by government and allied business interests. (Hall, 1986, p. 412).

Such a strategy is exemplified by the recently launched US $1.18 billion Grande Carajas Programme in the eastern Amazon region of Brazil. Based around development of the world's largest high-grade iron ore deposit at Carajas, the 840,000 km^2 programme zone would include development of 238,000 ha of mechanized soybeans, 12,600 ha of sugar cane, 417,000 ha of cattle pasture and 'enough rice to feed all of north-east Brazil'. As a result, most of the money and land will go to large landholders for mechanized agriculture, cattle ranching and even silviculture, which will also receive the bulk of rural credit and an infrastructure aimed at facilitating the export of agricultural products and the import of farm machinery and other inputs (Fearnside, 1986a; Hall, 1986).

Throughout the Brazilian Amazon, deliberate policy measures to promote this kind of economic development are estimated to have accounted for at least 35 per cent of all forest area altered by 1980; such policies include:

(a)   private capital investment in the Amazon region through tax incentives;
(b)   agricultural production through rural credits;
(c)   small farmer settlement in the Amazon region through directed and semi-directed colonization;
(d)   exports of Brazilian products through export subsidies (Browder, 1985).

Over the past two decades the Superintendency for the Development of the Amazon (SUDAM), along with its sister organization, Fundo de Investimento da Amazonia (FINAM), has been responsible for establishing incentive programme for attracting private investment to the Brazilian Amazon. Over the period 1965 to 1983 direct tax credit subsidies worth US $1.4 billion were granted to 808 existing and new private investment projects. Of these approx. 35 per cent went to 59 industrial wood producers (mainly sawmills), and over 42 per cent went to 469 livestock projects (virtually all beef cattle production). Other tax incentives administered by SUDAM included tax holidays and deductions for operating losses (*ibid.*). Such tax breaks have clearly accelerated deforestation by subsidizing both the initial project development and ongoing operations of cattle ranchers and the forest products industry in Amazonia.

For example, the cattle projects subsidized by SUDAM are estimated to have caused over 26 per cent of all forest cover alteration from 1972 to 1980. Not only have SUDAM-financed livestock projects enjoyed generous long-term financing, but at 49,500 ha the average size of the projects is substantially larger than the non-SUDAM average of 9,300 ha. Thus SUDAM projects not only have a greater financial capacity to clear forest, but they also cover larger forest areas. Yet because SUDAM tax credit funds are not allocated for maintenance, much clearing is not to increase the total net area in actual production, but to replace already degraded fields. Perhaps 20–25 per cent of the forest area of the Legal Amazon that has been cleared for pasture is economically inactive.[20]

Thus, without such generous subsidies, it is doubtful whether large-scale ranching in Amazonia would be economically sustainable. Recent findings in fact suggest that such projects are increasingly plagued by a low rate of implementation and with a high abandonment of pasture, which is attributed to the following economic factors:

1. Without real appreciation of land, no form of traditional ranching has a positive real rate of return in eastern Amazon – unless, of course, they receive the SUDAM incentives.
2. Without overgrazing, real land values must appreciate at the rate of 30 per cent before the investments become economically viable.
3. Even with improved pasture technologies, a real appreciation of land of 15–30 per cent a year is required to make the rate of return to overall investment resources positive;
4. Investors can maximize their private returns by using overgrazing; they cannot improve their returns by investing in pasture improvement (Binswanger, 1987).

Financial analysis of a typical SUDAM-financed ranch reveals that the discounted present value of net returns to the investor is US $1.87 million, nearly 2.5 times the investment outlay. If all subsidies were removed, however, the project would produce a net loss to the investor of US $0.65 million.[21]

Since 1970 the Brazilian government has subsidized directed and semi-directed programmes for small farmer settlement in Amazonia. In general, this approach has been portrayed as a politically more acceptable option than reform of the traditional agricultural lands elsewhere in Brazil. While there are substantial differences in subsidy rates among such programmes (e.g. a directed programme might spend US $13,000 per family in direct benefits compared to $3,900 per family in a semi-directed programme), there appears to be a positive correlation between the consumption of subsidized financing and the area of forest cleared. Moreover, the impact on reducing rural population pressure in the rest of Brazil has been largely superficial; the two largest programmes are in Rondonia where, by 1980, only 48,417 families had been given either permanent or temporary land titles. Yet these two programmes were responsible for an estimated 6.6 per cent of the forest area altered in the Legal Amazon (*ibid.*).

In sum, most of the extensive deforestation of the Amazon – over 15 million ha by 1987 – can be directly related to government-financed programmes and subsidies, particularly for ranching and colonization. In addition, certain general macroeconomic policies, such as the income tax, the land tax and land tithing regulations, are providing economic incentives for deforestation.

For example, a claimant who lives on an area of land has first preference to title for three times the area which he or she has cleared. This right is obtained if the claimant has used and lived on unclaimed public land for more than 5 years or has squatted on private land for a sufficiently long time without being challenged by the owner. Contrary to popular belief, as there are no vast areas of unclaimed land available for settlement in the Amazon, small farmers have difficulty in finding 'free' land for squatting. Only corporations and large ranchers have the capital to build their own access roads into the forest, whereas squatters need to stick close to public roads for access to health, education and marketing facilities. Thus, not only do the rules of land allocation encourage rapid deforestation by ranchers, as the final amount of land given legal title is a multiple of the area of forest converted to pasture, but clearing land also provides protection against squatters. This 'first come, first served' titling also ensures a rush to claim large tracts of land; plots of up to 3,000 ha are not uncommon. An unintended result of such land allocation procedures is that squatters are more likely to invade small forest reserves, which the forest service is finding increasingly difficult to guard.[22]

Similarly, as the land tax can be legally reduced by a factor of up to 90 per cent by converting 'unused' forest land into a more productive 'use', a farm containing forests is therefore taxed at a higher rate than one containing only pastures or cropland. Consequently, the land tax system provides an incentive to larger farms who are eligible for the progressive tax to convert their forests (Binswanger, 1987).

Finally, as agriculture is virtually exempt from Brazil's income tax laws, these laws provide additional incentive for land acquisition in Amazonia by wealthy individuals and corporations – i.e. in addition to the already high demand for land as a hedge against inflation and risky financial markets. However, because small farmers or other poor individuals do not benefit from this tax break, but do have to face the higher land prices that result from it, they are increasingly 'squeezed' out of the land markets. Consequently, those without land have to resort to squatting on the Amazonian frontier, and those who do own land will be tempted to sell out to larger landowners. As a result, the income tax

- tends to increase the demand for land in Amazonia, to speed up conversion of land for agricultural uses, and to raise the price of land;
- tends to increase inequality in land ownership holdings;
- increases the pace of migration of poor people to the frontier areas in search of land (*ibid.*).

Policies for sustainable development in Amazonia
Certainly, for the Brazilian Amazon at least, economic policies, incentives and investment strategies have accelerated the pace of deforestation and forest degradation. The two major sources of Amazonian deforestation, namely cattle ranching and small farmer settlement, can be traced to direct government subsidy programmes. The same can be said for the new phase of Amazonian deforestation of large-scale agricultural development based around increased mineral exploitation. At the heart of Amazonian deforestation, however, is a whole economic strategy that is biased towards large landholdings and commercial developments at the expense of small-scale ownership.

The first step towards a new strategy for sustainable development of Amazonia is to set aside areas of forest land that appear to have high protection or conservation value. The former would include areas that formed highly important watershed functions, particularly the regulation of water flowing to the highly productive alluvial plains and swamplands. Forests with high conservation value would be those areas with particularly notably concentrations of biodiversity. The latter could be divided into those in which recreational tourism – i.e. the national parks – is allowed, and those that are purely conservation reserves – i.e. the protected area. The latter should also include, where appropriate, sufficient areas to protect the livelihoods of indigenous forest-dwelling communities.

As some of these protection and conservation areas would straddle the frontiers of two or more Amazonian countries, international agreements on their establishment and management would be essential. In addition, as the Amazonian countries would forgo some benefits of developing these areas, whereas the rest of the world would be deriving important option and existence values from the establishment of Amazonian conservation and protection reserves, international financing of their establishment and management would be essential. The recent 'debt-for-nature' swaps implemented in Bolivia and Costa Rica might prove to be one effective type of financial arrangement (Hansen, 1988). However, this should not preclude direct donor assistance for establishing and managing parks and protected areas, training foresters and park officials and providing them with improved equipment and resources, and improving the monitoring and enforcement against illegal trade in protected Amazonian species.

The remaining Amazonian land should then be allocated to the best economic use, such as timber production, large-scale mineral, hydroeiectric and agricultural development, smallholder agriculture, including shifting cultivation and ranching. Here immediate priorities are required:

1. A land classification system that would distinguish forests of high production value from areas more suitably converted. For example, a forest highly valued for its timber would be an area with a high potential for regeneration and with good access for log disposal, whereas a low-value, secondary forest with low-quality standing stock and no possibility of regeneration regardless of access should receive higher priority for conversion.
2. The subsidies and other economic incentives that are encouraging inefficient and unsustainable forest conversion to ranching, large-scale development projects and commercial cropping should be ended. In late 1988 the Brazilian government announced the removal of some of the tax incentives for land clearance.
3. Economic analysis of large-scale development projects, such as the Grande Carajas Programme in the Brazilian Amazon and the many hydroelectric projects in Amazonia, should comprise an extended analysis that includes proper economic valuation of the environmental impacts of the projects. In a portfolio of projects, such as the Grande Carajas Programme, environmentally compensating projects may also have to be included to ameliorate any resulting environmental degradation (see Chapter 3).
4. Distortions in land registration, titling and purchases, as well as

income and other tax breaks, that encourage land speculation in Amazonia which particularly work against smallholders should be halted. In Amazonian countries, such as Brazil, where land distribution in non-Amazonian arable regions is highly skewed, land reform should be a more economically efficient and sustainable means of providing livelihoods to the landless and rural poor than opening up forest lands in Amazonia with poorer-quality soils.

In effect, what these policy changes call for is a new economic strategy that takes into account the total value of the Amazonian ecosystem. The current strategy underestimates this value by assuming that conversion of Amazonian forests is 'costless', and therefore that the value of the land is best maximized under some alternative use. This strategy extends to include the inefficient and unsustainable mining of Amazonian forests for timber, as well as the conversion of water resources to hydroelectric generation with little analysis of the environmental and social consequences. An alternative strategy for sustainable development of Amazonia must start with the proper economic analysis of its total values. Only then can the region's resources be optimally allocated to their best use.

Notes
1. The 'Legal Amazon' region of Brazil includes the country's traditional 'Northern Region' plus Mato Grasso and parts of Goias and Martanhao States (Figure 9.1). It comprises an area of approx. 5 million km², or 57 per cent of the country. In 1980 the tropical forest zone was almost 3.7m km², or approx. 67 per cent of the Legal Amazon; and moist forest proper covered almost 2.9m. km², or 57 per cent. In addition, there are another 1.3m. km² of tropical forests located in Amazonian regions outside Brazil – i.e. Venezuela has 0.31m. km², Colombia 0.27m. km², Ecuador 85,000 km² and Peru 0.6m km². This makes a total Amazonian forest area of about 4.2m. km²: see Pearce and Myers (1989).
2. Myers (1980) defines tropical forests as 'forests that occur in areas that have a mean annual temperature of at least 75 degrees Fahrenheit and are essentially frost-free – in areas receiving 2,000 mm or more of rainfall per year and not less than 100 mm of rainfall in any one month for two out of three years. They are mainly, if not entirely, evergreen'. Myers (1984) notes that all tropical forests are commonly called 'rain forests'; however, he suggests true rainforests are only those tropical forests that receive at least 4,000 mm of rain annually and at least 200 mm in ten months of the year. The more appropriate term for most tropical forests is 'tropical moist forest'.
3. For further discussion of the links between Amazonian deforestation and the greenhouse effect see Barbier (1989, ch. 6).
4. Repetto (1988, p. 74). For example, wood products account for more than a quarter of industrial output in four of the region's six states, exceeding 60 per

cent in Rondonia and Roraima, but the *entire* Brazilian wood industry, of which the Amazonian contribution is relatively small, accounted for only 12.9 per cent of industrial output and 4.9 per cent of foreign exchange earnings in 1980.

5. For example, although attempts have been made to develop commercial brazilnut plantations, many pilot projects have failed because the trees are pollinated by one species of bee that, in turn, requires other tree species for feeding when the nut trees are not flowering. Moreover, as the trees depend for germination on a particular species of rodent that chews and softens the seed coat of the nut, either brazilnut reserves need to be large enough to support a breeding population of this rodent or the seed coat has to be softened artificially: see Caufield (1982).

6. See Chapter 5 for a definition of option values.

7. For further discussion see Barbier (1989, ch. 6) and Houghton *et al.* (1985).

8. The common conception that existence value resides only in people 'outside' the resource-depleting nations should be resisted. There has been substantial outrage within Brazil, for example, over deforestation.

9. See FAO (1982); Fearnside (1986b); Myers (1980, 1984). The extent and rate of deforestation and degradation in these nuclei of intense activity can be dramatically illustrated by the case of Rondonia in Brazil (Pearce and Myers, 1989). In a vast state of 244,000 km^2, in 1975 only 1,200 km^2 of forest had been cleared. From 1975 to 1986, however, colonial settlement and other economic activities had increased the population by almost tenfold from 111,000 to over 1 million. Thus by 1987 a total of at least 147,000 km^2 of forest had been either degraded or deforested, or roughly 60 per cent of the state. If this exponential rate of destruction continues, the entire forest of Rondonia would disappear by the year 2000.

10. In stark contrast with existence or preservation values, user costs (as the name implies) are the stream of benefits forgone by any existing and potential users of an environmental asset as a result of its degradation or depletion.

11. For example, Sioli (1985, pp. 197–203) argues that when a certain percentage of Amazonian forests has been destroyed, the environmental 'threshold' effects 'will probably have a disastrous effect on the survival of spared forest areas which are intended as "nature reserves" or the like'.

12. For example, according to Caufield (1982), although Brazil's Indian population was an estimated 6–9 million in 1500, it had dropped to 1 million by 1900 and to under 200,000 by the early 1980s. Of the 230 tribes living in Brazil in 1900, only 143 survive.

13. See Vidart (1981); Butler and Schofield (1981, pp. 321–4) have also established a link between the conversion of forest to pasture and the spread of *chagas* disease, which has already affected 10 million South Americans.

14. For example, Sioli (1985) reports that the carrying capacity of converted pastures near the Belem–Brasilia highways decreased from 0.9–1 head of cattle on young pastures to only 0.3 head after some six years. Because of the declining soil phosphorous combined with soil compaction and weed invasion, cattle pasture is not sustainable under the low-input system in general use among ranchers in Amazonia. Thus by 1981 over 50 per cent of the pastures established in the Paragominas area were degraded, and the observed trend is for ranches to become uneconomic after 5–8 years under standard low-input conditions and after 12–14 years with 'adequate management' (Fearnside, 1986a). The same problem of nutrient loss faces cultivation on converted forest land, especially as many colonists are ignorant of traditional tropical cultivation skills, do not have sufficient land to practice shifting cultivation sustainable and often cannot afford appropriate fertilizers or crops. However, Fearnside notes that the poor

economics of pasture from converted Amazonian forest land is overrided by the
use of cattle pasture as a rapid and cheap means of securing claim to the land for
speculative purposes in the 'advance' of anticipated development and farmer
settlement. As is discussed below, the economics of cattle ranching are also
distorted by fiscal incentives through numerous subsidies.

15. For example, there is evidence that the annual floods experienced in Amazonia
since 1970, especially the high peak flows of 1981 and 1982, and the commonly
reported incidence of river flooding are connected with increased deforestation
of upland areas: see Salati and Vose (1984).

16. See Potter (1975); Potter (1981); Salati and Vose (1984); Sioli (1985).

17. For example, in the region of Manaus, the present dry period is at the maximum
that the local ecosystem can tolerate. Any lengthening of this dry season or
further reductions in rainfall at other times would induce irreversible ecological
changes: see Salati and Vose (1984).

18. See *ibid.*

19. Sioli (1985) and American Geophysical Union (1988); see also the discussions in
Barbier (1989, ch. 6) and Houghton *et al.* (1985).

20. Browder (1985, pp. 21–3, 29). Browder (n. 7) acknowledges that other estimates
of the average size of SUDAM livestock projects range from a low of 18,126 ha
(by SUDAM itself) to 28,860 ha. On the other hand, for the traditional North
region and Mato Grasso, the average size of cattle ranches is 872 ha.

21. Repetto (1988, pp. 79–80). It is also noted that only 20 per cent of SUDAM-
financed livestock projects market their timber, compared to 47 per cent of non-
subsidized ranches. For all projects, this equates to a potential loss of nearly
50,000,000 m^3 of roundwood, or an opportunity cost of US $100–250 million.
This is equivalent to one-eighth to one-third of all SUDAM tax credits distributed to Amazonian livestock projects from 1966 to 1983.

22. Browder (1985, pp. 16–20). Binswanger (1987, p. 18) also notes that 'small scale
squatters are frequently accused of contributing in a major way to the deforestation. While this may be of local importance in several regions, it is probably less
of a problem than the ranchers.' The exception would be in Rondonia, which is
the region for the major colonization programmes.

References

American Geophysical Union (1988), *Journal of Geophysical Research*, 93, 1389–95.

Barbier, E. B. (1989), *Economics, Natural Resource Scarcity and Development:
Conventional and Alternative Views*, London: Earthscan.

Barrow, C. J. (1981), 'Development of the Brazilian Amazon', *Mazingira*, 5, 36–47.

Binswanger, H. P. (1987), *Fiscal and Legal Incentives with Environmental Effects on
the Brazilian Amazon*, Discussion Paper, World Bank, Washington DC, May.

Browder, J. O. (1985), *Subsidies, Deforestation, and the Forest Sector in the
Brazilian Amazon*, Washington, DC: World Resources Institute.

Butler, E. H. and Schofield, C. J. (1981), 'Economic assault on Chagas disease', *New
Scientist*, 29 October, pp. 321–4.

Caufield, C. (1982), *Tropical Moist Forests: The Resource, the People, the Threat*,
London: Earthscan.

Dowling, G. J. (1981), 'Growing goodwill in Brazil', *Timber Trades Journal
Hardwood Supplement*, August, 27–9.

Fearnside, P. M. (1986a), 'Agricultural plans for Brazil's Grande Carajas Program:
lost opportunity for sustainable local development?' *World Development*, 14,
385–409.

Fearnside, P. M. (1986b), 'Spatial concentration of deforestation in the Brazilian Amazon', *Ambio*, 15, 74–81.

Food and Agricultural Organization (FAO) (1982), *Tropical Forest Resources Assessment Project*, FAO/United Nations Environmental Programme, Rome.

Hall, A. L. (1986), 'More of the same in Brazilian Amazonia: a comment on Fearnside', *World Development*, 14, 411–14.

Hall, A. L. (1987), 'Agrarian crisis in Brazilian Amazonia: the Grande Carajas Programme', *Journal of Development Studies, 24*, 522–51.

Hansen, S. (1988), *Debt for Nature Swaps: Overview and Discussion of Key Issues*, Environment Department Working Paper No. 1, World Bank, Washington DC, February.

Houghton, R. A. *et al.* (1985), 'Net flux of carbon dioxide for tropical forests in 1980', *Nature*, 16, August, 3124–5.

Mahar, D. (1988), *Government Policies and Deforestation in Brazil's Amazon Region*, Environment Department Working Paper No. 7, World Bank, Washington DC, June.

Myers, N. (1980), *Conservation of Tropical Moist Forests*, National Academy of Sciences, Washington, DC.

Myers, N. (1984), *The Primary Source: Tropical Rain Forests and Our Future*, New York: W. W. Norton.

Padoch, C., Chota Inuma, J., De Jong, W. and Unruh, J. (1985), 'Amazonian agroforestry: a market-oriented system in Peru', *Agroforestry Systems*, 3, 47–56.

Pearce, D. W. and Myers, N. (1989), 'Economic values and the environment of Amazonia', in D. Goodman and A. Hall (eds), *The Future of Amazonia: Destruction or Sustainable Development?*, London: Macmillan.

Posey, D. A. (1985), 'Indigenous management of tropical forest ecosystems: the case of Kayapo Indians of the Brazilian Amazon', *Agroforestry Systems*, 3, 139–58.

Potter, G. I. (1975), 'Possible climatic impact of tropical deforestation', *Nature*, 258, 697–8.

Potter, G. L. (1981), 'Albedo change by man', *Nature*, 291, 242–3.

Repetto, R. (1988), *The Forests for the Trees? Government Policies and the Misuse of Forest Resources*, Washington, DC: World Resources Institute.

Salati, E. and Vose, P. B. (1984), 'Amazon Basin: a system in equilibrium', *Science*, 225, 129–38.

Sioli, H. (1985), 'The effects of deforestation in Amazonia', *Geographical Journal*, 151, 197–203.

Vidart, D. (1981), 'Amazon roulette: destruction or development?', *IDRC Reports*, 10, 10–11.

Index